OUR BACKS WARMED BY THE SUN

Caitlin Press Inc.
8100 Alderwood Road, Halfmoon Bay, BC V0N 1Y1
www.caitlin-press.com

Text design by Vici Johnstone. Cover design by Sarah Corsie and Vici Johnstone

All images are from the author's personal collection unless otherwise noted. Cover photo 2008.023.775 Stevens Fonds, Touchstones Nelson: Museum of Art and History.

Edited by Meg Yamamoto

Printed in Canada

Caitlin Press Inc. acknowledges financial support from the Government of Canada and the Canada Council for the Arts, and the Province of British Columbia through the British Columbia Arts Council and the Book Publisher's Tax Credit.

Library and Archives Canada Cataloguing in Publication

Our backs warmed by the sun : memories of a Doukhobor life : / by Vera Maloff.
Maloff, Vera, 1951- author.

Includes bibliographical references.

Canadiana 20200225154 | ISBN 9781773860398 (softcover)

LCSH: Maloff, Vera, 1951- | LCSH: Maloff, Vera, 1951- —Family. | LCSH: Doukhobors—British Columbia—Biography. | LCSH: Doukhobors—British Columbia—History. | LCSH: Doukhobors—History.

LCC BX7433 .M35 2020 | DDC 289.9—dc23

OUR BACKS WARMED BY THE SUN

MEMORIES OF A DOUKHOBOR LIFE

VERA MALOFF

CAITLIN PRESS 2020

I dedicate this book to past generations of Doukhobor Spirit Wrestlers, to the children and those to come.

—ᴠᴠ—

I also dedicate this book to my Mother who has seen many changes in her lifetime.

As I finish writing this story, it is January 2019. I have returned from visiting Mother in the rehabilitation unit in Kelowna, where she is recovering from a stroke. Through her persistence and willingness to work hard, she has qualified for two to three hours of rehabilitation—physiotherapy and occupational therapy—a day. The wonderful staff in the unit hold her as an example of someone who, despite her age, can improve. She is relearning to sit up, rise from her chair to stand tall and take steps with a walker. And when the physiotherapist asks if she has had enough or is tired, she shakes her head and continues one step at a time.

And that, in itself, must surely be the motto for the peacemakers of the world, and perhaps for all of us to live by: One step at a time.

CONTENTS

Map of Area

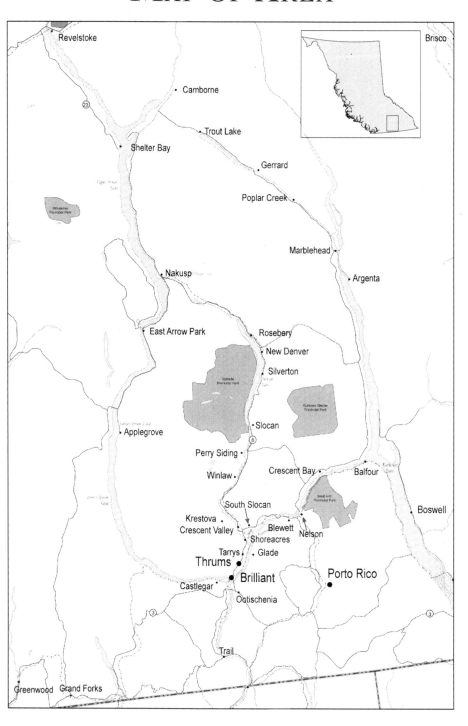

MALOFF–HOODICOFF FAMILY TREE

MALOFF

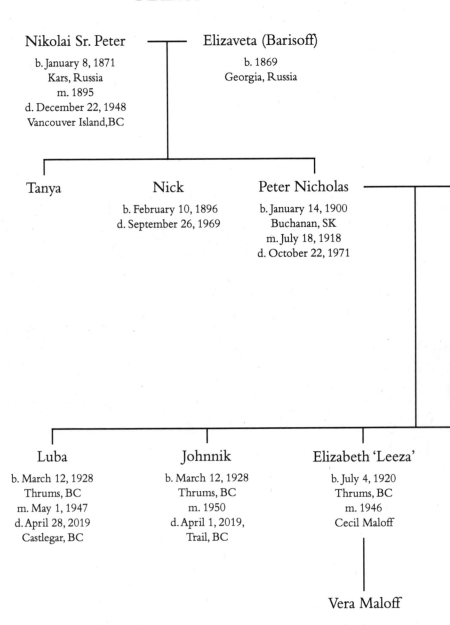

Nikolai Sr. Peter — Elizaveta (Barisoff)

b. January 8, 1871
Kars, Russia
m. 1895
d. December 22, 1948
Vancouver Island, BC

b. 1869
Georgia, Russia

Tanya

Nick
b. February 10, 1896
d. September 26, 1969

Peter Nicholas
b. January 14, 1900
Buchanan, SK
m. July 18, 1918
d. October 22, 1971

Luba
b. March 12, 1928
Thrums, BC
m. May 1, 1947
d. April 28, 2019
Castlegar, BC

Johnnik
b. March 12, 1928
Thrums, BC
m. 1950
d. April 1, 2019,
Trail, BC

Elizabeth 'Leeza'
b. July 4, 1920
Thrums, BC
m. 1946
Cecil Maloff

Vera Maloff

HOODICOFF

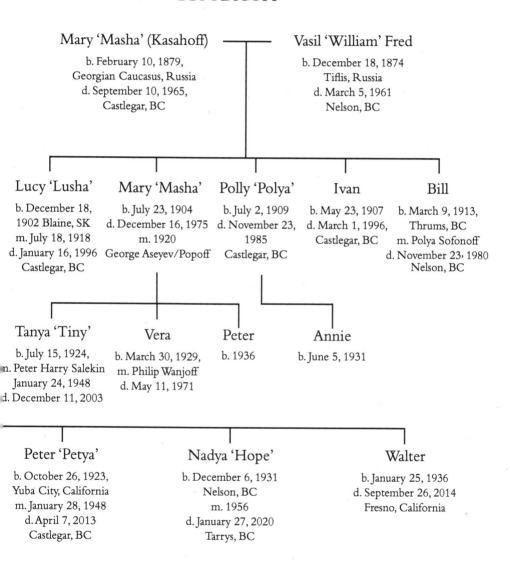

Mary 'Masha' (Kasahoff)
b. February 10, 1879,
Georgian Caucasus, Russia
d. September 10, 1965,
Castlegar, BC

Vasil 'William' Fred
b. December 18, 1874
Tiflis, Russia
d. March 5, 1961
Nelson, BC

Lucy 'Lusha'
b. December 18,
1902 Blaine, SK
m. July 18, 1918
d. January 16, 1996
Castlegar, BC

Mary 'Masha'
b. July 23, 1904
d. December 16, 1975
m. 1920
George Aseyev/Popoff

Polly 'Polya'
b. July 2, 1909
d. November 23,
1985
Castlegar, BC

Ivan
b. May 23, 1907
d. March 1, 1996,
Castlegar, BC

Bill
b. March 9, 1913,
Thrums, BC
m. Polya Sofonoff
d. November 23, 1980
Nelson, BC

Tanya 'Tiny'
b. July 15, 1924,
m. Peter Harry Salekin
January 24, 1948
d. December 11, 2003

Vera
b. March 30, 1929,
m. Philip Wanjoff
d. May 11, 1971

Peter
b. 1936

Annie
b. June 5, 1931

Peter 'Petya'
b. October 26, 1923,
Yuba City, California
m. January 28, 1948
d. April 7, 2013
Castlegar, BC

Nadya 'Hope'
b. December 6, 1931
Nelson, BC
m. 1956
d. January 27, 2020
Tarrys, BC

Walter
b. January 25, 1936
d. September 26, 2014
Fresno, California

Elizabeth Maloff 1940s

TENACITY

—⁓—

"I'm ninety-seven!" my mother, Elizabeth, chuckles. Her blue eyes sparkle and her weathered, wrinkled face lights up in a broad smile. "Caught up to Great-Grandmother Malasha! In Russia, she survived a flu that took her husband and son. Left her second husband, smuggled herself and two young children onto the ship bringing Doukhobors to Canada."

Malasha's tenacity is in Mother's blood. But winter has taken its toll. I sense the creeping whiff of decay, the smell of old houses. Still, the aromas of fresh bread and *peerahee* reassure me as I cross her doorstep. I often find her stooped over the kitchen counter, a kerchief tied around her crown of white hair, her large, efficient hands folding the *peerahee* dough over their fillings of cheese, bean, beet and sauerkraut. She shares these tasty pastries with all who visit.

Her kitchen is the family gathering place. It's a modest home, heated by a wood stove that she keeps burning fall, winter and spring. Having been brought up in a gardening family, she follows the seasonal rhythms of nature. In late winter she spreads the seed catalogues over her kitchen table and makes lists of seeds to order. In spring she starts the greenhouse, keeping the tomato and cucumber plants warm with a wood stove under the floorboards. She continues to plant a garden, intermingling flowers among the vegetables. Fragrant white alyssum—"Butterflies love them"—and sturdy asters and zinnias "for the table." Pink and purple petunias for their abundant flowers.

Her spirit gleams in the small triumphs: walks on a path skirting the mountain where she played as a child. At night when she can't sleep she gets up and checks the greenhouse, and when I chide her on this nightly vigil, she replies, "The stars were beautiful. Everything was so still. I breathed in the cool night air. I felt happy to be here, alive. And after, I got back to sleep."

Of her life she wishes to tell me the good things: skipping by her father's side to visit friends, riding bareback on an unbroken horse everyone else was afraid to ride. "Thought it would be faster to get to the other end of Thrums on horseback," she says.

She is the keeper of the family history. Her cousins ask, "Leeza, how come we didn't know that our father was born in Georgia?" Her sisters inquire, "Where did Grandparents live in Oregon and California?"

Her answer to me is "When they were young, they weren't interested in family history. But Great-Grandmother Elizaveta and I were close. I listened to her stories as I watched her bake bread and worked in the garden beside her."

There are dark stories that she keeps close to her heart. She is now the only elder who can tell me about the cabin where Grandfather served his house arrest during the Second World War—and find it. So, in early winter, before snow blocks the roads, we make a road trip to Blewett.

—m—

The road we follow is dusted white with the first snowfall, and our Subaru makes virgin tracks up the mountain slope through second-growth alder and poplar, and then the firs close in around us.

"It's all so different, Vera. It *could* be this place, but I'm not sure," Mother says.

My husband, Steve, reverses back down the narrow road and, at a log landing, jockeys the car around to point downhill.

I shift my gaze from the clearing that is being taken over by the forest and turn to Mother in the back seat. "Could it be the place where we went last time? That cabin looked like it might have been Grandfather's."

We retrace our steps and, instead of the left turn up Bird Road we had taken, we follow Fortynine Creek Road straight ahead. At an intersection of three driveways, we take the one to the right that leads to a collection of cabins and paddocks. A No Dogs sign is posted at the gate, and as we drive past it, an emu greets us. Last spring when I brought mother here, the rustic appearance of the place had intimidated us—whoever lived here wanted privacy— and we had turned around and gone home, but today we take a deep breath and follow the narrow rutted tracks.

On its side of the fence, the emu runs alongside us as we drive toward a menagerie of buildings, past a log cabin whose walls are propped up by posts, until we are met by three large dogs of mixed breed, barking loudly but wagging their tails. Mother and Steve stay in the car. I step out to walk the last ten metres to the largest building. Even before I reach the gate leading onto the front porch, a white-haired elderly woman opens the door and steps out.

"You lost?" she asks.

"Well, no." I explain to her that we are looking for the place where my grandfather lived seventy-five years ago.

"What's his name?"

"Pete Maloff."

"No one here by that name. Bought this place from Antifaeffs. Lived here fifty years."

I point to the shed we drove past. "That building over there looks like one he might have lived in. Could I take a picture of it?" I add, "He was under house arrest when he lived here."

This piques her interest, and she says, "There was a rumour that some old man lived up there on the mountain and that he was in some kind of trouble with the law. I walked all over this land when I first bought it, and there was an old cabin at the top of the next property."

"That must have been my grandfather's!" I say. "He wrote a book after he lived here."

"Well, I always felt that this was a tough place to be living all by yourself. Would have worked for house arrest, though. I'd like to read that book. Come back in the springtime. That cabin up the mountain fell in long ago, but the foundation should still be there. My shed … well … you could take a picture of it, but of course you can't go inside."

I see light bulbs shining in the windows of the shed and ask, "Does someone live there?"

But she doesn't answer and closes the door. This is the Kootenays. The illicit marijuana industry is prolific, and one does not ask to look into seemingly abandoned buildings. Still, elated, I run back to the Subaru and relay this confirmation of Mother's story about Grandfather's house arrest in Blewett. "That woman bought this property from the Antifaeffs fifty years ago."

Mother nods. "Antifaeffs built here after Father left."

"She told me she heard of an old man living up there who got in trouble with the law."

"Father was not old then," Mother answers. "He just looked old. The way they tortured him."

———*◆◆◆*———

Grandfather was forty when he lived in Blewett, but in pictures from that time, he is white-haired and thin. Mother is one of the few of her siblings who will talk about those years of growing up with her father, Pete Maloff, of his campaign for peace and resistance to registration during the Second World War—although, by the way her lips tighten when she speaks, I recognize she holds some memories back. I prod, insist, ask for more details, and for me, the family history she reveals is fascinating. For my mother, the tension of her whole body tells me these memories hold pain. "Some things I try to forget," she says.

When I asked my aunts about what happened in those years, they responded with, "Better it is all buried."

Aunt Luba's recollection of rowing across the Kootenay River to Blewett to stay with her papa and going for help to the Gorkoffs when he was so ill is intense, but she too changed the topic when I asked for details.

My aunt Nadya started to tell me, "I was walking home with my friends one day and passed a police car." She swallowed and continued as if this were happening before her eyes. "I see someone waving to me from the back seat of the car. I look closer. It's my dad." She closed her eyes tightly in an effort to make the vision go away. "I don't want to remember the past. I'm afraid of police and police cars to this day. Ask someone else."

Uncle Peter, who typed and retyped Grandfather's manuscript several times in those days before computers, has died. Did he tell his family anything of his past? Peter was in jail in the forties, but no one now remembers why. Mother said, "He went to Vancouver to look for his younger brother John, to keep him out of trouble. But Peter went to some kind of protest and ended up in jail for two years. John ran away and came home."

The youngest sibling, my uncle Walter, who was born in 1936, between his father's incarcerations, remained silent. He died like his

1920 Pete and Lusha Maloff expecting Elizabeth.

The Maloff family. Possibly just before Pete Maloff was arrested for refusing to register in the National Mobilization in 1941. Back row left: Nayda, Johnnik, Elizabeth, Peter and Luba. Front row left: Father Pete, young Walter, Mother Lusha.

father, on a trip to California. Before he passed, he did tell me about his hero, Volodya Meeralyubov, a Russian First World War veteran who came to live with the family. "It was so chaotic at home with people coming all the time to ask for help. I often went to Volodya's cabin. It was peaceful there against the mountain." Walter was fourteen when he built his cabin next to Volodya's.

What the family has rarely spoken of is the fact that Grandfather Pete Maloff was in trouble not only with the Canadian legal system, but also with some in the Doukhobor Sons of Freedom[1] community. An agitating element in that community wanted him to join them, and when he spoke out against their use of violence, the family home was hit with arson.

Only once, when the sisters were sitting around the table

---

1. A radical Doukhobor sect.

drinking tea and we cousins were playing in the background, did I hear Aunt Luba speak of the arson attempts. "I was walking home with my friends late one night, and as we got closer to our house, I saw it was on fire. I ran and screamed to wake everyone and then pulled heavy beds and couches out the door before they could burn." Luba stared at her hands in her lap and shook her head. "I don't know how I did it!"

The sisters did not notice that we stopped our game of pick-up sticks, our young ears big, our mouths wide, as we listened and watched. Mother clasped and unclasped her hands. "Before that, our woodpile was burned. That winter we heated our house with wet wood. Then Dad's trunk of books was set on fire." They looked into their teacups, sighed and were silent.

—— w ——

Through my mother's stories and the reluctant recollections of my aunts, through family photo albums and newspaper articles from the local papers of the time, I have pieced together a story of growing up in the Maloff household when my grandfather was active in the peace movement from the 1920s to the 1960s.

When I hear a verification of my mother's stories, I am delighted, and a chill goes down my spine in an "aha" moment.

Friends who live along the Kootenay River in Blewett tell me, "We met an old-timer who rowed across the Kootenay River to catch the local train."

"My aunt Luba took the train from Thrums to Beasley and then rowed across the river to Blewett," I say. "She almost drowned in that leaky rowboat everyone used!"

They nod their heads. "Come, we'll show you where they used to cross."

Some of what I am told is hard to verify and accept as true. A Doukhobor friend, Peter Sookavieff, whose father spent time in the penitentiary with my grandfather, tells me, "We visited the site of the BC Pen when it was being torn down. The friend I was with showed me the solitary confinement cells. He told me that your grandfather Pete was hung upside down by his feet in one of those cells."

Now, in 2018, in Canada, I find this hard to believe. But in 1932? What might have happened in a BC Penitentiary isolation cell?

THRUMS

—⁓—

The community of Thrums is located in a narrow valley in the Selkirk Mountains of British Columbia. It is on the sunny side of the Kootenay River; across the river the coniferous forested slope drops steeply down to the shore. On its west end Thrums is bounded by a steep bluff above the river, and on its east, by a rocky outcropping that delineates it from Tarrys, a community similar in size, geography and population. In between, the valley widens slightly where, in the past, small fruit and vegetable farms flourished.

Train tracks and a narrow road link Thrums to Nelson, thirty-three kilometres to the northeast. To the west, Highway 3A cuts through the bluff, proceeds thirteen kilometres to Castlegar and connects with Highway 22, which leads south to the smelter city of Trail. The railway track follows the river, and in my mother's time one could catch the twice-daily short-haul train to Castlegar and Trail. The long-haul train to Vancouver and Calgary also stopped every day to pick up mail and passengers.

Artifacts show that the Sinixt Indigenous People and their ancestors used this land, fishing for salmon and picking berries for ten thousand years, but those who named the locality Thrums were of English ancestry, and they developed the first farms at the end of the nineteenth century.

The Russian immigrant Doukhobor families who bought land here in 1908 were independent of the larger Christian Community of Universal Brotherhood (CCUB),[2] or Community Doukhobors, who settled in the surrounding area and were led by Peter Vasilevich Verigin—Haspodnyeey, "Lordly," Doukhobors named him. Many Independent Doukhobors,[3] including the Hoodicoff and Maloff families, respected and adhered to the suggestions of Haspodnyeey.

---

2.   The Christian Community of Universal Brotherhood was a communal organization of Doukhobors in Canada that existed to 1938.

3.   Doukhobors living independently on their own land and not in CCUB communities.

They retained the Russian language, prayers, pacifistic beliefs and agrarian lifestyle. For a generation, Russian was heard in the stores, on the school playground and in prayer, so that several sons and daughters of the English families learned to speak a kind of "Doukhoborese," a fluid combination of English and Russian.

Doukhobor leader Peter Vasilevich Verigin, 1902, on his release from Siberian exile prior to immigrating to Canada. Royal BC Museum and Archives, C-01443

Mother's grandfather William Hoodicoff and his brother Sava and sister Fenya bought land in Thrums. The families worked together to clear the fir and pine forest, develop gardens and build wooden houses, barns and the essential *banya*, or bathhouse. They had a workhorse for transportation, pulling stumps and plowing; cows for milk, from which they made butter and cheese; and chickens for eggs. What they didn't grow was available a few steps away at one of the three local stores. Together with their neighbours they built a school and a prayer hall.

Three generations of Maloff women—my grandmother Lusha, my mother, Elizabeth, and myself—grew up in Thrums. My brother and sister still live there, next door to my mother.

My earliest memory of Thrums is associated with a picture of Mother and me outside of our house. I am three years old, hands in my pockets, pockets full of pebbles collected from the clearing around our house. Mother has just hung up the laundry: my denim coveralls, her print dress, Father's long underwear and heavy pants.

She calls, "Come, Vera. Hot soup."

But I look down, searching for more stones. I hear the rushing of the creek in spring flood. My toes squish the soft sand. Water slips through my fingers grasping shiny stones from the creek. I bend, tumble, gasp. My breath is jagged, hurts. The water—cold.

Peter Vasilevich Verigin, Haspodnyeey (Lordly), was the spiritual leader of the large party of Doukhobors, (the Christian Community of Universal Brotherhood) from 1886 in Russia to 1924 in Canada, when he and several of those he was travelling with were killed in a train explosion. Royal BC Museum and Archives, C-01948

A three-year-old Vera in front of her family home in Thrums. Mother (Leeza) is on the porch.

Hands grasp, shake. I wriggle as Mother picks me up, carries me. Safe in her strong arms, I gaze up at the poplar trees silhouetted against the sun. Leaves are budding. Their resinous smell is sharp against my nose.

Mother lives in that same house in the clearing. The clothesline, the single-pane wooden windows and the three wooden steps up to the entrance are still there. The house foundation sits on wooden blocks. I remember the wind whistling through the floor and windows of that house. In winter Jack Frost left ferny patterns on the glass. I used my fingernails to scrape a hole in the frost so I could see outside.

My cousins all lived in the neighbourhood, and we roamed freely without regard for the fences except for the animal enclosures. Like my grandmother Lusha, when I turned five I went to elementary school and Sunday school nearby.

On Sundays, parents and children gathered in the basement of the community hall, where often the smell of *borsh* and *lapsha* lingered after a wedding or a funeral. After a prayer meeting, our parents took turns teaching us Christian beliefs—the Ten Commandments and Christ's declaration to love one's neighbour as oneself. They said that the spirit of God lives within each person and that human beings are all equal children of God, regardless of race, colour or creed. We learned about our Doukhobor heritage, our history of pacifism and vegetarianism.

Gathered around a table—on one side, us girls with kerchiefs tied under our chins, on the other, boys with clean faces and Sunday school clothes—we sat wide-eyed, shoulder to shoulder. Our parents, women on one side, men on the other, sat on benches behind us. One of our neighbours—Tyota (Auntie), we respectfully called her—sat at the head of the table and in her callused hand (every family grew a large garden) held up a picture of a huge bonfire. Doukhobor men were throwing guns into the flames, and women and men were gathered in prayer around them. "This is a painting of the Burning of Arms," she explained. "June 28, 1895, on the day of Saints Peter and Paul in Russia, in the Caucasus Mountains, our *pretkee*, ancestors, collected their weapons and set them on fire. They said they would not kill their fellow man and refused to serve in the czar's army. The czar sent Cossack horsemen to whip and drive our people to jail. They were exiled in chains to Siberia or to poor Tatar villages in the Caucasus. Their life was harsh. Many died."

A friend's father, Alex Markin, slowly stood and turned to us children. "Grandfather Greesha Sukherov [Soukeroff] was sent to Siberia. He was able to come to Canada after he served his term, and he lived in Thrums behind our place. He and my grandmother had a small shop where they sold sweets, fabric and lace. He showed me the scars on his back from the lashings he received."

My mother nodded her head. "Grandfather Sukherov visited us frequently. Father respected him for his stand against the Russian Cossacks and the czar. He wasn't a big man, but stocky. He must have been strong to survive."

Mother paused and then continued. "Grandfather Nikolai Maloff was imprisoned too, in a Tatar *aul*, village. Grandmother Elizaveta told me that when many men became so ill they couldn't work, the governor permitted their wives to join them and look after them. My grandparents lived with the Tatars right up to the time they immigrated to Canada."

We learned that the Russian author Lev Tolstoy and the Quaker community stepped in to help the Doukhobors. Through their efforts, Canada agreed to grant us exemption from military service and provide homestead land. Tyota continued, "In 1899, 7,500 Doukhobors sailed across the oceans on cattle ships that they cleaned and rebuilt so that people could sleep in bunks in the hold and cook on the decks." As our Sunday school group of children watched, Tyota traced the journey on a large map of the world—from the Black Sea port of Batumi, across the Mediterranean and Atlantic Oceans to Halifax, Canada, where the first ship landed in January.

Next, she displayed a photograph of our ancestors, warmly dressed in sheepskin coats and Russian felt hats, posing with the government officials who welcomed them. On a map of Canada, she showed how they continued the journey, by train to Winnipeg, Manitoba, and then to Saskatchewan, where they were given land. "We are fortunate to be living in a peaceful land here in Canada. In Russia scores of people suffered terribly and died during the wars that came later."

Many Doukhobors lived in British Columbia now, and my brother Ceral raised his hand and asked Tyota, "How did we end up in the Kootenays?"

Our Sunday school teacher told us, "Doukhobors lost their homesteads when they refused to swear an oath of allegiance to the king. They believed in having only one master, God. Furthermore, they wanted to live in villages and work the land together, but the rule was that they live and work on their plots individually. Their land in Saskatchewan had already been cultivated and their homes built, but everything reverted back to the Crown. The community borrowed money and purchased land in the Kootenays where we live now."

Now, when I tell a friend about the loss of the thousands of acres of land in Saskatchewan, he is incredulous. "That's dreadful! But you tell me this so matter-of-factly that it seems you simply accept this loss. How do you *really* feel about losing the land your grandparents worked so hard to develop?"

Then, when we were children, as we sat listening to our parents talk about our past, it seemed that loss was the price of acting on one's principles. After all, we were learning to sing a psalm that said "a person devoted to the sacred can have a hard time living in this world, enduring suffering and being called a fool, while a person with no awareness of the sacred can have an easy life—wealth, status and popular acclaim."[4]

—⁓—

As I grew up, while we worked in the garden or cooked together, Mother told me more of the family story.

My great-grandparents Nikolai and Elizaveta Maloff, their son Nick, Nikolai's mother, Malasha Androsoff, and her two young children, Vanya and Aksinya, all emigrated together. But Malasha and her children were stowaways on the ship because her second husband, who did not participate in the Burning of Arms, had refused to let her leave Russia. Mother said, "He hired police, and they searched the ship top to bottom and almost, *almost* found them, but Malasha and her children hid in the coal bins for three days until the steamer was well out to sea. They could hear the tramp of feet and the shifting of boxes and sacks as the police hunted for them. She's not on any register because she took the place of a woman who had died just before the ship's voyage."

I grew up in a house heated with coal and we had a coal shed in the backyard. The coal chunks were hard, dirty and dusty, and I could not imagine hiding there. Crossing the oceans in the month of January on what had been a cattle ship, and living and sleeping in the dark hold—would it smell like our barn did? Did the ocean waves toss the boat around and crash on the deck?

My grandfather Pete Maloff was born January 18, 1900, in Saskatchewan. "In a barn, because the house was crowded," Mother said. Later I read that during the Doukhobors' first winter in Canada, many families lived in dugouts until they were able to build log shelters. I shuddered at the thought of surviving the winter in a dugout. How did they keep warm and clean?

At first the Maloff family lived in a community with other Doukhobors, but Nikolai wanted his children educated in the public schools, and when Nick and Pete were of age, he sent them to the local school. The CCUB Doukhobors believed that government indoctrination was part of the school system. Nikolai was shunned by many in the community for sending his children to the English

---

4. Translated from Russian by Natasha Jmieff.

school and was asked to leave. He felt he had no other choice than to take the oath of allegiance to procure a homestead, but all his life he felt guilty for betraying his principles. He became an Independent Doukhobor with land of his own, but shortly after, Nikolai moved his family to Oregon with a group of Doukhobors who started a co-operative farm in the Willamette Valley. Then, because of a poor purchase agreement and mismanagement, the land they bought was repossessed by the former owner. My great-grandparents, together with Grandfather Pete, moved farther south to California. When the United States entered the First World War, Nikolai and Elizaveta sold their farm there and returned with their family to Canada, where their sons had conscientious-objector status.

Mother smiled and said, "While their parents were busy wrapping up their affairs in California, Dad and Uncle Nick came to British Columbia. At first, they went to Grand Forks, then to the Kootenays, where they met their future wives. Imagine how young they were! Father was eighteen when he met Mother, and she was only sixteen years old! Mother said that right away she knew she would marry only him. They wed in 1918, and I was born in 1920 at home in Thrums."

My maternal great-grandmother Masha Kasahova and great-grandfather William Hoodicoff married in Saskatchewan and established a farm there. Four of their children were born on the farm, but they refused to take the oath of allegiance and as a result lost their land. The family moved to British Columbia at the same time the Community Doukhobors did. Deciding to live independently, the Hoodicoff family purchased land in Thrums. Their children, including Grandmother Lusha, attended government school right next to where we lived in Thrums.

That was the short version of our family saga. I was to eventually learn much more.

—⁓—

I attended school in the next-door community of Tarrys, where the majority of students were of Doukhobor ancestry. I did not know about our parents' struggle to make sure their children wouldn't be indoctrinated with respect to the military, that Doukhobor students would be excused from participation in Remembrance Day ceremonies. We were permitted to stand outside the classroom, in the hallway, when the national anthem was sung or when teachers read the Bible. Still, I heard that speaking Russian in school was punished with the strap, though some classmates continued to speak Russian while hiding in the washrooms.

In the early 1960s I noticed the absence of two grade-five classmates, twins, who sat in the row behind me. I heard whispers that they had been taken with other children from neighbouring villages to a reform dormitory in New Denver. Why? What had they done? We heard that perhaps it was because their parents refused to send them to school. It seemed to me that those boys had been in my classroom just days before.

Then there was a protest trek by the Sons of Freedom sect. We watched from the roadside as a parade of cars and trucks drove past our house and on to the village of Agassiz, far to the west, where many of their brethren were imprisoned. It was confusing. There were troubled voices, but I don't remember an adult explaining to us children what was truly happening. All I knew was that I was glad to live at home with my extended family nearby, that I liked school, and as I grew older, I cringed when all Doukhobors were blamed for burnings and bombings in the Kootenays. Weren't we a peaceful sect?

———

Today as I visit Mother we share memories and look at pictures together. It is spring and again the creek is running high. Yesterday Mother slipped on the bridge over the creek and fell. Luckily her granddaughter saw her and my sister helped her out of the cold spring runoff. Her mishap reminded me of how, decades earlier, she pulled me out of that same creek, and she then tells me of the time she almost died in Waldie's pond by the Columbia River. I want to hear all her stories. So she begins.

LEEZA: I was born to a Doukhobor family in 1920 on a small market-garden farm in Thrums. My grandmothers, Masha Hoodicoff and Elizaveta Maloff, were the midwives, and my father, just turned twenty, assisted them. My *babushkee* inspected me, declared that I was a healthy baby girl, swaddled me in soft homespun linen and gave me to my eighteen-year-old mother to nurse. I was the first grandchild born in the Hoodicoff family and the second in the

The Hoodicoff family at their home in Thrums, possibly 1913. Standing: Mother Masha, daughters Mary, Polly, Lusha; in front: Father William, sons Bill and Ivan.

Maloff family; my cousin, Nina, had been born two weeks earlier. All the aunts and uncles came to congratulate my parents, Lusha and Pete Maloff, to peer at me in my little wooden rocking cradle, gently pull my ears and whisper a prayer for me to grow healthy and strong. The prayers must have worked, for here I am, Elizabeth Maloff—though most people call me Leeza—living in a house next door to where I was born.

My Hoodicoff family lived just across the road from our house, and in the mid-1920s my Maloff grandparents moved to a small cabin next to us. My grandmothers were happy to snuggle me and rock me to sleep, and my mother's sisters, to entertain me. As I learned to walk I happily wandered between all their homesteads, across the dirt road and railway tracks, which had little traffic then. My grandparents would invite me in, sit me on a bench, give me an apple and ask me to sing for them. I learned at a young age to entertain them and their visitors with Doukhobor songs Mama had taught me.

I was two when I almost died. Papa worked at Waldie's Sawmill in Castlegar, and most of the year he biked to work early in the

Lusha with three-year-old Elizabeth in California.

morning and back in the evening. In winter, when the road was nearly impassable, Mama, Papa and I lived in the workers' cabins next to the sawmill. Mama had bundled me up in layers of wool—wool stockings, skirt, jacket and toque—and sat me on a sled to watch as they skated on the frozen pond beside the sawmill. At the edge of the river the ice was still thin, although their skates slid quickly over this crust. I sat for a while, watching Papa, Mama and their friends gliding, then wiggled out of my cocoon and tried to slide on the smooth ice with my rubbered feet. It was fun: a few feet toward Mama, wobbling back a little toward my sled. Then I was in the black water.

The next thing I remember was coughing, shivering and Mama sobbing as she stripped off my heavy wet clothes and started rubbing my chest, arms and legs with her hands. "Leeza, dear, *darahaya*, *doch*, open your eyes! Look at me, Leeza!"

1923. Elizabeth with her baby brother Peter.

Papa wrapped me in his rough jacket and I felt his heart pounding as he ran with me toward our cabin. After that fright, Mama worried any time I left her sight, and in spring we were happy to move back to Thrums, to our large family, our garden and our animals, where Mother could relax her vigilance again.

In Thrums, we knew everyone. There were the English-speaking *anhlyeekee*: the Johnsons, who owned the general store and post office; the Bakers, who ran a confectionery across from our house—four of those little teddy bear candies I craved were a penny; the Chalmers, who raised chickens and sold eggs; our neighbours, the Pratts, who had beef cattle and butchered meat; and the McLeods, whom I remember for the beautiful singing voices of their daughters. Everyone else was Doukhobor and spoke Russian.

When I was three and a half, in October 1923, my brother Peter was born and Mama was busy with him, so Papa often took me wherever he went, walking the railway tracks as everyone did, since the dirt road was dusty in the summer and muddy in the spring and fall. I hung on to Papa's rough, callused hand, skipped railway ties and tried to keep up with his long strides. Orchards of apples, pears and plums, fields of strawberries and raspberry and black current bushes bordered the track, all destined for the jam factory in Brilliant. In spring the flowers gave off a heady, promising scent of the fruit to come. The road and railway allowances were used for grazing cattle, and as we walked along we could hear the cattle bells clang. Sometimes when we walked by the Drazdoffs',

Mr. Drazdoff would call, "Tyunkya, Hapka, where are you?" and if we hadn't known they were his cows, we'd have thought he was calling his daughters.

As we passed Johnson's store, Charlie Johnson or his son, Norman, would be loading the horse-and-wagon teams parked outside the storeroom with hundred-pound sacks of bran, oats or wheat, or barrels of kerosene for lanterns. Occasionally, noisy Chevy pickup trucks chugged past, but few people in Thrums besides the Johnsons owned a vehicle. Most walked, and Papa would stop and talk to friends and acquaintances from the neighbouring villages: Brilliant, Glade, Shoreacres and Castlegar.

It was a treat when, on a Saturday, Papa and I set out to Pepin's place on the riverbank. There, Fyodor Pepin gave those assembled a haircut. I listened to the hum of men's voices and watched Fyodor's scissors snip quickly around the ears and collars of Father's friends so that many different colours of hair covered the wooden floor. Then it was my turn: I would sit up straight and quiet on top of the apple box that Fyodor put on the chair. He would put a towel around my shoulders and take extra care to shape my thick blond hair in a short bob around my face.

"*Krasyeewa*, beautiful. Good girl for sitting so still," Fyodor said as he whisked the towel off. I was so proud to have a haircut from a barber, like my handsome papa.

Years later, when Norman Johnson came to visit my mother and me—he knew Mother from school days—we'd sit on the swing under the apple tree and talk. He told me about the beach just below Pepin's.

"It was a white sandy beach like no other in Thrums," he said. "The sand went so far out into the river, and in the summer everyone, especially we teenagers, swam there. But we were not unsupervised. As soon as elderly Mrs. Saliken, who lived next door, saw us coming, she'd head out to the beach too. She'd sit on a patch of grass, wave her cane in the air and assign swimming spots. 'Boys to the left and girls to the right.' The reason was that few of us had bathing suits. Nobody told her to be the boss of the beach, but there she sat all day, her long skirts tucked up around her knees and stockings rolled down around her shoes, until we all left." Norman paused, a faraway look in his eye. "That beach got flooded when the Brilliant dam was built. A shame. Those were the days." Norman shook his head and continued. "I hung around with all the teenage boys, Doukhobor and *anhlyeekee*." He laughed at my surprised look when he used our slang word for English-speaking people. "It was in style to carve whistles. We all had pocket knives we sharpened using our dads' whetstones. We'd cut a branch of a willow tree and hollow a short piece for the whistle. Well, one of us usually cut our finger. Blood running everywhere!"

"What did you do?" I asked Norman.

"We knew where to go. Polya Kinyakina, a *lyeekarka*, a healer, lived toward the mountain behind our store, and we ran through the fields to her house. We'd knock, and as soon as she opened the door and saw the bloody fingers, she'd tell us, 'Quickly, quickly, pee on those cuts.'" Norman laughed uproariously and slapped his knee. "Imagine," he said, "what the doctors would say about that now. But no one got any infections."

Norman loved talking about those days in Thrums when he was a teenager and in love with a Doukhobor girl, Helen Boolinoff. Helen drowned in the Kootenay River one day in early May when there was a flash flood. The clay bank she was standing on collapsed and she was carried away by the raging water, down to where the Kootenay River joins the Columbia. Norman was devastated. Eventually, though, he did marry Kathy, one of his own, a girl who worked and lived in a small store at the end of Thrums. He said they had a good relationship and trusted each other. He told us how she met my uncle George Aseyev.

"Kathy got around Thrums by cycling, but her bicycle was so dilapidated and squeaky that one could hear her coming from a long distance. One day, as she was cycling home, she saw a neighbour she recognized as George Aseyev standing in the middle of the road. Unusually for George, as he was always seen puttering around in his shed, he was simply standing there. Kathy slowly approached George, her wheel wobbling and squeaking more than ever. George waved her down.

"'Stop,' he barked. 'Get off!' He flipped the bike over, took the oil can he was holding and oiled the gears until all the squeaks were gone. Finally satisfied, and rubbing his greasy hands on his coveralls, he told her, 'Give it a try.' Kathy got on and George gave her a push.

Brilliant, BC, in October 1924. The funeral procession for Peter V. Verigin, after he was killed in a train explosion. Royal BC Museum and Archives, C-01670

'Away you go.' Kathy told me that bike never squeaked again." Norman chuckled. "I guess George got tired of listening to that racket, but he sure scared Kathy at first. She thought he was angry at her."

Norman visited several times, and when we met on the street in Nelson, he always stopped and talked to me—in Doukhobor Russian of all things, as he kept our language.

The most tragic thing happened when I was four. I didn't know the date at the time but it is etched in Doukhobor history: October 29, 1924. Our household was in an uproar, Mama sitting crying, Papa pacing and questioning, "How could this happen? Why? Who?" I couldn't understand what was happening and rushed across the road to Babushka Hoodicoff's. But I was sobbing so hard and couldn't say a word; no one there could figure out why I was crying. "Leeza, what happened? Are you hurt? Did someone die?" It was only when Babushka crossed the road to our place that she realized the awful truth. Someone had indeed died: the Doukhobor leader,

Peter V. Verigin, and eight people with him were killed in a train explosion.

After this tragedy, a pall fell over our family and our community. Everywhere we went there were hushed voices, shaken heads, disbelief and sadness. The evidence of the murders—the torn clothing, the shattered bodies—was hard to absorb. Papa must have gone to the funeral in Brilliant, where there were thousands of people, but I mostly remember the feelings of despair.

—⁓—

Now I think about my mother's memories in the context of these historic events. The death of the Doukhobor leader left the community in turmoil and without direction in a time of trouble. Directors of the CCUB searched for a new leader, a process that took them back to Russia to meet with Haspodnyeey's son, Peter P. Verigin. With the leadership in disarray, and Lusha having health problems, Pete Maloff took his young family back to California, where he had lived previously and knew many in the Russian community.

CALIFORNIA INSPIRATIONS

—⁓—

When I ask my mother about their trips to California in the 1920s, she tells me of things a child remembers.

From Nelson they travelled on the SS *Moyie* sternwheeler to the end of Kootenay Lake and then took a train to Spokane. There, she watched her papa out of a hotel room window as he went across the street to buy a Chevrolet that had a wooden steering wheel, a rumble seat in the back and folding windows that buckled down. That Chevy became their home as they toured Oregon and California. Molokan friends the Dobrinins in Oregon and Doukhobors the Verishagins in California greeted them with hugs, meals and soft beds.

They moved on to Los Angeles, where they lived in the Russian Jewish district. My mother tells me, "Mama got treatments for her bad headaches; Papa worked. I remember sitting on our doorstep and watching children roller skating down the sidewalks. How I wanted

Pete Maloff (on left) in Oregon visiting friends.

to join them, but Mother said we didn't have money to spend on extras. One of our outings was a walk and a picnic on the beautiful white-sand beaches just outside the city."

Grandfather Pete Maloff and his friends decided to rent a farm near Yuba City, where they harvested grapes, pomegranates, peaches, plums and nuts. Mother says, "Papa and Mama were busy on the farm, but my life there was wonderful. I always had friends to keep me company, and Petya, my brother Peter, was born there in California."

I learned of Grandfather's early life in California by reading his book, *Doukhobors, Their History, Life and Struggle*, printed in Russian. Thankful for my early years in after-school and weekend Russian classes, I slowly read, and as I became more fluent, I was enchanted by the language. Later, rummaging through his papers, I discovered the loose pages of his manuscript translated into English; his son had laboriously typed several copies. One of these copies I located in the local Selkirk College library, on the top shelf of Special Collections. Grandfather Pete had hoped to publish this manuscript in his lifetime. It was not to be.

In my eyes, this find—the exploits and thoughts of my grand-father—was a treasure.

As I read his manuscript, I learned that he and his family lived in Oregon and California during several different periods in their lives. First it was in 1913 that my great-grandfather, Pradedushka Nikolai Maloff, and his family migrated from Saskatchewan to a co-operative farm close to Peoria, Oregon. There, they joined other Doukhobor families setting up an agrarian Christian democratic community they called the Colony of Freedom. In a reaction against the authoritarian way in which Peter V. Verigin led the Christian Community of Universal Brotherhood (CCUB), they decided that everyone was to have a voice. For four years they successfully cultivated the farm and observed Doukhobor practices of prayer. Then, dissolution: their one thousand acres had forty owners, and the documents were drawn up so that if one defaulted on his payment, all lost the land. After a lengthy trial, the verdict: everyone was to vacate. Nikolai's family purchased a farm farther south, near Orland, California, in the northern Sacramento Valley. There, almonds, walnuts, persimmons, pomegranates and citrus fruits flourished. For vegetarians like my great-grandfather and his family, this was Eden.

Many CCUB Doukhobor families of the time did not send their children to school, but in Oregon Nikolai's sons, Nick and Pete, completed high school. Subsequently Pete worked as a surveyor's helper, briefly trained to be a telegraph operator and then, through his father, secured an apprenticeship with a Russian journal, *Veleek-iy Okean* (*Great Ocean*) in San Francisco.

He started in the mailroom as an errand boy. The editor, Anton Petrovich Sherbak, took an interest in this Doukhobor lad who had joined the company. Sherbak introduced Pete to other Russian expatriates, socialists and intelligentsia and encouraged him to read widely and to revisit his Doukhobor roots. Pete boarded with a Molokan family, establishing lifelong connections and friendships among this pacifist religious sect that originated in the same area in Russia as the Doukhobors.

I admire the frankness of my *dedushka* Pete's writing. In 1914 America was in a recession, and after nine months of working for little money at the journal, he was convinced by a couple of young Russian immigrants that he could make better money farther south in Los Angeles. Pete joined these adventurers, contributing his meagre cash to help tide them over until they got to the "promised land." As many hobos did at that time, they attempted to ride the rails, catching trains in the middle of the night and hiding in boxcars. Their escapade landed them in a cold cell. His newfound friends deserted him, and Pete was left scavenging for food and sleeping in barns. He learned about the perversions of man, as he called it, when a "sodomite" attempted to rape him.

Steinbeck's *The Grapes of Wrath* describes the Great Depression of the 1930s; Pete's attempts to find work were as hopeless in 1915. I found it hard to believe that Pete's family allowed him such freedom, but perhaps at the beginning of the twentieth century, other fifteen-year-olds wandered throughout America and survived by their wits.

Finally, his pride shattered, Pete requested help from his brother, Nick, who sent him fifteen dollars with which he returned to San Francisco. He found a job in a Spanish restaurant delivering enchiladas and tamales to other restaurants and centres of amusement, some for wealthy families and some for the San Francisco underground scene.

Pete eventually summoned the courage to approach and apologize to Anton Sherbak, whom he had left without word. Sherbak chastised him. He had taken in this Doukhobor teenager and had been like a father to him, clothed him, gave him spending money and even took him to the world's fair that was in San Francisco at the time. Sherbak told Pete that the life he had enjoyed at the printers was over and Pete would not be able to resume work at his militant paper. Sherbak was returning to Russia, where he would dedicate the rest of his life to supporting the plight of the common people. Throughout his life, Pete felt he had missed a great opportunity, and he yearned to follow his mentor to Russia. Years later, he learned that Sherbak had died amid widespread starvation in Stalinist Russia in the 1920s.

The United States entered the First World War in 1917, and my great-grandfather Nikolai worried about compulsory military service for his sons. Pete had been arrested during a roundup of men the police suspected of supporting migrant farm workers who were striking for better wages. The sheriff threatened to register him in the army, refusing to believe this tall youth was not yet of age. He was freed only when the sheriff's daughter understood that he was truly underage and requested he be released. Pete had burst into tears and blubbered, "Do what you like with me, even kill me, but I will never join the army."

The family returned to Canada, where an agreement with the government qualified Doukhobors as conscientious objectors. There, Pete met and married Lusha Hoodicoff, an attractive, lively daughter of an Independent Doukhobor family in Thrums. California had also captured his heart. Throughout his lifetime, he travelled back to California to reconnect with friends and correspondents who often had innovative—radical, for the time—ideas, and for solace in healing his body and spirit.

In 1923 Pete returned to California with Lusha and young Leeza. In his book, Grandfather wrote that his previous correspondents welcomed his family hospitably. In their discussions, he became a kind of unofficial missionary in explaining Doukhobor life concepts. Furthermore, the vibrant California culture of the 1920s provided opportunities for him to meet philosophers, writers, peace activists, spiritual leaders and dedicated vegetarians.

1923 Elizabeth (left) with her childhood friend Tanya Wlasoff (right) in Yuba City, California, on the cooperative farm their parents worked jointly. They were to meet again at the BC Girls Industrial School in Vancouver where they were held for a year in 1932–33.

While Lusha received treatments from Dr. Phillip Lowell, who specialized in fasting cures, Pete worked odd jobs and in his free time immersed himself in the libraries and cultural events Los Angeles offered. This was his higher education: lectures in the Vegetarian Dining Room on nutrition and health, free forums on international subjects and labour problems on Saturdays, lectures at the agnostic centre on Sundays and visits with theosophists and Hindu mystics. He attended the Russian Cultural Club and renewed his friendship with the Molokan brotherhood. He said of the Molokans that they treated his Doukhobor family as kin, that their inner warmth of heart was unequalled. To be their guest was the greatest of privileges.

J. William Lloyd, poet, writer, scientist and anarchist, and his friend Dr. Leroy Henry, a publisher of a satirical magazine, had moved in 1922 to a ranch near Los Angeles that they called Freedom Hill. Pete was introduced to them through a correspondent, A. Wagner, who had been part of the Beilhart community that sought "the essence of spiritual existence."[5] They met in Lloyd's modest home—a kitchen, bedroom and study with a huge library, a collection of music and a fireplace that Lloyd built himself. Pete transcribed a lively discussion he had with Lloyd and Henry.

Lloyd asked about Doukhobor relations between men and women and was surprised when Pete answered that marriage was a Doukhobor custom, though some in the Sons of Freedom sect had tried a "free love" community and it ended in disputes and unhappiness.

Dr. Henry's viewpoint was that marriage itself caused suffering and confusion.

Lloyd's philosophical response was "Woman, as mother of the race, is the center of life, but man has enslaved and exploited her. The sex problem is the most important social problem. Its solution would disentangle if not all, at least many human complications."

Both agreed, "If one loves another, they can live together. If not, nothing should force them to continue that way of life."[6]

I found it amusing: Pete thought it was tiresome that these men, both in their late sixties and bachelors for the last twenty years, were so consumed with the question of male and female rela-

---

5. Maloff, *Doukhobors*, pt. 2, chap. 9.
6. Maloff, *Doukhobors*, pt. 2, chap. 9.

tionships that their whole discussion that day focused on this topic.

—⁓⁓—

Peace activism in California in the 1920s was a hazardous activity that nevertheless was finding fertile ground. Among the numerous people Pete visited, Mr. Greenfield and Fanny Bixby Spencer stand out. Pete was welcomed as a fellow "peacenik" by Mr. Greenfield, a Protestant missionary in Santa Barbara. Pete wrote,

> He lived almost in the center of the town and his huge house and garden occupied a whole block. He had trees, which he had collected all over the world. We met our host in his garden without shirt and barefoot. Sechsauer (a vegetarian correspondent from Santa Barbara) introduced us: Doukhobors from Canada. Greenfield rushed to us, as if we were coming from another world and said, "I love the Doukhobors. Their heroism is unsurpassed." Mr. Greenfield surprised us and made a great impression. His house was several stories high, all sparkling with silver and marble, but he, as we heard from his own lips, had the Doukhobor movement on his mind.[7]

Greenfield had written a small book against war, *Ethics of Killing*; however, on attempting to promote it, he was heavily fined and imprisoned and had his right to vote taken away. The US government burned several hundred copies; still, Greenfield was able to conceal two books, one of which he gave Pete in honour of Doukhobor pacifism.

Pete had exchanged letters with Fanny Bixby Spencer, and during this trip they met at her orphanage in Costa Mesa. Their discussion that afternoon ranged from the cause of justice for women and the education of children to the equality of all races, Doukhobor philosophy, socialism and anti-militarism. At the end of the afternoon, she gifted Pete her book *The Repudiation of War*. Researching on the internet, I found out Spencer, one of California's richest women, was under government surveillance for standing up

---

7. Maloff, *Doukhobors*, pt. 2, chap. 9.

for peace. Under the influence of her abolitionist grandfather, she became a social and political activist, supporting women's suffrage and child labour issues. This strong, principled woman left a deep impression on Pete.

When I mention this visit to my daughter, she asks, "Did Grandmother meet Mrs. Spencer? Was she in the conversations? It doesn't impress me otherwise." I hope that Pete included Lusha in these discussions. Mother does not remember, and Grandfather does not mention it in his book.

Pete attended the international centre for Self-Realization Fellowship that Paramahansa Yogananda had established in Los Angeles to bring meditation to the West. Jiddu Krishnamurti also lived in Los Angeles in 1925. At this time Krishnamurti was being groomed by the theosophist Annie Besant to be the new World Teacher, a messiah. Annie Besant had been for a time the president of the Indian National Congress party. This connection served Pete well. Thirty-five years later, he was able to travel to India, where he met with members of the Congress party and Prime Minister Indira Ghandi. With them he shared his love of, and correspondence with, Mahatma Ghandi.

Pete met Ilya Lvovich Tolstoy, with whom he had corresponded for several years, after a lecture on Russian art at the Los Angeles city library. Pete said that the son was the "image of his great father." Comparing internet pictures of Lev Nikolayevich Tolstoy and his son Ilya, with their bushy beards, broad noses and deep-set eyes, I see the close resemblance. Ilya had moved to Hollywood in 1926 to help stage his father's novel *Resurrection*.

When they met, Ilya patted Pete on the hand and gave a strict order: "Tomorrow with whole family and without fail, come to see us!" On Sunday morning Ilya was waiting for them in front of a Spanish-style mansion and greeted them warmly. They spoke of Lev Tolstoy's support of the Doukhobors. "For my father, Doukhobors were a symbol of spiritual wealth. ... They were blessed with the natural ability not only to see the truth, but to live according to the truth."[8] Ilya and Pete developed a close friendship, and he vowed to come and stay with the Doukhobors in Canada. Sadly, he

---

8. Maloff, *Doukhobors*, pt. 2, chap. 9.

1927 California. This photo was taken just before Pete, Lusha, young Peter and Elizabeth leave California for British Columbia. Grandfather Maloff stands tall beside his wife. It is a rare photo of Babushka Lusha without a *platok* covering her hair.

died a few years later without this journey having taken place.

My mother was six years old on this visit with Ilya. "Tolstoy's wife looked like a princess," she said. "She was dressed in a beautiful rose-coloured velvet gown and wore sparkling jewels on her fingers and around her neck."

Mother remembers the family stopping to visit an acquaintance in the San Quentin prison who had been incarcerated for some provocation against an insurance company. Of that visit Pete wrote, "I was profoundly shaken by what I saw in this walled world and as I was leaving the prison was overcome with deep foreboding."[9]

———

Ninety years after meeting Peter Cassidy, the mention of his name lights up my mother's eyes and brings a wide smile to her face. The Maloffs met Peter Cassidy at a Sunday forum in a local park in Los Angeles where he strummed his guitar and spoke out against war. Cassidy was a forerunner of the hippie movement in the truest sense of the word. In his fifties at the time, he was long-haired and barefoot, ate only nuts and fruit that were being discarded from markets and lived in a small tent. "Money is evil," he said. Despite this man's peculiar appearance, Pete valued him as a child of nature who seemed to be imbued with an incomparable love for humanity and took pleasure in simple things. Pete attended lectures at an agnostic society Sunday evenings with Cassidy. Cassidy's response to the learned scientists and philosophers who lectured there was "All your

---

9. Maloff, *Doukhobors*, pt. 2, chap. 9.

knowledge is worthless. Leave the cities and go out to till the soil." Pete always maintained that his work as a market gardener was an honourable way to make a living.

Though the Maloffs were invited to join several spiritual communities in California, Cassidy agreed with their idea to return to British Columbia to support the Doukhobor movement. At the end of 1927, when they were ready to do so, Cassidy begged to join them. Years later, Pete would write, "His pleadings still burn my heart. I am sincerely sorry that we did not take him along. Each time I remember him, I feel guilty that I did not care enough for the purity and sincerity of his soul. Two years after our departure he died in an old men's home."[10]

Pete and Lusha left California in 1927, inspired and energized to work for peace. They did not yet know that the consequence of speaking out was to be incarceration, sometimes for years at a time. The time of prisons and of children taken from their home was to come.

---

10.   Maloff, *Doukhobors*, pt. 2, chap. 9.

NIKOLAI AND ELIZAVETA

I know my great-grandfather Nikolai Maloff through pictures, Mother's stories and his woodcarving. I hold a spoon carved by my *pradedushka* that is over eighty years old. It has a chipped edge, a faint crack along the bowl, and the finish is worn thin where the spoon rested. I stroke its soft patina. It is a well-used piece, for mixing and for eating *borsh* and *plow*. I imagine Nikolai grasping the raw cherry wood, turning it, deciding to create this spoon.

Prababushka Elizaveta was the midwife who delivered my mother. Lusha and Pete gave their first-born her name, Elizabeth. Grandmother and granddaughter stayed close; they shared many stories. Mother tells me, "Babushka was two years older than her husband but she was youthful, and everyone told Nikolai, 'What a young wife you have!'" They were born, grew up and married in a part of Georgia that is now ceded to the country of Turkey. They lost a daughter when she was two years of age. Then their son Nick was born. It was during the time when Doukhobor men were laying down their weapons and refusing to serve in the Russian army. The repercussions were harsh. Nikolai, along with others, was indentured to work in Tatar villages that could barely provide for their own needs. Elizaveta and young Nick sheltered with relatives, moving from house to house. When many of the men began to die from disease and starvation, the Russian government allowed the wives to join their husbands in exile.

Elizaveta and Nick reunited with Nikolai in a Tatar village. She learned to sing some of the Tatar songs and a treatment for thick lustrous hair—mare's urine. The Tatars loved young Nick's light brown hair, his fair Russian features and lively attitude. They wanted to adopt him and told the parents that he would become a *hlawniy*, an important man, in their village. Elizaveta was terrified they would steal him, not an uncommon practice at that time. As a three-year-old, Nick had no idea of the danger and dashed about

Great-grandfather Nikolai Maloff was well known for his skill in carving utensils—ladles, forks, knives, spoons—that he sold.

the village playing and chasing dogs. Elizaveta constantly kept an eye on him and even slept holding on to him.

In 1898 the czarist government gave Doukhobors permission to migrate. Released from indentured servitude, Nikolai and Elizaveta joined the Doukhobor migration to Canada, with four-year-old Nick safely in their arms. They settled in Saskatchewan, close to the village of Buchanan. After this exodus from the land of their birth, no place held them long, and they moved to Oregon, California and then British Columbia.

Nikolai built rock foundations, a skill he mastered in the Tatar villages. He sang as he worked, a favourite hymn, "Slava Slava Tebe Hospadyee":

> The heaven Thou hast created,
> The earth for habitation,
> Glory, glory to Thee our Lord!
> The living earth rejoices,
> The heavens sing praises to Thee.
> *Slava Slava Tebe Hospadyee.*
>
> (translated by Eli Popoff)

He loved to be outside and from spring to fall slept in the open air. When Babushka Lusha needed someone to watch over the children, she asked him.

I have not in person seen Elizaveta's plaited rag rugs that are displayed in the photograph. They were woven from old clothes she cut into narrow strips, braided and sewed together to make a colourful splash on the wood floor. The colours reminded one of what they had worn—Lusha's yellow apron, Pete's sturdy grey work pants, the bright blue strand of a loved dress, the orange and green patterned curtain that used to hang in the bedroom. Nor are there pictures of the hats Elizaveta stitched from leftover scraps of fabric. She stiffened the wide-brimmed hats with wire and added a ribbon and trim in colours that matched.

Elizaveta planted flowers—pink Livingstone daisies, red California poppies, tall blue phlox—and herbs such as chives, mint and camomile. She left gardens behind her whenever they moved. But there were no flowers like the ones Elizaveta remembered from the

Nikolai and Elizaveta Maloff in front of their crafts in 1947. They were preparing to leave for Vancouver Island where they joined a Doukhobor community in Hilliers.

high alpine meadows of Georgia. She was the shepherd of the family, wandering the hills of the Caucasus, coming home in the evening to find a space beside the *pech* for her to warm, to eat and to sleep. She was raised in the Barisoff household and took their name even though her father was a Lazuneen Rilcoff, she was told. Still, the Barisoffs treated her well even after her mother died young. Those were good years.

I want to remember the sound of Elizaveta's voice: the backbone in it when she told the Tatars of that Georgian village, "You may not have our son!" I imagine it loving but determined when, in the Saskatchewan village, she told the man who loved her and whom she loved too, "It's only a dream that we could run away, start a new life together. Think of how we'd hurt our children, our spouses." Did she rail and shout against Nikolai's religious ideas? Ultimately was her voice accepting when his dominated? She yielded when he donated money from the sale of their land in California to the Doukhobor Christian Community of Universal Brotherhood, when they moved to build a community on Vancouver Island even though they were elderly and Nikolai was not as strong as he once was. Nikolai died in the new community of Hilliers, and Elizaveta returned to Thrums.

Did Elizaveta feel she had a choice, or did she believe a woman ultimately needed to support her husband? It led her to a life of poverty and without a place of her own at the end of her life. In summer she slept in a tent, in winter on family couches, and then she moved in with her daughter Tanya in Mission, where she knew no one.

Prababushka, you matter. I want to tell her: I have your blood running in my veins.

This is Mother's story about Nikolai and Elizaveta Maloff, her grandparents, when they lived next door to them in Thrums.

LEEZA: We returned from California to Thrums in 1927. Uncle Nick, his wife, Tyota Hannah, and cousins Nina, Helen and Olga had lived in our house while theirs was being built in Castlegar, and they moved to their farm there. Dedushka Nikolai and Babushka

Elizaveta at Nikolai's gravesite in Hilliers, BC.

Elizaveta had lost their home in Shoreacres after Haspodnyeey died, and they moved into a cabin beside our house.

In spring, our big, burly *dedushka*, who built the rock foundation for our house, decided to make his home in a tree.

"Nikolasha, it's still cold," Babushka Elizaveta discouraged him. "*Nyet*, I'll just cover up more."

He built a platform in a large poplar tree. The branches and green leaves made the walls, a canvas tarp, the roof. Otherwise it was open to the wind, sun, moon and stars. He brought up a warm wool-filled mattress and quilt.

As soon as Dedushka Nikolai let us, my brother Petya and I raced up the stick ladder to his eagle's nest. We were as high up as the birds! We could see everything: the *sennyeek* waiting for the hay crop; the shed for our Jersey cow Tyunya, the goat and our workhorse Dan; our house that was being added on to because the twins were born; and the gardens. We could join Dedushka, sleep and watch the stars with him! We'd pull our blankets up there too! But Mama pointed out that the platform was just big enough for Dedushka.

Dedushka slept in that tree until fall. He'd wake with the birds, pray and start work— cutting firewood, hoeing in the garden or carving his wooden ladles, spoons and knives— singing as he worked.

We loved visiting Babushka Elizaveta. We were sure to get a slice of her freshly baked bread or the sticky fruit leather she made from the plentiful apples, pears and plums, and while talking to us she gently rubbed our backs and shoulders. Babushka was a buxom woman, with hips and a bosom

The Maloff family back in British Columbia where Pete Maloff became attracted by the spirituality of the Sons of Freedom community.

as generous as her spirit. In the summer we'd find her in the garden wearing a beautiful, wide-brimmed, decorated cloth hat she had learned to fashion in Georgia. She usually went along with Dedushka's ideas, moving with him several times in their lives, though she considered some of his ideas extreme.

Mama sewed my clothes, but when it was time for a new dress or a *platok* to cover my head for prayer meetings, it was Babushka Elizaveta who took me to Abrosimoff's dry goods store next to the barber Fyodor Pepin. Abrosimoff's store stocked bolts of cotton, satin, rayon, wool and brocade. Babushka knew that mother liked yellows and browns in fabrics that were durable. I stroked the shiny blue taffeta and tried to distract her. "Babushka, isn't this beautiful!" Instead she chose serviceable cotton I had to be satisfied with. While I wandered between aisles of china dishes, cutlery, pots and pans, she purchased embroidery thread and a flower pattern to trace onto a light rayon or a fine woollen material for a *platok* to wear to prayer meetings. "Leeza, you should know how to embroider these *platkee*. All the girls are learning. I'll teach you when you're older," she said.

Babushka Elizaveta introduced me to Polyusha and Fedya Streliev, who lived at the west end of Thrums, where the bluff met the Kootenay River. Babushka had a toothache for days, put cold compresses on her jaw and chewed on cloves, before she finally agreed the tooth would have to be pulled. She rolled up a few coins in a handkerchief, pinned it under the waistband of her long skirt, took her wooden cane and set off. I was welcome to come if I wanted to, and of course I did. She walked briskly; I trotted by her side.

Fedya had a special room where he kept all sorts of interesting pliers and tooth pullers. Babushka didn't even look at them but sat down in his chair, adjusted her kerchief around her head and pointed to her swollen gum and painful tooth. "It has to come out," she sighed. Fedya rolled up his shirt sleeves, washed and dried his hands and gave Babushka's shoulders a squeeze. Before he pulled her tooth, he cradled Babushka's jaw and gently vibrated around the sore tooth. I stood open-mouthed and watched as Fedya placed huge pliers in Babushka's mouth and pulled. There was a loud crack, and Fedya triumphantly turned to show me the long root and the rotten hole in the tooth.

Elizabeth's uncle Nick Maloff and his daughter Helen on their farm in Castlegar in 1927. During this time, the brothers Nick and Pete became estranged when Pete supported the Sons of Freedom ideals.

"Not like your shiny new teeth," Fedya said. "Eat your apples and carrots, Leeza. You'll have strong teeth like a horse." And he gave me a carrot to munch on.

Babushka lay down on a small bed, and Fedya set glass cups on her back. I watched as the skin under those cups puckered up in red bumps. Babushka said it helped with her high blood pressure. We walked home, and Babushka rested in bed for a few days before she was up gardening and cooking again.

At five o'clock on Sunday mornings, spring and fall, Dedushka Nikolai gently roused us and helped us bundle into our coats for *malenyeeye*, a prayer meeting. "Wake up, dears. We're going to have a morning walk, pray and sing, and then we'll have a good breakfast."

I loved those early Sunday mornings with Dedushka. In spring, as Dedushka, Petya and I walked to *malenyeeye*, I breathed the freshly washed air and felt the earth alive beneath my soft *laptyee* shoes. Birds sang out and frogs croaked their noisy springtime songs. In winter we gathered later, but it would still be dark. Dedushka lit his big coal oil lantern and held it high above his bearded face, and as Petya and I plowed through the snow he'd say, "We'll just walk slowly. Enjoy the snow." The lantern lit up our little group, and our shadows shone blue on the snow as we sleepily followed Dedushka. Before the brick-lined Thrums hall was built, we gathered in living rooms to recite prayers and sing psalms. As we approached a home, we could see the moving lanterns of other Doukhobor families walking to the meeting, the Vanins, Danshins and Lebedoffs. Lanterns inside the open door beckoned us in.

Babushka Hoodicoff would already be at the prayer meeting. "When we say our prayers," she'd remind us, "God will protect us for the rest of the day. Morning is the most important time to pray." My favourite prayer was a short children's one that Mama helped me memorize: "Lord, give us Thy blessing. Hope nurtures me. Love brings me to God. Where there is love, there is God. Our God be praised."

After we said our prayers, we sang psalms and hymns, our voices blending. As my brother and I grew older, I learned the soprano voice and he the tenor.

After that early morning we looked forward to a breakfast of *borsh*, bread and hot buckwheat. Again we recited *Otche*, the Lord's Prayer, with Dedushka prompting us: "We must thank God. Many are not as fortunate as we are to have food and a safe place." Our family, Papa, Mama, Babushka, Petya and I, bowed our heads, while Dedushka led the prayer, his head bent, his bushy beard flowing over his homespun shirt.

THRUMS 1928

On Sunday afternoons, Mama often asked Dedushka to look after us children, while she went to the large Doukhobor gatherings in Brilliant where the new leader, Peter Petrovich Verigin[11]—Chistiakov, "the Cleanser," Doukhobors named him—talked about Christ's teachings. Dedushka agreed only if she would tell him in detail everything that went on in the meeting. Mama and her friends walked all the way to Brilliant, singing as they went.

Sometimes they rode with Norman Johnson. Then a teenager, Norman, whose family owned the general store, used the store truck to drive everyone to Brilliant and Shoreacres. Mama paid him a dime and climbed into the back of his pickup with other kerchiefed women in long skirts and men dressed in their best Cossack-style shirts and trousers. I could hear them singing as the truck swayed over the bumps and around potholes in the dirt road.

Mama came back and ate a little, and then neighbours started filling our living room, sitting on benches against the walls and on the floor. Mama recalled Chistiakov's discussions in detail. Even those who had been to the meeting wondered, "Lusha, how could you remember everything so clearly? What a good memory you have."

One Sunday afternoon when Mama came home I could tell she was excited and happy by the liveliness in her walk. She gathered us around and announced, "Chistiakov told us, 'Let us go forward and teach our children. Let Doukhobors become professors, yet remain Doukhobors.'" Since Petya and I were now of school age, five and eight years old, Mama had started to teach us at home and she was happy to hear that Chistiakov approved of education.

Dedushka Nikolai was especially pleased. "That's the best news yet about Chistiakov," he said, thumping his fist on the table. In Saskatchewan, before they moved to Oregon, he had taken a huge step in leaving the Doukhobor community to send Papa and Uncle Nick to school. At that time Community Doukhobors rejected government schools. But Dedushka even built a little house next to the Buchanan school for them to live in during the school year, as their farm was four miles away. When Papa was eleven or twelve,

---

11.   Peter Petrovich Verigin, son of Peter Vasilevich Verigin, arrived from the USSR to become the leader of the Christian Community of Universal Brotherhood in 1927.

he believed he was unjustly strapped by the teacher, and he refused to go back to school. Dedushka said, "Oh, yes, you will. You know how hard it is to live. I'll drag you there on a rope if I have to, but you'll go to school, all right!"

Now, years later, many of our neighbours agreed. "We need to educate our children. But we should have our own schools. Government schools teach what the government wants."

As I sat crowded into the warm living room, surrounded by my family and neighbours, the conversations washed over me and I listened with interest. I liked learning. Papa had stacks of books in his room upstairs that I was eager to read.

In those days in Thrums, Papa and Mama, Babushka and Dedushka welcomed everyone. Some visitors came to ask Papa to write letters or petitions for them, others to discuss Doukhobor philosophy, and some to help. When Papa's friends from Grand Forks, the Wlasoffs, or our uncle Nick's family from Castlegar visited, Mama and Babushka cooked big pots of soup or *borsh* and bread, and everyone pitched in with the gardens, the animals or building on to our house.

Summer evenings we sat out on the porch and ate sunflower seeds, pinching them out from the big sunflower heads if they were freshly harvested. In winter, visitors came walking with lanterns, and as they crowded around the stove, the smells of steaming wool, smoky kerosene and freshly cut apples filled the house.

I often shared my bed with cousins and friends, all of us sleeping sideways, giggling into the night, and next door I heard echoes of joyous laughter also far into the night, especially when Papa and George Wlasoff recollected their boyhood in Oregon and California. Papa was usually serious and philosophical, but he and George knew how to make each other happy and lighthearted, laughing at the curious situations they had found themselves in.

Mama's sister Masha married George Aseyev and moved farther west in Thrums to the Aseyevs' farm. The Aseyevs' home resounded in singing, and when Mama wanted me to study a new psalm or hymn, we went to learn the melody and harmony from Uncle George or his mother, my great-aunt Masha, who had a large repository of songs in her memory. As I grew older I picked strawberries and raspberries at the Aseyevs' until my hands and mouth were red with sweet berry juice, and all the time I was surrounded by singing and stories.

The Thrums school on the property next to ours was built by my grandfather Hoodicoff, his brothers and all our neighbours. The two large classrooms were kept warm with a big barrel-shaped stove, tall windows let in light, and large blackboards hung on the walls. Mama said that when she went to the school, they took turns carrying pails of water from a concrete cistern to fill the water barrel and bringing in armloads of wood for the stove. She learned English songs that she sang to us: "Jesus Loves Me" and "Mary Had a Little Lamb." Mama told us stories about Christmas concerts and parties, about her classmates, about the Johnson children and about how Ernie Pratt liked her in school, but after she met my papa, she wouldn't even look at him.

This was the school that I would have gone to, but Mama taught my brother, Petya and me at home. We learned to read Russian through alphabet books, *azbukee*, and through our songs and beautifully illustrated Russian children's books. English primers and storybooks were brought by the school inspector, who visited regularly. The inspector would ask Petya and me to read, write and add and subtract some numbers, and I heard him tell Mama, "Good job teaching your children, Lucy. I'm pleased with their progress. They are very well behaved."

Babushka and Dedushka were happy we were learning too. I could read the English newspaper to them. I was happy with our peaceful life in Thrums, with our large family and our many friends and neighbours, but in 1929 change was coming.

1929

They were so small. Johnnik was five pounds and Luba under four pounds. I imagine the scene: Thrums, the Maloff house, on March 12, 1928.

It would still be cold, the wood stove burning, but warm enough. Mother said that they had already planted the early peas and asters in the garden that year. Did the midwives—Babushkee Elizaveta Maloff and Masha Hoodicoff—know that twins would be born that day? Or was it a surprise when Luba followed her brother Johnnik? I ask Mother, "How did they know how much they weighed?"

"They used the market balancing scale. I heard them talking. The *babushkee* didn't think Luba would live, she was so weak, but Father wouldn't hear of it. 'Of course she'll live. Don't say such a thing!' They wrapped Luba in a woollen quilt and placed her close to Mother and twin brother Johnnik on the couch by the stove.

"Tyota Masha brought a mother hen with chicks. 'Enough beans and buckwheat,' she said. 'Now, with all these children, you need good strong food.' Papa got a cow and a goat for milk.

"As the eldest, even at eight, I was expected to help with five-year-old brother Petya and the twins," Leeza says. "My days of visiting grandparents and playing with cousins were over. My relationship with Father grew strong. Mother was busy, but Father always found time to listen. Even in later years when I approached Mother with a question or a problem, she'd tell me, 'Talk to Papa.'"

A year later, in 1929, Leeza's father, Pete Maloff, was imprisoned. What had he done to land in jail? It is a story Leeza, my mother, does not readily talk about, and I know very little regarding this era of Doukhobor life. In Pete Maloff's book, *Doukhobors, Their History, Life and Struggle*, he wrote that after the arrival of the Doukhobor leader Peter Petrovich Verigin—Chistiakov—in 1927, "fate threw him into a whirlpool of events."[12] Pete promised a sequel to explain and record those events. Questioning Mother, I learned that Pete was very involved with the leader of the Christian Community of Universal Brotherhood (CCUB). Although Pete was not a member of the CCUB, Chistiakov visited him often and they talked late into the night. The Maloff family was vegan at the time, and despite the chiding of her sisters, Lusha prepared a vegan *borsh* for him, without the usual heavy doses of cream and butter. Chistiakov praised the *borsh* highly.

Pete Maloff (1929), was a strong voice in the Anti-War movement. His involvement eventually led to charges and jail time.

On learning that Pete was acquainted with the Molokans, Chistiakov asked Pete to lead a group of Doukhobors to meet with them. In the spring of 1929, Pete took a choir of young men and women chaperoned by Lusha's younger sister, Polly Hoodicoff, and a respected man, Mr. Babakaiff whom Chistiakov selected. In those years, crossing the US–Canada border was a simple affair not requiring passports, but still they were worried about Babakaiff, who had been born in Russia and immigrated to Canada when he was very young. The group kept telling him, "Make sure you do not say you were born in Russia. Just say you were born in Canada." Babakaiff was so confused and stressed that by the time they reached the border and the customs official asked where he was from, he blurted out, "Came from Russia! Born in Canada!" The rest of the choir was allowed to continue on to California, but first they returned Babakaiff to his home.

---

12. Maloff, *Doukhobors*, pt. 2, chap. 9.

Pete Maloff (back row, centre) with Doukhobor and Molokan men in California. The bus they travelled in (rented for them by Molokans) is in the background.

The family photo albums of the time contain many pictures of this choir with their Molokan brethren, arms linked in camaraderie. I distinguish Molokan women from Doukhobor women in the photographs mainly by how they wear their *platkee*—the Molokan *platkee* cover their heads and the ends are draped over their shoulders, whereas the nine Doukhobor women have theirs tied in the front. Molokan men were more apt to have full beards; the Doukhobor men are clean-shaven. A note in the photo album suggests that the Molokans hired a bus to transport the Doukhobor choir to California.

In the same year, the choir toured settlements in Saskatchewan where Doukhobors lived. When I ask Mother how they travelled there, I am astounded to hear that they sat on benches on the back of a farm truck. It would have required fortitude to sit on wooden benches, bumping along for hours through the mountain passes of the Rockies and out onto the prairies on the rudimentary roads of the 1920s, for the two-day journey. Fourteen young women dressed in pastel-coloured Doukhobor suits—long skirts and wrist-length blouses, heads covered in *platkee*—pose with their chaperone, Polyusha Streliev.

As we browse through these pictures, drinking tea and talking about those times, Mother tells me Polyusha Streliev was asked to participate by Chistiakov. "She was a big woman, and her husband was smaller. He was the *lyeekark* in Thrums who pulled teeth." I recognize her standing beside the choir members, a portly woman wearing a black *platok*. Five years earlier her youngest daughter had died in the train explosion that killed Chistiakov's father, Peter Vasilevich Verigin.

The fourteen men photographed with Grandfather Pete Maloff are dressed in white shirts and dark pants, and many are holding fedoras. Pete wears a suit with a vest and a string tie. In the background is an old truck with a covered back similar to that of a panel van. The choir members had many relatives in the villages in Saskatchewan and they were hospitably billeted with their kin.

In 1929, the twins would have been a year old. I ask Mother why Grandfather was on the road when the babies were still small.

"He was spreading the word,, *prapavedawal*, that there was a big war coming and that the Doukhobors needed to shout from the rooftops against warfare," she tells me.

The Second World War did not start until 1939, but from the 1926 California meetings Pete attended I recalled that he had written about the evil of "Prussian militarism." I searched through his manuscript and on page 471 I found the information. He wrote,

> We listened to the brothers Rolas who had just arrived from Germany. They told the story of the German revolution of 1923 when Hitler made his first and still insignificant appearance. How ardently they spoke in describing the danger, which was darkening Germany's horizon. What a terrible evil was Prussian militarism. This they predicted would grow to monstrous proportions.[13]

In 1948, when Pete wrote his book, he was able to speak with hindsight.

> What seems so strange now, is the fact that such warnings were taken by the public in a very light

---

13. Maloff, *Doukhobors*, pt. 2, chap. 9.

mood. They were even met with laughter. Such a serious man as Thomas Bell made fun of the brothers Rolas. "Your fears have no foundation," he repeated. "Hitler is no more than a soap bubble. He will inflate himself and burst."[14]

Pete had heard the warnings about a war on the horizon, and Chistiakov, who had lived through the horrors of the First World War in Russia, would have had the same fears. I began to understand: Pete was fervently inspired by the Doukhobors of the preceding generation who had burned their weapons. His experiences in California with pacifists and activists further strengthened his resolve to act. I had listened to Grandfather Pete speak when I attended Doukhobor meetings in the 1960s, and though I was barely in my teens, I was moved by his passionate oration. Koozma Tarasoff, in his book *Spirit Wrestlers Voices*, described him as "an enthralling emotional speaker."[15] At twenty-nine with a young family, Pete could be trusted to supervise the youth choir. Chistiakov chose a willing and reliable man.

But I still wondered. "How were you all able to manage with the babies?"

"Chistiakov told my mother, 'No one will be ill. The children will all be looked after and healthy.' And we were. Vanya Perepolkin brought us Paranyusha Voykin to help with Luba and Johnnik. She was a small woman. Her husband had been a strong, big man, able to carry her on his shoulders when she tired on one of the treks in Saskatchewan, but he died in the Prince Albert jail because he refused to eat the meat they were feeding the prisoners. The guards forced hot soup down his throat after he had been fasting, and it burnt his throat and stomach." Mother shakes her head as if to shake the thought. "We loved Paranyusha. She was like a mother to us. She was so gentle and kind."

Mother was nine years old the summer of 1929. I think of my own nine-year-old granddaughter, secure with her loving family and dancing, skiing and playing hockey like many of her classmates. This was not the life Leeza lived. Her father was absent for

---

14. Maloff, *Doukhobors*, pt. 2, chap. 9.
15. Tarasoff, *Spirit Wrestlers Voices*, p. 45.

Six of the nine so called "ring leaders" who were sent to Oakalla for a peace march on Baker Street in Nelson. They were officially charged with "obstructing a police officer." The nine men were Larry Chernenkoff, George Dutoff, Mike Hadiken, Pete Maloff (second from the left), Vladimir Meir, Peter Perepolkin, Alex Popoff, John Relkoff, and Paul Vatkin.

weeks, months and years at a time, and they were eking out a living through market gardening.

Women were so often left to look after the children, gardens and households. I remember hearing a story of a husband who left his wife just after she had a baby. He had held the baby, changed her diaper, kissed his wife and then departed to participate in a peace trek. Another man was building dams on the Kootenay River, but when he was asked to go with the group to Saskatchewan, he quit and joined the choir. Such was their devotion to pacifism. But the missing fathers left an emotional gap, and their families suffered.

In the Maloff family, my uncle Walter was angry that his father was absent during his youth, that his beliefs and peace activism took precedence over the well-being of the family. Other siblings wondered, "What good did Father's protests do? All those years he spent in jail! For what?" Leeza supported her father, telling Walter, "We did not understand Father. He was striving for a greater cause. We should have learned from him and followed his footsteps." However, I have seen the toll on the family through the generations, a tension and anxiety we all have carried from childhood.

—⁓—

I try to piece together the events of 1929. This was the time of the stock market crash. What I know of Doukhobors of the time is that most were living on farms, growing grain, fruit and vegetables for the local markets, or they were in the labour force. The stock market crash hurt them too. The newspapers of the summer of 1929 reported that strawberry farmers were requesting government aid because of the collapse of the soft-fruit market. There was a permanent injunction against shipping cherries by the Doukhobor CCUB as they refused to take out a licence from the produce marketing board.[16] The Doukhobors were fined a total of $2,100 plus costs in 1928, a huge sum in those years. I marvelled at their tenacity to stand up for their beliefs. This must have been one of the original anti–marketing board protests that continue to this day.

As I explain to Mother what I have learned from the newspapers, she nods her head and sips her tea. I haven't found any reference to Doukhobor events that would have landed Grandfather in jail. Before starting to sort through all the newspapers of 1929, I ask her what time of year Grandfather and the choir left for their trip to the prairies.

"It must have been in spring. Father said a Saskatchewan farmer complained, 'These gatherings are disrupting our work. We have to seed the fields. Time you British Columbians went home.'"

I laugh at the frank criticism. "Good thing there were some practical Doukhobors."

Now I have a timeline, so I continue my search through the *Nelson Daily News* archives in the Nelson museum and the papers in the local collection at the Selkirk College library. When I find articles to corroborate Mother's stories, my first reaction is a hurrah; then as I read further—shock.

---

16. "Injunction Is Taken against Doukhobors," *Nelson Daily News*, August 26, 1929.

A truckload of Doukhobors arrived in Kamsack
Saskatchewan on Friday evening. The fire fighting
equipment was brought into force today to dispel
a parade of 150 members of the Sons of Freedom
cult. The paraders were given a thorough soaking.
Kamsack citizens, their ire aroused by the spectacle
of Sons of Freedom following a banner down the
street and singing songs, determined to put a stop
to the demonstration. Two lines of hose were speedily laid to the meeting grounds and the water was
played over the Sons of Freedom. The fire truck was
run through the parade but it formed again. The
banner carried by the Sons of Freedom was torn
from the grasp of the man who held it. This encounter marked the end of the riot, as the Sons of
Freedom moved out of town.[17]

Although Saskatchewan Doukhobors must have joined the
"paraders" to swell the ranks to 150, this article refers to the sing-
ers I had been looking at in the family photo album, in the picture
labelled "Grandfather's Party to Saskatchewan." Several were just
teenagers, neatly dressed in the costumes of a choir, such as sixteen-
year-old Nellie Denisoff, who had been chosen for her beautiful
singing voice. What a clash of cultures. Doukhobors speaking out
for a peaceful resolution of conflict, versus other citizens of Kamsack, some of whom undoubtedly had relatives who fought and
perhaps sacrificed their lives in the First World War. They lived in
the same villages and nearby farms. The tension between these dis-
parate groups must have been explosive. In the past, imprisonment
of Doukhobor martyrs had become almost a rite of passage, a sign
that one was steadfast in one's beliefs, but to be sprayed from a fire
hose by fellow Canadians!

It seems that Chistiakov protested this treatment. The July 27,
1929, Saturday morning *Nelson Daily News* stated,

Verigin passed through this town on the train for
Winnipeg. He stated to some of his followers who

---

17. "Fire Hose Is Turned upon Sons of Freedom," *Nelson Daily News*, July 22, 1929.

met him that the reason for his visit to the Manitoba capital was to obtain legal advice as to the law in respect of parades, the clash between the Sons of Freedom, of which Verigin is the head, and the towns people a week ago being the reason for seeking this advice.

The following Monday's paper quoted a Doukhobor official who stated that "Verigin's journey had been inspired by threats to have him expelled." Chistiakov had been under threat of deportation. Was it to avoid expulsion that Chistiakov requested that Pete Maloff rather than he himself lead the group of Doukhobors to California and subsequently to Saskatchewan? Pete, feeling that Doukhobors needed to take a strong stance to declare their opposition to war, would have taken on the challenge.

"What did Grandfather go to jail for?"

Mother describes a protest in Nelson where Pete was arrested for leading an unauthorized march through the streets. I find a picture in our photo album that attests to that. Pete is striding along with many marchers, all men, dressed in suits, long coats and white shirts, many with ties, walking through the streets of downtown

This protest march against the use of taxes for military spending resulted in harsh sentences for the nine organizers. Pete Maloff leads in the middle (fourth from right, above).

Nelson. They look intent and serious. The post office, now Touch-stones Nelson Museum of Art and History, is in the background. The picture is labelled by Uncle Walter "May 1, 1928, Father Leading Anti-War Party in Nelson." I wonder if he had the right date? Or were there several such protests? Reactions to the demonstrations were escalating. The August 2, 1929, *Nelson Daily News* reported that a Doukhobor "parade had started when a fire hose manned by stout firemen was trained on them. Mayor R.D. Barnes warned the paraders that they could not enter the city displaying banners preaching sedition. They could not parade the streets and obstruct traffic. ... It was when a large fire hose amply manned was turned in the general direction of the 65 to 70 would be paraders that the attempt was brought to an end."

Was this why the "paraders" had such determined and grim faces? Why they wore long coats and jackets in the summer? And what did the banners say? I continue to delve into the dusty stacks of the *Nelson Daily News*, and in the edition dated August 26, 1929, I finally discover the message on the banners. They carried a banner inscribed with the following seditious message:

> "We are followers of Christ, therefore we cannot serve two masters. We cannot pay taxes on which firearms and ammunition are constructed."

> "We cannot see our brothers being confined in prison and tortured to death."

> "You have taken our outer clothes. We will render to you our underclothes."[18]

Mother says that it was because her father, Pete, was in jail that her Maloff grandmother and grandfather, mother and siblings all joined the protest at the South Slocan tennis courts. They didn't know how else to be heard. This was the beginning of what became the arrest of Doukhobor men and women and their incarceration at the Oakalla Prison in Burnaby.

A day later, the protest camp in South Slocan was in the news. It appears that the police were prepared for trouble. The banners provided the flash point.

> Three provincial police officers passed all Sunday night and yesterday at tennis courts at South Slocan guarding the road above to see that no attempt was made by the Doukhobors encamped there to form into parade with the seditious banner.[19]

I was amazed that the police were so worried about a peaceful parade that they hung around a day and a night waiting for the possibility of

---

18.   "Police Halt Doukhobors," *Nelson Daily News*, August 26, 1929.
19.   "Community Leader Verigin Tells Fanatics Must Obey Law," *Nelson Daily News*, August 27, 1929.

a "seditious" banner being unfurled. There was more. A headline in the August 30, 1929, *Nelson Daily News* reads, "Doukhobors Land in Jail after a Fracas Near Here [South Slocan]." And in the *Rossland Miner*:

> Six months imprisonment with hard labour in Oakalla prison at the coast, was the sentence imposed on 104 Doukhobors of the Sons of Freedom element … arising from the nude demonstration at South Slocan, August 29.[20]

Nikolai Maloff, my great-grandfather, had been arrested and imprisoned for that demonstration. The police records verify the incarceration: on September 7, 1929, Nikolai Maloff was sentenced to Oakalla for indecent exposure.

The September 27, 1929, edition of the *Nelson Daily News* reported that on the previous day, nine Doukhobor "ringleaders … found guilty of obstructing a police officer in the dispatch of his duties, were sentenced to six months hard labour at Oakalla prison, at the coast."[21] Pete Maloff was one of the nine.

Mother tells me that her father, Pete, liked to dress appropriately. He was not one to protest using nudity, but his father had been arrested for such an offence. It is true that some of the Sons of Freedom used nudity to attract attention to their message: "If you will take everything from us, and do not let us live by our beliefs, then take our clothes also. We will stand before you naked in the world, but strong in our values." As with so many Doukhobor families of the time, there was a split in beliefs about nude protests. This dispute caused grief and heartache, as it did in many Doukhobor families.

Pete's brother, Nick, disapproved of his family's activities altogether and, in the next few years, moved to Langley, in the British Columbia Lower Mainland, away from the turmoil in the Kootenays.

The nudity was sensationalized by the news media, and it became a way for the justice system to incarcerate and silence many of the Sons of Freedom. Oakalla Prison had long had a reputa-

---

20. "Oakalla Jail to Be Filled with Douks," *Rossland Miner*, September 12, 1929.
21. "Nine Leaders Douks Sent Oakalla Jail," *Nelson Daily News*, September 27, 1929.

Nick Maloff with wife Hannah, and daughters Nina, Helen and Olga on the banks of the Columbia River in Castlegar.

tion as "a hard place to do time." I search the internet and find the *Runagate Pictures* blog on memories of Oakalla Prison, which says, "On the Pacific coast no prison was more 'infamous' than Oakalla."[22] The numbers of hangings, suicides, attempted suicides and riots are shocking. Beatings and isolation in underground cells were common.

Imprisonment traumatized not only the prisoners who spent that winter in the "infamous" Oakalla doing time with hard labour, but also children, men and women who were subsequently confined at Porto Rico in the Kootenays. The harsh treatment also created a radical movement of Sons of Freedom Doukhobors who over the next few years proceeded to get more extreme in their reactions to government repression.

These protests marked the beginning of the Porto Rico internment in an abandoned logging camp for many of the families whose relatives had been arrested and sent away to Oakalla. Lusha

22. "Documenting Memories of Oakalla Prison 1912–1991," *Runagate Pictures*, July 2, 2009, http://runagatepictures.blogspot.com/2009/07/documenting-memories-of-oakalla-prison.html.

Maloff and her children, nine-year-old Leeza, four-year-old Petya and one-year-old twins Luba and Johnnik, spent a long cold winter in that abandoned logging camp, policed by guards. No one was allowed to leave or to bring food or clothing, though Leeza said that her uncle Nick managed to elude the blockade and bring them a truckload of supplies.

Pete Maloff's book ends before the era of Chistiakov, and the promised sequel was never written. It was only by following a picture and newspaper trail that I was able to glimpse into the life of Mother and her family and the "whirlpool of events" in that year of 1929.

Interned at Porto Rico. Lusha with her children; Elizabeth who was nine, the twins, Johnnik and Luba at a year and a half and Peter was almost six years old. 150 men, 171 women and 216 children were interned at Porto Rico in the winter of 1929–1930.

PORTO RICO

It is the beginning of October. The nights are cool, the air crisp. We sit in Mother's living room, a fire crackling in her wood stove, a box of photographs labelled "For Leeza" on the table beside her floral couch. I pull out a large, 16½-by-5½-inch, professionally photographed picture. A piece is torn out of the bottom and it is stamped "Geo. A. Meeres, Nelson, BC." There is a jagged crack that looks like a lightning bolt from the top of the picture toward the crowd below. Those gathered at the bottom of the picture are dressed warmly in jackets and sweaters, lined up in four to five rows. In the front row sit toddlers, many in toques and boots, their legs spread in front so that I see the soles of their boots. Behind them stand women wearing kerchiefs tied under their chins, long skirts and sweaters. Young school-aged boys and girls are dispersed among the rows, neatly dressed, patiently posing. Strong, handsome fathers hold babies; white-haired, bearded grandfathers stand next to their families. I try to count the faces, but past 150 I get lost as my eyes dart from row to row.

"Where is this, Mom?" I ask. "Why is everyone lined up, all so serious?"

Mother takes the picture in her large gnarled hands and looks intently at the gathering. She turns to me, purses her lips and says, "This is in Nelson, in front of the *zhuzhaleetsa*, the place where the steam engine trains dumped their spent coal."

The dusty grey slag heap of the burnt coke towers behind the crowd, making up the picture's distant background. Just behind the group, sheets are strung between poles, like the makeshift tents I used to make in our backyard. An old Model T stands to the right, and two power poles dwarf the crowd.

We peer at the faces, small circles in the picture, and she finds her mother, a tall, slim, good-looking woman, her head covered in a white *platók*. The twins, a year old, are there: Luba, held by a tall man, and Johnnik, sitting in the front row, his head turned, seeking his mama in the back. Mother fetches a magnifying glass, and as she slides it from figure to figure, she identifies dozens of people, a list of long-ago friends and acquaintances: Vanya Androsoff, Great-Grandfather's brother, in that brown cap he always wore; Varyusha Dutoff, who still lives in her own house at ninety-nine; George Wlasoff, Grandfather's friend; Piscoon Popoff, nicknamed so because of his high-pitched voice; the Koftinoffs, Slastukins, Popoffs, Podovinikoffs and Postnikoffs.

"There's Pavel Skripnik, the cook at the camp," Mother says. He is standing in the back, a handsome man in a white shirt and a shock of white hair falling over his forehead. She points to another man. "Here's George Nazaroff and his family. He helped make a room for us in Porto Rico. Where did you find this picture, Vera?"

My uncle Walter recently passed, and we were clearing out the electrical shed behind his cabin. I tell Mother, "It was tucked in behind the fuse box, wrapped in this plastic bag." I hold up the Hefty One Zip jumbo storage bag that kept the picture dry. "What a place to keep it!"

"Walter hated the idea that our parents were involved with the Svobodniki back then," Mother says, using the Russian word for the people called Sons of Freedom or Freedomites in the newspapers. "He thought protesting against government was a lost cause. 'Foolish. Why do it?' he said. Maybe that's why he hid the picture." She shakes her head. "My friend Tankya Wlasoff told me, 'Why hate what our families did back then? That was the time.'"

Mother clears her throat, looks at me and says, "It was a long time ago. I was only nine. I try not to think of that time." She frowns. I lean forward, and as she holds the picture she starts to tell me what happened over eighty-five years ago. Her voice becomes younger, and her parents, long dead now, are Mama and Papa.

LEEZA: It all started here in Thrums. The old Svobodniki Doukhobors lived next to George Aseyev's place in a community against the mountain. That summer of 1929, Petya and I sat on our front porch and watched as the Svobodniki walked along the road in Thrums, holding poles supporting large banners that said, "Land should not be bought or sold," "Land belongs to God alone," "People must not pay taxes for land" and "Taxes support war." There

A makeshift camp of Doukhobor families protesting the arrest of over 128 Doukhobor men and women in South Slocan. Geo A. Meeres

was such a commotion all along the road; it was exciting to watch. I could feel their energy and fervour. Papa didn't pay the taxes either, so our land was taken away. Like the Svobodniki, Mama and Papa were also against an education that promoted militarism and capitalism.

To begin with I really wanted to go to school. The school was right here! Almost in our front yard, and everyone walked by on their way there. All my playmates went, and I dreamt of going to school, I was so enthusiastic. But my parents said that the government schools taught about war. The students had to sing for the king, and they said that is why we had all the fighting. So Mama told me, "Leeza, you can learn with your brother at home. I'll teach you. We have school books with lots of stories."

I started to read and write, and I still remember that funny story, *The Little Red Hen*, about the chicken that did all the work and there was no help from anybody. Mama said that the chicken

was like her, trying to get us to help her more. Mama was a good teacher. Strict. She taught Petya and me Russian and then English every morning.

But we had so many visitors. People came to ask Papa for help writing letters and making signs. The old Svobodniki said that all books needed to be burnt because they were written by man, not God. Papa loved books and had quite a collection, so he was afraid, especially when Nastya Zaroubina came around, that they would burn his books. When those Svobodniki showed up, Papa didn't have the heart to send them away, but first he made sure he hid his books. So my education didn't quite turn out; it was hard to learn with so much disturbance all the time. I had to understand these things.

We had just started to live a little better. Papa worked in the Okanagan in the spring and made a little money. Mama would write letters to Papa, a quick letter so that Papa would feel better. She would say that she was managing and all the children were okay. I would run to the post office. Charlie Johnson owned the Thrums store and post office, and he would already be carrying mail to the train station. He said, "You're fast. Run quickly, get a stamp, then catch up to me." His wife would sell me the stamp—three cents for a stamp; imagine all that trouble just for three cents—and then I'd run after Mr. Johnson.

Charlie Johnson was a returned soldier from the First World War. His feet were damaged in the war, so he limped badly. He said that he could have bought all the land in Thrums for taxes when people weren't paying, but he didn't because he understood what the rallies and protests were about. He supported them and gave people credit when they didn't have money for groceries. Each person paid him back, he said.

Everyone gathered to protest on the old road in South Slocan. Our leader, Chistiakov, had prophesied that a big war was coming. "You have to feed the dogs before you go hunting, so that they will follow you," he said. People believed this meant they had to let the government know that Doukhobors wouldn't participate in the war effort—they wouldn't pay taxes that go toward war or teach their children about patriotism and fighting for one's country. Papa was in jail already because he had been leading a protest in Nelson, but the rest of my family was there: Mama, Dedushka, Babushka, Petya, Luba and Johnnik. There were many other families, too. Right away, though, the police came with trucks and buses and arrested many men and women, including Dedushka. We were left with Mama, and there were other kids with their mamas. We didn't know what to do. I was scared.

Then a big group joined us. A friend of mine, Varyusha, came. Her family had driven from Grand Forks and stayed in our house in Thrums on their way. It was like that then; friends would drop in, eat, stay overnight without question. When they arrived in South Slocan, we were so happy! We were energized. Mama, too, was full of inspiration. She said we were speaking out for everyone taken away to prison. We started on a march, a *pakhot*, to Nelson to protest the jailing. On the way, we stayed overnight in a barn in Bonnington. I was so tired that I didn't even notice where I slept. When I woke up I saw that I had been sleeping on rocks.

We got to Nelson the next day. I wanted to see my papa and *dedushka*, but the police herded us toward the *zhuzhaleetsa*. After a few days there, we learned that all the arrested people were charged with disobedience and sent by train to Oakalla Prison in the Lower Mainland. We camped for three weeks next to that *zhuzhaleetsa*. People brought food and the men set up tents for sleeping, though many slept outside. For cooking, there was a big pot over a fire. The cook, Pavel Skripnik, was a friend of Papa's. He was from the Ukraine and had studied to become a priest, but he supported the Doukhobor cause. He was tall and thin, and so kind and caring. We would line up with our bowls and he would ladle soup into them. Paranya Voykin and Mr. Pereverzoff helped with the twins. Mr. Pereverzoff always carried Luba—she barely walked yet. I kept an eye out for them too. There was no place to get clean and it was so dusty, but we children didn't care about that; we ran around and played together. There were a lot of friends. People would come and go, but we stayed. With Papa and Dedushka in jail, where would we go?

Then the police rounded us up, and the women and all of us children were moved to the Salvation Army building. We were frightened, remembering what happened to Papa and Dedushka. The people there gave us a little soup, and we slept huddled together on the floor. After about four days, the police took us to Porto Rico, a logging camp up in the mountains close to Ymir. The men who hadn't been arrested were at the site already. It's funny, I don't remember how we got to the camp. When you try to forget something, not all the memories come back right away.

When we first arrived in Porto Rico, I was wondering how we could possibly live there. Porto Rico had been a large sawmill owned by the Doukhobors, but it was abandoned when the trees were all cut down, and then a fire went through. There was a big old barn, a kitchen and some bunkhouses, but many of the buildings were falling down and there were no doors or windows on them. That first night everyone slept on the floor of what I think had been the eating area. The men had a lot of work to do to make it livable. Porto Rico is in a rainy, snowy area. It gets very cold there in the winter.

We were lucky. George Nazaroff prepared a room in the bunkhouse for his family—made it a little more weatherproof, found firewood, built bunk beds—but he gave the space to Mama because he respected our papa, and since Papa wasn't there for us, he helped out. He put a pot-bellied stove in our room, one of the ones that the police had given us. But still, to keep warm, Petya and I slept in one bunk, on the boards, and Mama with the babies in another. The men did the cooking, and everyone shared. Mama would go to the kitchen and bring soup for us. There wasn't much.

George Nazaroff organized a school and, though he wasn't trained, became the teacher. And he was good. Every morning he would sit us down and ask us to be quiet and listen. There were lots of children, but he made sure we were peaceful. He was a peaceful fellow himself, and it didn't matter how disturbed others were; he stayed calm. We didn't have books, paper or pencils, so we learned our prayers and sang psalms and hymns. Our homework was to memorize a prayer for the next day.

I remember Mr. Nazaroff and his family well. He was a heavy man and his wife was a small, thin woman. His daughter, Grace—Hrunya—was two years older than me, but her brown hair was still in braids like mine. Later we would talk about what happened, and she reminded me how her dad helped us out and gave us their room. Sam, Syomka, was the same age as me, and boy, he was rambunctious, and a tease. We each had a different prayer or song to remember, and he would often memorize what I was supposed to, just for a joke. Mary, the youngest, was a baby.

We came to Porto Rico at the end of September, and at first it was warm. We played tag, and the older boys built a raft that they used to cross the creek, pushing it back and forth with long poles. We girls stood on the bank and watched. It seemed like so much fun. Sometimes they invited us to stand on the raft and take a trip across the creek, but I only got a chance to do that once. I had to help Mama with the twins.

We had a picture taken there. Mama got all of us organized. The photographer, Mike Voykin, was just learning how to use the camera, so we'd be sitting there and he'd say, "Just a minute, I have to fix something." It was hard to keep Johnnik and Luba still, but finally he took the picture.

At first, we were allowed visitors. Friends and relatives brought us food, and we greeted them with such joy. Then the police told us that we couldn't have any more company. They set up a blockade on the road to the camp and stopped everybody. Somehow, my *dyadya* Nick got through. He asked everyone he knew in Ootischenia to give food, blankets and clothing, or "they'll all perish," he said. He filled his truck with a huge load and came. Everyone was surprised he got through the police blockade. He teased us, "Here you are, you devils. Eat, or you'll die like rats." He was kind-hearted but liked to tease. He didn't stay long; he was afraid he wouldn't get back out. I think that Babushka went with him, because after he left, she was gone too.

Then the snow came. There was so much, it piled up to the roofs. The nights were cold and long, and in the mornings we woke to frost on our blankets. Mama brought us food and we ate huddled together. Maybe people got together in the evenings, I don't know. We stayed in our room. We couldn't leave Luba and Johnnik alone.

Babushka Elizaveta with her grandchildren in the Porto Rico internment camp. Her son Nick "smuggled" her out of the camp before winter set in.

Somehow we got through that winter, and in the spring the police allowed people to leave. Mama's brother, Ivan Hoodicoff, came to pick us up, and we went home. There was still a lot of snow in Porto Rico when we left, but in Thrums it was planting time. Mama said we had to plant a garden so that we would have food. Papa came home from Oakalla later that spring.

I heard that they found three graves by the logging camp, and some people knew who died, but I was a child and I don't remember that. I always tried to block that life out, but gradually it is coming back. The main thing is that I pulled through.

I often asked Papa why we had to have such a hard life, why he had to be so outspoken all the time and why he had go to jail. He told me that we could have had an easier life, but he spoke out against war so there wouldn't be any cripples or orphans, so that children would have their dads, and that there must be a better way. But there was a price to pay.

—⁓—

My mother, Elizabeth—Leeza to her family—is now in her nineties. We children did not know about her Porto Rico internment until recently when we found pictures of the men, women and children camped in Nelson and she began to tell us what happened when she was nine years old. In the eighty-plus years that have passed, the reasons for the protests of the time have become blurred, and the internment in the isolated, barely habitable logging camp, Porto Rico, is something that few remember; those who do, do not speak of it.

Wishing to learn more about the internment of Doukhobor men, women and children in Porto Rico, I search through the local newspapers of the time. A story in the *Rossland Miner* of September 5, 1929, headlined "Doukhobors Jailed When Take to Nude [*sic*]," gave a description of arrests made August 30 of Doukhobors in South Slocan. The situation began with the police demanding that the Doukhobors deliver four men who had previously "paraded nude" along the highway in South Slocan, but quickly became a struggle as 128 Doukhobor men and women were arrested. The police officers were organized and prepared.

> Starting from Nelson in cars and buses of all descriptions commandeered for the purpose, the 60 special constables under the leadership of six provincial police officers drove quickly out to a point around a bend in the road about 100 yards from the South Slocan tennis courts where the fanatics were encamped. There they stopped while Inspector Cruikshank and other officers went on ahead to make the arrest of the four Doukhobors charged with indecent exposure. Sergeant Gammon explained [to the special police force] that they were required to stop any attempt made by the fanatics to prevent the arrest of their fellows and to arrest any of the Doukhobors who were stripped or started to strip. They were to arm themselves with switches and use them on any stripped members of the sect or those who showed fight. ...

Plying their switches viciously and dragging screaming Doukhobors along the ground, the police officers went to work, to bring the crowd over to waiting buses, cars and trucks. ...

After about an hour all the Doukhobors were herded over to the trucks and nobody was left on the former camping site but some of the younger women most of whom did not disrobe, with the children.

From an article titled "Oakalla Jail to Be Filled with Douks" in the September 12, 1929, edition of the *Rossland Miner.*

One Hundred and four were given six months for indecent exposure. The protesters were tried five at a time with the judge saying, "I feel that it is time you people had a lesson." Speaking through an interpreter, he continued, "Tell them they have had a fair trial. ... They will receive the full term imposed by the act for this offense, six months with hard labour." ... When one man protested that he was not satisfied with the trial, the magistrate commented "I feel it is a waste of time to explain matters to you."

Mother and I have pored over this picture in front of the *zhuzhaleetsa.* In a family album, we find other photographs of the family in Porto Rico. Babushka Lusha, Leeza and Petya are standing beside the twins sitting on a bench. All are neatly dressed, Mother in a white sweater, dark skirt and leggings, the twins in coveralls, Petya in a woollen jacket. In the background are a few scrubby trees that have lost their leaves—what is left of a logged-out forest. During a recent visit, Mother says, "Take these pictures. I don't want to see them anymore."

A Spy in the
Doukhobor Midst,
1932

—⁓—

Mother is very nervous about sharing information on Sasha Keersta, especially how the evidence he collected was hidden and passed on to the Doukhobor leader, Chistiakov. She wonders if this information could still get people in trouble. Eighty years after Keersta, Mother continues to distrust the Canadian government, saying, "It is now as it was then."

Stories of spies in the Doukhobor midst are pervasive. My grandparents Pete and Lusha Maloff were an easy target for espionage; particularly if the newcomers said they were associated with the peace movement or the Communist Party, or of Russian heritage, Grandfather was a generous host. This fraternity with some who it turned out were government informants led to serious consequences for Pete and his family.

Pete was not a Communist but believed in their ideals of sharing and equality. He corresponded with Tim Buck, who was the general secretary of the Communist Party of Canada (CPC) from 1929 to 1962. Mr. Buck visited Pete and Lusha in Thrums. Nigel Morgan, the leader of the Communist Party of British Columbia, also visited regularly. When Pete was travelling to the Soviet Union in the 1960s, Mr. Morgan wrote a reference letter to the authorities there. These associations, and his past history of speaking out against government orders he saw as against his conscience, put his name on a watch list for government surveillance. Furthermore, although he was against the violence some agitators in the Sons of Freedom community resorted to, he had been associated with Svobodniki previously.

I remember a visitor my grandparents had in the 1970s, a tall, gregarious man who made himself useful. He helped around my grandparents' farm, visited the property we had bought with my husband and gave suggestions for building. An excellent listener, he would nod his head and encourage confidences. It turned out that rather than being associated with the CPC as he claimed, he was connected to the RCMP Security Service.

There were many other instances. Mother tells me that her father corresponded with Mahatma Ghandi, and that is why, when he visited India, he received an audience with Indira Ghandi. "Where are those letters from Mahatma?" I ask her. "They would be amazing to read!"

Her answer: "Grandfather was always followed. One time when he was in Calgary his briefcase containing the letters was stolen." Mother also recalls a White Russian visitor who arrived at Grandmother Hoodicoff's place in 1933. She and her siblings had just returned from the orphanage and industrial school they had been placed in when her parents were jailed. Having seen him as a frequent visitor to their home, she was not surprised when he took all five children to Nelson to buy shoes. "We were so happy with our new shoes. We didn't have any and winter was coming. Later

The Maloff residence. Pete and Lusha welcomed many visitors including communists, back-to-the-landers, draft resisters and those who they were later to learn were spies.

we found out that this man worked in the courts as a translator and a guard. Did he buy us those shoes out of guilt?"

John J. Verigin, the leader of the Union of Spiritual Communities of Christ,[23] was much more adroit in dealing with spies. When one of the Russians who was known to be an informer met him and suggested, "Dyadya, Uncle, let's have a chat," John Verigin would quickly say, "Yes, good idea, we'll do that." But as soon as the Russian turned around to talk to him, he was gone. "I can never get to talk to John Verigin," he complained to my grandfather.

Mother can remember when Sasha Keersta appeared among the Doukhobors in the early 1930s. Her story comes alive as she tells it.

LEEZA: It was an early March morning. Outside, a driving rain was lashing our window, and the seven of us felt cozy and happy to be together. Mama was nursing four-month-old Nadya in a rocking chair next to our cookstove, the four-year-old twins, Luba and Johnnik, were at the table, tapping their wooden spoons, and Papa was lifting a steaming cast iron pot out of the oven. I elbowed my brother, Petya, sitting next to me on our school bench. "Let's go over that song again. Mama and Papa like it, and we could sing it for Easter."

Petya, who had just turned eight, tweaked my braid and made a face. We could smell the fragrant *kasha*, but not everyone was at the table yet, so with a sigh he agreed. "*Kharasho*, Leeza, one last time."

> God loves the little sparrow
> Saving it from death
> And if God so loves the little birds,
> I know he loves me too.

"Very nicely sung," Papa said. "Now read it over so you remember the words."

I propped the Russian song in front of us and looked at Petya. "You first."

---

23.   The Union of Spiritual Communities of Christ (USCC) succeeded the Christian Community of Universal Brotherhood as the voice of the Community Doukhobors in 1938. John J. (Ivan Ivanovich) Verigin became the secretary of the USCC after his grandfather Chistiakov died in 1939.

Mama threw a towel over her shoulder to burp Nadya and spoke softly to Papa. "Petrunya, I had quite the dream last night."

"Oh?" Papa answered.

Mama would sometimes ask us about our dreams, and we wanted to hear hers. We slid on the bench closer to her.

"In my dream, it was dark, the moon just rising, but as I looked outside, I saw a shadowy creature creeping toward us." Mama shivered involuntarily. "It came so close I saw its rotten teeth, smelled its nasty breath."

Papa frowned. "Lusha, what are you talking about?"

"It woke me up, that dream. I am afraid we're in for some trouble," Mama said even more quietly.

"Lusha, that's all behind us." Papa put the hot buckwheat on the table and turned around to give Mama's shoulders a squeeze. "We're home, safe."

But Mama's dream made me shiver, too, and my stomach knotted. I couldn't forget Porto Rico.

Mama patted Nadya on her back and shook her head. "That Sasha Keersta who keeps coming around here. I don't trust him."

Papa replied, "Sasha's friendly enough, and he's got interesting stories about Russia. He worked for Czar Nicholas as some kind of security person."

Sasha Keersta was unlike our other visitors. When he showed up, each time with a different car and driver that he hired, all of us kids would run out to the front of our house to watch him. The driver would open the door for him, and first we would just see his shiny shoes, then his stylish felt hat covering his dark, short-cropped hair, and as he stepped out we could see his tailored suit. This was during the Depression, in 1932, but Keersta was always *naryazheniy*, well dressed, not like us standing watching him, Petya and Johnnik in coveralls that were patched at the knees and Luba and I in cotton dresses Mama had sewn. And then the cane—a shiny black one that he twirled as he walked. When Petya said that he had heard the handle of that cane was made from a penis of some animal, I believed him.

Keersta would dismiss his driver, bring out some papers and then come into our living room to talk to Papa. Mama didn't like Keersta, but if he came at dinnertime, as he often did, she fed him.

Then she left the room, but Petya and I would watch him. His Russian was different from ours. He had a honeyed voice, my mother said, and I knew she meant not in a good way by the way she wrinkled her nose. If we didn't have a job to do, we'd gather in the living room, Luba and Johnnik too, and listen to his Russian stories, but when he started asking Papa about his friends and what was going on with Doukhobors here in Canada, we'd run off.

Mama didn't often disagree with Papa, but now she raised her voice. "Petrunya, I wonder what he did for the czar's family. He's *not* a friend." Mama passed Nadya to Papa and ran her fingers through her long, light brown hair. I watched as she expertly braided, coiled and pinned it neatly in a bun at the back of her head. "He comes here way too often, asking for information about people. Be careful!"

Papa shrugged. "I noticed that too, but we have nothing to hide. I just change the topic." He motioned to us. "Leeza, Petya, come and eat."

At the table, we bowed our heads and said a prayer. Mama spooned the steaming hot *kasha* into bowls and poured warm fresh milk into our cups. "I've heard about his visits to Vanya Perepolkin."

Vanya Perepolkin and his wife lived down the road from us in Thrums, in a little village against the mountain together with other Svobodniki. He often came by in the evenings to sit with us, eat sunflower seeds and talk. Papa said that Vanya had a unique view of life. He believed one's conscience was a connection to God. He said there would be no need for police and governments if humans listened to their consciences. Vanya didn't even like that Mama was teaching us to read because reading would take us away from God's word.

Mama poured cups of hot mint tea for herself and Papa, then continued, "Vanya and Nastya figured out a way to get rid of Sasha Keersta permanently."

"I heard. Something about the Bible?"

"Keersta's always promoting the Bible, saying that it has the answer for everything."

Papa raised his eyebrows. "Vanya wouldn't take to that too well, even though he tries to be kind to everyone."

"Petrunya, Sasha left his Bible for Vanya and Nastya to read, 'to mend their ways,' he said. You know the one he always carries around—a fat one, embossed in gold."

"I can't see Vanya being interested in that."

"No, and then Nastya used Keersta's Bible for fuel in her stove to bake bread. She said it baked very good bread."

"Keersta's Bible! Burnt to make bread!"

Papa put his teacup down, wiped his face and shook his head in disbelief. He loved his collection of books upstairs and often told us to be very careful with them.

"And to add to it," Mama replied, "they used to invite him to share a meal, but this one time Vanya told him, 'Keersta, you don't plant a garden and you don't work. We've prepared food that we've grown with our own hands. But you, you can eat your books.' Keersta did not return. Petrunya, you must stay away from him!"

After Mama's warning, Papa was not as welcoming, but Keersta persisted in visiting, sometimes even twice a week. I'd be busy helping Papa wash clothes on our washboard—there were always so many—and there he was.

"I have something very important to talk to Pete about," he would say.

It was the end of March when everything began to change.

It was an early spring, warm during the days. Frogs were already croaking in the pond, and the leaves on our cherry trees were budding. We'd been preparing our garden and planting our early crops. Nadya was asleep in a basket by the garden, Papa was guiding the plow, our gentle horse, Dan, was pulling, and Mama and Petya were raking the soft soil and making the rows with the *prawadyeelka*—Mama liked straight rows, neat and parallel to each other. I was showing Luba and Johnnik how to drop the early peas and sunflowers seeds into the soil. Johnnik would make roads in the soil, pretending he was driving a truck, but sister Luba loved to plant, and I told her that soon we'd have green peas to pick fresh off the vine. We squatted over the brown earth and grinned at each other in anticipation.

Toward evening, as had become usual, Keersta was there talking to Papa. Then his driver arrived, and off he went in a flourish, donning his hat and flapping his coat open to sit, we thought, like a czar in the back seat.

Petya noticed Keersta's notebook first. He picked it up and nudged Papa. Notebook in hand, Papa waved at the retreating car, but Keersta didn't look back. Absent-mindedly Papa flipped the pages open, then looked more carefully. I could tell from his ashen face that something was wrong. Before I could ask him what it was, Papa walked into the house, holding the notebook as if it were a poisonous snake. "Lusha, look what Keersta left," Papa said as he showed the pages to Mama. They bent their heads over the writing, studying the notes.

After a page or two, Mama said, "Hide it at my parents', not here. He'll come for it." Papa shoved the notebook into a bag with the seeds we were taking to my grandparents and in the early twilight hurried across the road and the railway tracks. After a quick look at the notebook, Dedushka Hoodicoff buried it under the hay in the barn.

A frantic Keersta returned shortly. "Pete, I left a very valuable book here—one with my insurance receipts and the names of everyone who bought insurance from me. I must find it." While Papa and Mama kept busy feeding the animals and milking the cow, we children watched quietly. Keersta looked everywhere: under the table and couch in the living room, upstairs in the library and in the yard, retracing his steps. I could tell he was angry—he looked something like brother Johnnik did when he got upset—and a huge scowl was on his red face as he stomped around from room to room. But Keersta didn't find anything and finally left with his driver.

That night as I lay in my bed, Luba cuddled next to me, I heard Papa and Mama talking on the other side of our bedroom wall. Papa said that the notebook contained information about Doukhobor activities and particularly about Chistiakov. "You were right, Lusha. What an idiot I was! I trusted him to be what he said he was—a Russian immigrant, just trying to make a living as an insurance salesman. What was I thinking?" Their voices trailed off. I hugged sister Luba close to me and knew there was going to be trouble.

Early the next morning four policemen banged on our door. Papa and Mama were ordered to stay in the kitchen with Nadya. Luba and I huddled next to our parents, but Johnnik ran off to

Babushka Hoodicoff's, with Petya and two policemen following him. We sat silently, barely breathing, holding hands, Nadya whimpering, while those police tramped through our entire house. We could hear their heavy tread go up the narrow stairs to Papa's room, then heard the thump of books and papers falling. Downstairs they shuffled through every cupboard and drawer Mama had organized, and as they rifled through the rest of the house we could hear beds being overturned, the scrape of furniture being shoved aside. Then they went across the railway tracks to help their partners at Babushka and Dedushka Hoodicoff's home, turning their house inside out. They even dug in the barn through the hay, but just, *just* missed finding the book. Finally, they left, their grim faces telling me this wasn't over yet.

As soon as he could, Dedushka smuggled the notebook, hidden at the bottom of a knapsack, to Chistiakov. Chistiakov was not surprised that Keersta was an informer; many Russian and Canadian undercover agents had spied on him.

Later, when we were taken away—Mama to the Piers Island prison, Papa to the penitentiary and we children scattered to the orphanage, an industrial school and a foster home—I would remember this early morning, the reassuring routine and warm feeling of being together suddenly jarred by Mama's dream of the creature with sharp teeth.

That summer of 1932, Sasha Keersta turned up at the Piers Island Penitentiary. He had taken a job as a translator and guard and was known to be very vindictive to the jailed Doukhobors. He said to Mama, "Too bad I lost that book. I'd have you in even worse trouble." But one day, while tying his shoelaces, he keeled over, dead of a heart attack in that same prison where those he had spied upon were incarcerated.

—*m*—

The Doukhobor inmates composed a song about Sasha Keersta. Eighty-five years later, her face knotted in concentration, my mother, Leeza, sings this song. [24]

---

24. Translated by Katya Maloff.

Скончался один покоритель
Сомкнул свои очи уста
Прощай бывший наш посетитель
Шпиончик друг Саша Кирста

He's dead now, our oppressor
His mouth and his eyes, they are shut
Farewell to the Russian swashbuckler
Our "friend," the spy Sasha Keersta.

In Russia you battled the enemy
You won through that horrific time
And the reward for your loyalty
Was gold from Czar Nikolai.

Those people you so tormented
Amongst whom were some clever folk
From your homeland you were banned
By the Bolsheviks that you did so provoke.

You keeled over without warning
In this jail in which we are kept
Farewell, there will be no mourning
For the two-faced Sasha Keersta.

As the final notes recede, Mother folds her hands and closes her eyes.

IVAN PEREPOLKIN,
A CHRISTIAN ANARCHIST

—ɯɯ—

I know Ivan Perepolkin from my mother's stories, my grandfather's writing and a photograph next to my computer. In the picture it is winter; snow covers the shed to the rooftop, and Ivan is elderly, slightly stooped, but appears strong and wiry. He is wearing a brimmed felt hat on top of a knitted *kalpak*, a toque. Probing eyes peer out from under his hat, and high cheekbones and a strong nose dominate his face. Wide lips sit above a soft-looking curly white beard. He is wearing an oversized wool jacket, on which a button has been moved to make the jacket tighter, and canvas pants that snow has stuck to. Ivan's stance and the expression on his face hint at his character: firm, determined, a man of strong opinions but at the same time kind and thoughtful. I believe his penetrating gaze would have intimidated me.

Grandfather Pete called him Vanya, and they spent many evenings in discussions while sitting on the porch of my grandparents' home in Thrums. Grandfather believed Vanya was a genuine Christian anarchist. In his book he wrote, "Ivan was a person of great spirituality. He always impressed me with his dynamic thought, his curiosity and his trustworthiness. His expressions were picturesque and reflected keenness of observation and knowledge of life. He seemed to be a true copy of Diogenes, completely devoid of greed and a man certain of his needs." Through the many talks with Vanya, Grandfather Pete learned of the values of the early Sons of Freedom movement: freedom, simplicity, seeking satisfaction in the Spirit, independent thinking and refusal to submit to unjust human laws. Grandfather wrote that Vanya was the first person among the Canadian Doukhobors to protest using nakedness and was nicknamed Czar of the Nudes.

I ask Mother about her memories of Vanya, and she settles in to explain.

Ivan Perepolkin. Pete Maloff considered him the "Professor of the Sons of Freedom."

LEEZA:Vanya Perepolkin owned land next to the Aseyevs in Thrums. I'd go down to the Aseyevs' barnyard to pet the calves and wave at Vanya, who was often working in his garden on the other side of the fence. He was short, and his first wife was a big woman. Papa told me about Vanya's philosophy. Vanya believed that the main evil and injustice of the world was based on property ownership. He said, "Selling and buying of Mother Nature is an abomination," so he invited several other couples to join him on his land. The settlement grew to include about twenty people with several small houses around a bigger communal house where they had guest rooms and gathered to share their meals, pray, sing and have meetings.

Vanya's community was vegan and avoided using animal labour. They turned the soil with their own hands; refusing to use leather, they set up workshops for making *laptyee* shoes using rubber soles and crocheted hemp uppers. Vanya told Father that he dreamed of living in a warmer climate where he could live on fruit and wear only cotton. "But in Canada," he said, "woollen socks and sweaters are necessities."

While munching on handfuls of sunflower seeds on our porch, I heard Papa tell Vanya, "Everything is good with you and your friends in *one way*—you don't eat meat or use animals for work. But this experiment of yours, free love"—Father frowned and sniffed—"is not a good idea."

Vanya shook his head vigorously. "Petya, I disagree with you. It's unjust to own a wife or husband. Relationships need to be free."

"People have passions, Ivan. Wives, husbands get jealous and angry. I don't think you and your friends are above this."

"We have talked about this, Petya. Men and women, both. We all agreed that we would only exchange partners with everyone's consent."

Eventually Vanya separated from his first wife, who moved in with another man in the community. We called her new partner *chorniy*—black Vanya—because he was swarthy, tall and big like her. Our Vanya became *beliy*—white Vanya—who lived with his second wife until he was an old man. He always told us what a good Christian his wife's former husband was, as he did not get angry at his wife for leaving him. Vanya, on the other hand, was always outspoken. He would tell people very bluntly if he saw they were doing wrong—living a *raskoshniy*, a rich, wasteful lifestyle, or killing animals for food, or enslaving them for work, or in any way violating God's law.

Vanya Perepolkin's land was where some of the first Doukhobor Sons of Freedom protests started in Thrums. On Sundays, many gathered there to hold prayer meetings and discussions. My grandfather Nikolai, curious to see what was going on, told Grandmother, "I'll just see what they are up to." Grandmother Elizaveta begged him not to go. Father was already in jail for leading a protest in Nelson, and she knew that with Grandfather Nikolai's passionate character he might join the protesters. When Nikolai was arrested, Mother and Grandmother sighed, shrugged their shoulders and decided, "We may as well join them."

—⁓—

In reading *Plakun Trava*, Koozma Tarasoff's historical book on the Doukhobors, I learn that 1931 to 1935 was a turbulent time for Doukhobors. Christian Community of Universal Brotherhood (CCUB) property, along with several government schools, was burnt down. Instead of investigating the crimes, government authorities levied a charge to the CCUB community to replace the schools.[25] They demanded that all Doukhobor children be sent to government schools and that births, marriages and deaths be registered. Additionally, the BC government barred Doukhobors from voting in elections.[26] A new federal-provincial law, which seemed to be written to deal directly with the nude Svobodniki protests, stated that those convicted of public nudity would receive a three-year sentence in a federal prison. In an attempt at appeasement, Chistiakov expelled CCUB members who "burned and stripped and forced people out of school" and those who did not pay CCUB dues. Tarasoff writes that most of these joined zealot settlements in Thrums and Krestova. Though the proof was often circumstantial, members of the Sons of Freedom were generally blamed for the criminal acts.[27]

I go back to reading Grandfather Pete Maloff's book. In the chapter on the Sons of Freedom he recorded conversations and

---

25.   Tarasoff, *Plakun Trava*, p. 129.
26.   Tarasoff, *Plakun Trava*, pp. 151–52.
27.   Tarasoff, *Plakun Trava*, pp. 131–38.

described many of their principal personalities, including Ivan Perepolkin. Using this and local newspapers as sources, I imagine the discussion at Perepolkin's property in Thrums the day the arrests took place.

—m—

The morning prayers finished, children scatter, playing hide-and-go-seek, skipping and playing marbles. The adults sit on the grass under the shade of the blossoming apple and pear trees. In front of them the dirt road, still muddy from spring rains, runs parallel to the Canadian Pacific Railway line. Below, the Kootenay River flows swift and clean.

Ivan Perepolkin, dressed in a white homespun linen Cossack-style shirt and pants, starts the conversation. "We have to listen to our conscience and our own intelligence."

Alyosha, a tall, red-headed man, nods his head in agreement. "I agree; conscience is our guide, not human laws or governments."

A woman, clearly agitated, stands up with her hands outstretched in an appeal. "But what are we to do? When we protested against taxes being used for the war effort, our lands were taken away. We are farmers. How will we live?"

Ivan shakes his head. "We are Svobodniki, Sons of Freedom. We fight for spiritual, not material gain. We must care about truth only. It is the most important thing in the world. Everything else has no value at all."

Another answers, "Our forefathers gave up much in our dear motherland for the truth. Shall we not do the same?" ·

A man waving a local newspaper announces, "Here is the latest from the *Nelson Daily News*: Chistiakov is sentenced to jail in Prince Albert for three years, and the court proceedings and appeals we have undertaken have done nothing to free him. We must support him."

A portly woman cries out, "Remember, they bombed our leader Haspodnyeey in 1924. Who knows what lengths they will go to, to silence our voice."

The consensus is that they need a peaceful way of demonstrating against the social injustice they see.

Masha, a large motherly woman, suggests, "If they rob us like that, we may as well show that they have left us naked."

In heated agreement, Fenya pipes up. "Since they have taken our outer garments, let them take our underwear too."

A young mother objects, "It is shameful to be seen naked by the whole world."

Ivan replies, "It is up to each to do what they feel is right. But God created nothing shameful. We feel ashamed of our bad deeds, nothing else."

A tall bearded man stands and speaks. "You know me. I have participated in many protests, walked with many of you in *pakhoti*, peace walks, against payment of taxes that go to support the war machine, against sending our children to schools where they are made to sing 'God Save the King,' even though kings create wars and send soldiers as fodder to the battlefield." Men and women nod their heads. "You also know that I have not agreed with you about public nudity, not out of shame, but because being naked is a private matter. The RCMP have been arresting nude protesters, but when those police trucks come, I will listen to my conscience."

Many others rise. "We must make a stand. If removing our clothes is the only way we can make our point, then that is what we must do."

"But remember Porto Rico! We may lose all! Our homes! Our children! We have gardens to tend, animals to feed!"

This discussion might have carried on for some time, but along that dirt road, a police car is slowly making its way toward the crowd, the police scrutinizing the gathering at Ivan's place. Quickly, without thinking, Ivan and a slight, quiet *babushka*, a woman of many sons and daughters, act on their inner voice, by undressing. They begin a prayer song, and the entire gathering joins in.

Down the road, from the east, more police trucks and cars begin to arrive, special constables driving each vehicle. The Svobodniki protest the way they feel is right; they protest to gather attention to their cause. Men begin to take off their shirts, their pants. Women unroll their stockings, unbutton their blouses, their skirts, helping each other. Children, wide-eyed, huddle around their parents. Police intrude on the gathering and arrest everyone. Parents carry their babies; toddlers and older children grasp their hands and follow them into the trucks.

One man dressed only in his cap and shoes offers to drive the truck to jail. "I have my licence. I see you may be short of drivers."

There never was such an orderly arrest. The Svobodniki men, women and children calmly climb into police trucks. They are ready to lend their bodies to this peaceful protest, no matter what the consequences, since many of their ancestors lost not only their freedom and their land, but their lives as well.

The protesters are taken to the Nelson provincial jail yard, which in the next few days fills up with over five hundred men and women and many children. There isn't enough room in the jails. Nine tents are set up in the prison yard, and barbed wire is coiled on top of the existing fence to keep the prisoners in and the visitors out. The warden orders a camp kitchen to be constructed outside. The prisoners cook their meals in shifts.

When they are taken to court, there is no leniency, no clemency. The presiding judge gives the adults three years of internment in a specially built federal prison camp on Piers Island in the Gulf of Georgia, where the men are separated from the women. The judge expresses his regret when the old and the infirm come before him, but he maintains his resolve to follow the newly created law for indecent exposure and sentences everyone to the three-year prison term. Over three hundred children, most under fourteen years of

In 1932 children and adults were incarcerated at the Nelson provincial jail yard. Eventually the families were separated and sent to a variety of institutions throughout the province. Vera Aseyev is the small girl on the right standing above the baby.

age, are taken from their parents and sent to institutions, orphanages and foster homes.

Nikolai Maloff and his wife, Elizaveta, are imprisoned on Piers Island for three years. Pete Maloff, Elizabeth's father, my grandfather, is jailed in the BC Penitentiary, in solitary confinement for lengthy periods for "disturbing the peace" when he led a peaceful protest march in Nelson to speak out against using land taxes to support war efforts. Pete's family is scattered, his wife Lusha sent to the Piers Island internment centre, and their five children dispersed among foster homes, orphanages and the Girls' Industrial School, a reform school for juvenile delinquent girls.

———

Ivan Perepolkin is not on the government website list of people arrested and imprisoned on Piers Island, and Mother, who was eleven years old at the time, does not remember what happened to him. She recalls that he did lose his land for non-payment of taxes and that a neighbour, Polly Postnikoff, whose husband had died, invited Vanya and his wife to live in a shack on her property. It wasn't much, but they lived out their lives there.

When Ivan lay dying, his wife asked, "Shall I light the lamp?"

His answer: "God will find me in the dark."

BC GIRLS'
INDUSTRIAL SCHOOL

—◁◈▷—

A shock ripples through me as I hold the letters that my mother's cousin Annie Malahoff has brought this morning. I had asked to talk to her about growing up in the Hoodicoff-Maloff household, and she responded by bringing these letters that have been in a shoebox at the back of her closet for many years. I unfold the yellowed paper, and the letterhead—"Children's Aid Society of Vancouver, B.C."—leaps out at me from the top of the page. I hold my breath as my eyes scan the letter.

CHILDREN'S AID SOCIETY OF VANCOUVER, B.C.
Member of Vancouver Welfare Federation
                                    Vancouver, B.C.
                                    August 22, 1932
Mrs. Mary Hoodekoff,
Thrums, B.C.

Dear Mrs. Hoodekoff,

Your grandchildren Tania and Vera Popoff are with the Children's Aid Society and they are quite well and happy. Hope (Nadya) Maloff is also with us. She is growing and is very well. Elizabeth Maloff is at the Industrial School, and Pete, John and Love (Luba) are at the Alexandra Orphanage in Vancouver.

Yours Sincerely,
Zella Collins
Manager

This letter from the manager, Zella Collins, to my great-grandmother Mary Hoodicoff is terse and to the point. With the children's parents in jail, she had to dictate hundreds of these letters to their relatives. The children were taken from the makeshift tents in the Nelson provincial jail and loaded on trains to Vancouver in May. The date of the letter is August 22. Would the families have known where the children were in the meantime? I imagine my grandparents' anxiety. Or perhaps they put their trust in God that the children would be looked after, as the early Doukhobors did when the czarist government in Russia separated parents from their children? I hope the latter, though that would take a great faith I didn't have. After their sentencing, the parents were transported by train and then by ferry across the Strait of Georgia to the federal Piers Island Penitentiary built especially for the nude protesters. Baby Hope (Nadya) had stayed with her mother, Lusha, for a short time, but by August, at eight months old, she was in foster care.

I look at Annie, at Mother. Their lips are pursed, brows furrowed, and I feel the tenseness of their bodies. They do not say anything but look down at the table set with tea. Feelings of sadness and outrage course through me as I think about the impact of this action on their innocent young lives.

The second letter is handwritten in pencil, and every inch of the paper is covered in the neat handwriting that I recognize as Mother's. The date is October 31, 1932: Halloween. Halloween, in my elementary classes, meant the children would have a party with costumes, food and games. In the industrial school in 1932, Mother was allowed to write a letter to her aunt. Mother does not look at this letter she sent more than eighty-five years ago. Instead, she looks down at her hands while I start to read the letter aloud.

800 Cassiar St.
Vancouver, B.C.
1932. Oct. 31.

My Dearest Aunt Polly,

I am very very lonesome for you. Dear Aunt I received your pictures and I was very glad. Dear Aunt I have no picture to send you. Dear Aunt please tell Betty Hoodicoff to write me a letter. I am very lonesome for her. I have just two of my friends here.

Dear Aunt tell grandmother Hoodicoff to come and visit me. I am very very lonesome for you Aunt and for grandmother. I am crying every day about my little sister and about brothers and about Luba.

Dear Aunt send me some material for handkerchiefs and please send me some silk to embroider. Dear Aunt you were asking what size shoes I wear. 3½.

I am very very lonesome for you Aunt and for Mother and father and for grandmother. I write this letter in school. Dear Aunt they let us write in three weeks two letters.

Dear Aunt we have a meeting every Sunday and say our prayers and sing, and we sing every evening after supper. Dear Aunt you know how I am geting [sic] along here.

Dear Aunt the big girls are cooking and baking the bread they cook in the morning porridge and we eat in morning bead [sic] with jam at dinner we eat peanuts and macaroni and potatoes and soup and rice In supper we eat oranges and cooked fruit and dates.

Dear Aunt tell uncle John to write me a letter if he is lonesome for me.

Dear Aunt I kiss you many many times and your children and Best regards for you and for your children. So good by your niece, Elizabeth P. Maloff

to Betty Hoodicoff,

Dear Betty

I am very lonesome for you. I received from you 1 letter so please write me a letter and I will write to you. Dear Betty I will kiss you many many times. Best regards for you and for your sister Annie. Your friend Elizabeth P Maloff

Please give my best regards to my Grandfather and Grandmother Hoodicoff and to all Saliken family and please tell them to come and visit me.

from Elizabeth P. Maloff

Mother's anguish and lonesomeness leap out of the page. I do not finish reading but look at Mother and Annie through a veil of tears. Mother folds and refolds a paper napkin, her hands restless. She sighs, "I had put away those memories. There was enough to think about in those days." Annie nods in acknowledgement.

Here is Mother's story.

LEEZA: The matrons take Petya, Luba, Johnnik and me from the Nelson jail, where Mama, Babushka and Dedushka are, to the train station Sunday evening. There are many of us, over a hundred girls and younger boys;[28] the older boys were taken away a few days earlier. I barely have time to say goodbye to Mama, and when we go through the tall prison gate, I look back. She doesn't seem like my strong mama at all, but small, clinging to the high wire fence around the prison yard. I want to call out, "Mama, I'll look after everyone. Mama, don't cry. Mama!" but the matrons hustle us away.

We board two special coaches attached to the end of the regular Canadian Pacific Railway train, and I help Luba, Petya and Johnnik find seats and tuck our little bags around us. Mrs. Westman, the head matron, walks through the coaches and calls out our names from a list. She wears a white uniform, and when I look up at her, she is so tall and stern looking with her short hair and glasses that I am scared of her. There are other matrons on the train too, in blue or green uniforms. All the kids are running around, excited, but I have to care for my brothers and sister. "Johnnik, Petya, Luba, come, sit. Let's stay together."

As the train heads west, we see the villages we know so well—Shoreacres, Thrums, Brilliant and Grand Forks—pass by the window. The train stops at these communities and people get on and off, but we can only peer out the windows and wonder what will happen to us. Into the night the train travels west, and in the morning we wake and see strange rivers, towns and mountains.

The trip is long; we are tired and hungry when we finally reach our destination, Vancouver. When Petya's and Johnnik's names

28.   Three hundred fifty-two Doukhobor children were placed in government care from 1932 to 1933: 71 in the Girls' Industrial School, 91 in the Boys' Industrial School, 114 in foster families, 75 in orphanages and 1 in a mental health institution. Lapshinoff, "Sons of Freedom Children."

are called, they climb down the train steps, sullen looks on their faces, and obediently gather with the younger children. Luba clings to me and whispers, "I'm scared, Leeza. I want Mama and Papa. When will they be here?"

"Luba, I won't leave you. Here, hold my hand." I hug her, but even as we step out of our coach, a matron firmly takes Luba's hand from mine and places her in the lineup of children going to the orphanage. Luba reaches out her arms to me, but I am also herded to another line and can do nothing but watch as tears stream down her face. My family has always been around me, and I always looked after my brothers and sisters, but now I am alone with strangers.

More than seventy of us Doukhobor girls are assigned to the British Columbia Girls' Industrial School. As we are driven up to a large, white, three-storey building, I see thick walls, barred windows and a tower in the middle; I think we must be going to jail. We learn that girls on the first two floors are sentenced to live here because they have done something wrong. So that we don't mix with the juvenile delinquent girls, we climb a metal fire escape on the outside of the building, three storeys up to get to the attic where our dorms are. Some of the girls complain that the stairs are steep and when it rains they are slippery, but we are young and it doesn't matter. I am never afraid of the height. Up and down the stairs, I always like it—I can see far and I feel free.

Inside the attic are two long rooms with high ceilings and sloping roofs. Sunlight, when there is any in this rainy city, comes through windows at the ends and through a dormer in the middle. From the north window, two storeys down at the front of the school, I notice a circular driveway, a lawn and an entrance patio. Magnolia trees, the branches laden with huge white blossoms, grow on both sides of the wide porch, but we never go there—it is outside the fence. Through the dormer window, I look at a big backyard, fenced in by a solid six-foot fence, and all along the fence, pink roses are blooming. There are chickens and gardens where the regular girls work. On the other side of the yard is a gymnasium. We spend all day there. We eat and do our lessons in an added lunchroom, and when it isn't raining, we play outside in front of it.

The fourteen-to-eighteen-year-old girls sleep on the other side of the building, and I am with the ten-to-thirteen-year-olds

Elizabeth Maloff (second row, fifth on the right), together with seven-ty-one Doukhobor girls, was housed in the attic of the BC Girls' Industrial School for a year.

on this end. Four smaller girls who are six to eight years of age share a room in between the two attics. Two matrons sleep in a room just off the hallway. There are rows of beds for the thirty of us on our side—mostly two beds pushed together so that two girls share the top blanket. A few girls have single beds.

I wish my sisters were with me. Until now I have always shared a bed with Luba, but she is four and Nadya six months old—both of them too young to be here. The matrons tell me that Luba and my two brothers are at the Alexandra Orphanage and that Nadya stayed with Mama in the jail for a while, but now she is in a foster home somewhere in Vancouver. Every night before I go to sleep, I think about them and about Mama and Papa and say a prayer to keep us all safe.

There are bathrooms with three toilets and showers for our dormitory, though we can't use them at night because our doors are locked. In the morning a matron unlocks the doors and there is a rush to line up for the washrooms. Thirty girls wait for the bathroom each morning, and some of the girls are always pushing to be first. The younger girls can use the bathrooms any time, as their room is unlocked and close to the bathrooms.

In an effort to re-educate the children to a different way of life and provide recreation, Luba, Peter and Johnnik were taken to Summer Camp Alexandra. (Luba second on the left, above, Peter first on the right, below)

Malasha Savinkoff is my partner. She's a few inches taller, but skinny like me. Her light brown hair is cut into a short bob; mine is long and blond and I braid it myself. The youngest of three brothers and two sisters, Malasha is from Grand Forks, and her parents have been sentenced to Piers Island Penitentiary where my mama, *babushka* and *dedushka* are. She is a good partner. We never fight. We take turns making the bed every day and changing it once a week. She tells me, "Leeza, let's stay together. See how well we get along? In the daytime we can go with anyone we like, but at night, don't go with anyone else." Some girls quarrel and I avoid them, but Malasha knows how to change the atmosphere and make everything less serious. The girls next to us are cousins and they bicker sometimes. Malasha says, "*Hlyan', payekhalyee!* There they go again! What are they arguing about? Everyone is the same here." Malasha tells them, "That's enough. It's getting late. Time to go to sleep." She is so *bistraya*, she quickly lets everybody know what she thinks, but she's easygoing and never means to offend anyone. She even gets some of the matrons to laugh at her jokes.

A few other girls help make life here acceptable. Hrunya Nazaroff, whose dad helped us in Porto Rico, is one. She is in the dormitory for the older girls. On our side is Natasha Barabanoff, a tall, skinny, pleasant-looking girl with medium-length hair, who is always jovial and cheers us up if we are sad. Even early in the morning I hear her chatting and laughing. Then there are the Wlasoff girls—two sisters, Tanya and Florence, and a cousin, Polly—who share a blanket.

My papa is best friends with Polly's papa, George Wlasoff. We lived together in a co-operative fruit farm in California before moving back to Canada. Polly is younger, and I like to tell her about our papas, about how when they used to visit, we would hear them talk and laugh all night. I tell her about a drive we took in the farm truck through the rolling country roads in California. Our papas had so much fun driving those roller-coaster roads that they said "Let's do it again," turned around and drove up and down those dips and hills once more just for the joy of it. We laugh and laugh, imagining our papas together. Polly and Tanya invite me to move over to their side of the dormitory, but I am comfortable with Malasha.

At first, food is a problem. For breakfast we are fed *kasha*, and that is good. But at lunchtime, oy, the food isn't at all what we are used to! We are vegetarian, and the big English cook doesn't understand this. She insists on adding meat bones to the soup, and when we complain, she comes out of the kitchen, her apron smeared with what looks to us like blood, and loudly smacks the table with her ladle. "You girls don't appreciate good food! You're lucky to have some meat. It'll make you strong and healthy." But I smell meat in the soup and my stomach heaves. All of us leave the soup on the table uneaten, so for our next meal she gives us a slice of bread that is starting to get mouldy, adding a little peanut butter or jam on top. I don't want to eat that smelly mouldy bread either and, together with most of the girls, refuse to eat it. The matrons punish us, making us stand outside on the concrete until our legs ache and our heads spin. They want us to study our lessons, but we say we won't if they force us to eat meat. Some of the older girls are taken to the detention cells in the basement for this protest.

Finally, we win. The senior girls take turns working in the kitchen making soup. There isn't much variety, but, oh, we are so happy to eat our Doukhobor soup again. After a few weeks they bring some turnips. We devour those cut-up raw turnips down to the last *kusok*. There aren't any greens, and we are used to eating fresh vegetables from the garden. I notice dandelions, which we used to eat in springtime, growing in the grass and start to dig them up with my hands. It is hard to dig them, but I wash and eat them, roots and all. Malasha, Tanya, Polly and Natasha look at me and dig the dandelions too. In the fall, there are big, fat rosehips all along the fence, and I eat those. The girls join in, and we strip the rosehips from those long rows of rose bushes.

We wear the same clothing we came in, and though relatives have brought some extra clothing, after a few months we look ragged and our blouses are tight and uncomfortable. A few of the older girls get their periods here, and that is a problem—too few bathrooms, and they are locked at night.

We are allowed visitors, but we don't know many people in Vancouver. Dyadya Nick and his family live in Langley, across the river from Vancouver, but they don't come to see me because Dyadya and Papa don't agree about protests against the government.

My cousin Helen is just two weeks older than me, and I think of her when it's my birthday. I turn twelve at the school, but it's a regular day. We don't celebrate birthdays here.

Then one of the girls has a visitor from home, and the news is bad. That night, the girls in our dormitory huddle, whispering, and I see them looking over at me. Finally, Polly walks up to me and says, "Leeza, I don't know if it's true, but everyone is saying that your papa died." I look at her, shake my head and whimper, "It can't be true. It just can't." I cry and cry. I don't sleep. I look up at the slanted ceiling and hear pigeons cooing in the rafters above me, and I think about how Papa and I used to go everywhere together. We would walk the railway track for miles to Shoreacres to visit Dedushka and Babushka, and I would never complain that my legs were tired; otherwise he might not take me next time. Mama was always busy with the twins and baby Nadya, but I could talk to Papa any time.

And I think about how Papa moved the gophers. We had gopher holes all over our farm, and they would come out at night to eat our vegetables. Papa made traps so that when he poured water in one hole, the gophers would pop out of the other hole and get caught in a burlap bag. He rowed those gophers across the river— the Kootenay River was swift in those days—and released them in the forest on the other side. When we asked where he freed those gophers, he said that he let them go in the same place in the forest, so they would stay together as a family. How could we be a family without Papa?

In the morning, I am red-eyed, my braid is awry and my clothes a mess. The matron in charge looks at me and takes me down to see the head matron in her office. Mrs. Westman sits behind her desk; I stand in front of her, head bent, rubbing my eyes trying to stop my tears. Through my sobs, I tell her that I heard my papa died.

Mrs. Westman says, "Who told you such a thing? I haven't heard anything. I'll find out at once if this is true."

—⁕—

Papa hadn't died. Years later he told me that instead of being imprisoned on Piers Island with Mama, Babushka, Dedushka and other Doukhobors, he was incarcerated in the BC Penitentiary for "disrupting the peace" in a protest that he led through the streets of Nelson. The judge labelled Papa an "instigator" and sentenced him to the New Westminster federal maximum-security prison for three years. There he was placed in solitary confinement for three months in the "black hole," where the prison guards intimidated him with threats of execution. Only an old Chinese orderly who delivered Papa's frugal meals kept his fear at bay by whispering to him, "They can't do that to you. They don't have anything against you."

A friend of Papa's heard that he was being badly treated at the penitentiary and thought of a way to help him. The friend placed Pete Maloff's picture and an announcement in a popular Canadian Russian workers' paper, the *Kanadsky Gudok* (the Canadian Whistle), stating that he had been tortured and died in the BC Penitentiary. (Many Doukhobors read this paper; Dedushka Hoodicoff always told Babushka, "Don't come home without the *Gudok*.")

The news spread, and everyone got riled up. There were telegrams and phone calls of protest to the jail and the government. Papa was released from the black hole into the regular jail, and after a while, he got to work in the jail gardens.

—————

I get a letter from Mama saying she is okay but she misses all of us. My auntie, Tyota Polya, Mama's younger sister, also writes. Her family is staying in our house while they are having theirs built. She says that the garden Mama planted before we were taken away is very good and the peas are abundant. I don't hear from Papa for a long time, and even though now I know he is alive, I worry about him. At night I hug my pillow tightly and try not to cry.

When I finally receive Papa's letter, it is like getting a huge present. I keep that letter under my pillow and reread it so often that the paper becomes soft from handling it and the ink fades. He writes that all this will be over one day and tells me to be patient and that we will be together. I am allowed to write two letters every three weeks, and I write back and tell Tyota that I miss her and everyone dreadfully, and to come and visit me if she can. I tell Papa that I love him and I will try to be patient. I write to Mama and tell her what we are doing at school and about the food that we eat.

Mama taught me, so I know how to write. But the reading and writing instruction at the institution isn't very good. I learn later that Mrs. Westman wanted all girls in the school to have a good education, to be trained in a trade, so they could have jobs after they left, but the government didn't want to spend the money—these were Depression years. The only training was the sort to prepare the girls for domestic service or farm work.

That summer, we get more bad news. Three babies who were in foster care have died.[29] The older girls organize special prayers. They tell us to get down on our knees and pray for our parents, our brothers and sisters and the babies. Though we've never said prayers on our knees before, we cave in and do what the girls say. We recite Doukhobor prayers our parents taught us.

> "Dom Nash Blahadatniy"
> Lord Give Us Thy Blessing.
> Our haven of refuge, that giveth us blessings, is our
> trust in God.
> In this sacred trust, Christ Himself dwelleth
> And His Holy Spirit is ever on guard.
> In all our undertakings may God be with us.
> Our God be Praised.[30]

When we pray and sing, the matrons come to watch, but they let us have our prayers.

I am worried about my baby sister Nadya, who is in a foster home. Matron Westman brought her to see me one time, and she looked skinny and cried all the time. I ask to see her again, but a matron just shows me a picture of her. She's small and isn't smiling. I wonder if she is learning to crawl, to walk, to talk? Is anyone giving her hugs and kisses? Does she remember me?

Luba, Petya and Johnnik come to see me once also, and a matron supervises us as we sit stiffly on chairs in a room downstairs. They are not the boisterous Johnnik and the cuddly Luba I remember from home. Petya, too, is different; in a serious way he asks what

---

29.   Babakaeff, Shlakoff and Postnikoff babies died in government care in July 1932. Lapshinoff, "Sons of Freedom Children."
30.   Prayer translated from Russian by Eli Popoff.

we eat here and who cooks for us. He thinks there is meat in their soup at the orphanage. After a while, Luba comes to sit on my lap and tells me they have been to the ocean and found seashells, while Johnnik nods, makes the sounds of the seagulls and says that the ocean is salty. I tell them to say their *pasalomcheekee* every night and that I will too. And then our visit is over, and a matron from the orphanage walks away with them.

In the evenings, we get together in our dormitory to sing. A Russian hymn we often sing is "Akh Chto Zhe Ti Ptashechka."

> Little bird, oh why so sad
> You are sorrowing, lamenting,
> And no joy you seem to show.
> And no nest you try to build,
> As from tree to tree you go.
> And the little bird replied:
> "Where can I build my nest?
> Birds of prey are all around:
> Giving me no rest.
> Their harassment will not cease,
> And they give my friends no peace.
> But I'll help them bear their cross
> As a true and faithful friend,
> And will ever be their helper
> From beginning to the end."

(translated by Eli Popoff)

A children's song we sing is "Akh Popalas Pteechka Stoy" about another bird that children caught in a net and imprisoned in a golden cage. The children want to keep the bird in the cage, feed it candy, tea and crunchies, but the bird replies that even though the cage is golden, it is still a prison and in a prison she will die. We feel like those sad birds.

Once a month, the matrons take us younger girls for a walk outside the schoolyard. We march two by two along the sidewalk to Hastings Park, and sometimes we walk down to the ocean. We play in the sand and collect small rocks to use when we play jacks. I look out over the ocean and think of Mama, Babushka and De-

dushka on an island far away in that same ocean. I look up at the seagulls circling and swooping around us and wish I were a bird and could fly away to my family.

Four-year-old Johnnik (above) and Luba (photo on the right) in the overcrowded Alexandra Orphanage.

I stayed in that school for a year. Some of the matrons were friendly; some were strict. I felt Mrs. Westman was kind-hearted and well meaning. Once she was away for almost a month, and things weren't the same. When she was present there was a better relationship and communication with the matrons and everyone.

In April of 1933, I heard we were going home. We would be staying with relatives or other Doukhobor families that agreed to take us. As I looked around our dorm, all the girls were smiling, jumping on their beds, hugging each other and wondering, "Who will we stay with? Who will invite us?" I just knew that Luba, Nadya, Petya, Johnnik and I would stay with Babushka Hoodicoff. She would always welcome us.

With overpopulation in the institutions and a shortage of caregivers, many children needed to look after one other. Years later they always recognized each other, but many did not speak of their internment to their families.

We girls didn't see each other much after we returned to our homes. We'd always recognize each other, the girls who had been in that school, but we didn't talk. We were part of a silent club. It was as if we were ashamed that we had done something wrong.

When the girls got older, many moved away from the Kootenays. Malasha lived in Grand Forks. She married and had a son, but she got sick with cancer, moved back in with her parents and died young. Tanya Wlasoff married a *nyee nash* and moved to California. She was always proud of what her parents did, standing up to the government, and when we talked on the phone, she would say, "It was the right thing to do." When she came back to British Columbia, she dropped in at my house, but sadly I wasn't home.

—*—

Mother's hands caress the worn cloth on her table. She heaves a sigh. "I have to change channels and come back to this world. It takes a while." She picks up her now tepid cup of tea and looks at Annie and me. "You can't live in the past and you can't change it," she says.

HOMECOMING,
SPRING 1933

—ᴧᴧ—

The institutionalization of Doukhobor children whose parents were interned at the Piers Island Penitentiary in the Gulf of Georgia raised protests in the Doukhobor community. The majority of children had been placed in existing orphanages and industrial schools that became overcrowded with the influx of the large group. Despite what might have been the best intention of the directors, many suffered from lack of personal attention. The youngest were fostered with families.

With the continuation of the Depression and the expense of caring for the children becoming a public issue, the Doukhobor leader, Chistiakov, was able to persuade the government to return the children to relatives or to other Doukhobor homes. A year after they were placed in government custody, they began to return to the Kootenays.

This is mother's story of the children's return to their Hoodicoff grandparents' home in Thrums.

LEEZA: We come, escorted by matrons, from every part of the city of Vancouver, streaming into the Vancouver Canadian Pacific Railway station. We come from the BC Girls' Industrial School, from the Boys' Industrial School, from orphanages and from foster homes throughout the city, and many of us have not seen each other since that day almost a year ago when we were taken off the train at that same station and assigned to our detention centres. Now we are going back, not to our own homes, but to relatives and willing families in our Kootenay villages.

There would have been 352 of us children waiting for the train this day, but some found homes previously and left on an earlier train, a few children do not have sponsor families yet, and three died in the BC Children's Hospital. Matron Westman, who is in charge of this transfer, is organized and efficient.

We sit on wooden benches, surrounded by our bags in the cavernous station, where murals of Canadian landscapes peer down at us from the ceilings. Tags labelled with our name, the name of the family and the town we are returning to hang around each of our necks. Matrons try to keep us organized, but we are young, and soon joy bubbles up as we see brothers, sisters, friends. Hundreds of us hug, kiss, cry, hold hands.

I search for my family: baby Nadya, twins Johnnik and Luba and brother Petya. Will they be able to go home? Will we be on the same train? And then, coming out of the rain through the tall doors, is, *Hospadyee Bozhe*, Nadya—all skinny arms and legs, crowned by wispy white hair—Nadya who was not yet crawling when I saw her last, now walking, though unsteadily, holding the hand of a matron. Then my heart pounds as, in the group of children from the Alexandra Orphanage, I glimpse Luba, clutching a doll, followed by Johnnik. Petya appears, carrying their bags, peering warily around for a familiar face.

I run, reach for Nadya and kneel beside her. Luba finds us and then Petya and Johnnik clasp my hand. In the middle of that swirling crowd, for a timeless moment we cluster together like rocks in a fast-flowing stream.

Our hug is broken as our Popoff cousins find us. Grinning from ear to ear, little blond Vera dashes to us and shouts her welcome. "Leeza, Luba, Nadya! You're here!" Curly-haired Tanya—Tiny—joyously joins the group hug. Then she inspects our tags and pulls hers out. "Mary Hoodicoff, Thrums. Yay! We're all going to the same place. To Babushka's. The seven of us going to Babushka's." Tiny, with Vera in tow, runs on to see who else is boarding the train.

Matron Westman, in her white nurse's uniform, stands tall amid the flow of children and matrons. She settles everyone with a whistle and a stern look. In a ringing voice she directs us. "When I call your name and the town you will be going to, line up at the boarding platform." She starts to read the roster of names.

Androsoff, Peter, Polly—Grand Forks
Antafaeff, Mary, Hanna—South Slocan
Arehoff, Nick—Brilliant
Babakaeff, Helen, Fred—Shoreacres
Beresoff, Helen—Grand Forks

> Beresoff, Nita—Tarrys
> Bloodoff, Tina, Netta, George—Brilliant
> Bullonoff, Alex, Pauline, Peter, Kate—Thrums[31]

Grouped with siblings and by destinations, children start to gather on the boarding platform as Matron continues to read the lengthy list. It is finally our turn:

> Maloff, Elizabeth, Petya, Luba, Johnnik, Nadya—
> Thrums

When we board the train, Matron puts me in charge of my brothers and sisters. I find our seats and try to settle my family around me, feeling like a mother hen. Nadya sits on my lap; I jostle her up and down, but she is crying, her tears mixed with a runny nose. Petya and Johnnik walk off to see who else is in our compartment. Luba thankfully snuggles up to me. Everyone is excited and wants to visit. I listen to the clamour of many voices.

"Annie, Nastya. How are you?"

"Florence, I am so glad to see you."

"Sam, Bill, where have you been?"

"Were they good to you?"

"Were they strict?"

"What did you eat? Did they make you eat meat?"

The hubbub around us continues. Nadya's whimpering also persists—she wants someone familiar, and I am unable to ease her loss. I, too, want to talk to friends I haven't seen. Finally, in the evening, as the train approaches the mountains, Matron Westman says, "You have a rest, Elizabeth. I'll look after Nadya for a while." She rocks her and Nadya falls asleep in her arms.

I sit with Luba cuddled up to me and my brothers kneeling on the benches across from us, their noses pressed to the window. The train travels slowly as water rises on both sides of the railway track from the spring floods.

In the train that night, we curl up, Luba and Nadya's heads lolling against mine, Johnnik and Petya huddled together. The rumble of the train is rhythmic, comforting. In the night, Luba mumbles in her sleep, Johnnik kicks out, Petya wakes and rubs his eyes, Nadya cries.

---

31. Lapshinoff, "Sons of Freedom Children."

Matron Westman, who is in a seat next to us, comes and picks her up again. "Sh, sh." I become accustomed to the noises of my family. But there is an empty space. My mind swirls with the thought: How did we end up here without our mama and papa?

Our family had been like peas in a pod. First there were Mama, Papa and me. We lived in Thrums and all our relatives lived close by—Babushka and Dedushka Hoodicoff across the road, dyadyas, tyotas and cousins all around us.

When I was three, Papa decided to visit friends in Oregon and California. When Petya was born there in California, I was so happy to have a brother.

We went back to Thrums, and I was free to wander everywhere. My cousins, neighbourhood friends and I would play together through the fields and barns, skipping, hiding, climbing trees and sliding down the skinny branches, never paying attention to whose place it was. Life was fun and full of possibilities.

Mama taught me songs, and I felt special and important when Babushka and Dedushka Hoodicoff asked me to sing for their guests. My favourite was a sad song, "Spokoyno Stoyala Ona Pred Sudom," about a beautiful Roman girl who chose death rather than deny she was a Christian. As I sang, I would act brave and then shed tears as I imagined her walking to her death to be torn apart by ferocious animals.

Papa would send me to Johnson's store in Thrums to pick up the mail. The Johnsons all knew me and would ask about my family. "How is your mom? How are the twins? Are they getting bigger?" The whole neighbourhood came by to see the twins.

And then the trouble started. Johnnik and Luba were still babies, a year old, when Papa was put in Oakalla Prison for leading a protest in Nelson against taxes for war. Mama, Johnnik, Luba, Petya and I demonstrated with the rest of the families, camping outside Nelson, and then we were interned by the government in an abandoned Kootenay mountain logging camp, Porto Rico, that winter. At least we were with Mama. In the spring we came back to Thrums and Papa came back from Oakalla. He found work picking cherries and apples in the Okanagan while we stayed in Thrums, but it was okay. Our *dedushka* and *babushka* Maloff moved to a cabin beside our house. Great-Grandmother's brother George and his wife, Hannah Kabatoff, who lived next door, also helped us. Nadya was born that December. Then, in the spring of 1932, again, there were protests and jail.

This time, Mama and Papa are sent away for three years. I have a hard time understanding why they are in jail. They didn't hurt anyone.

Now, it is hard to put us back together again once we have been shelled out of the pod, each one of us landing somewhere different. We are strangers to each other.

In the morning, cousins Tiny and Vera sleepily stand beside us. "We're all going to Babushka's," they repeat, and Luba and I move over to make room for them on the bench.

"Where were you?" I ask.

"With our foster mom and dad." Tiny pulls a picture out of her bag of a kind-looking older couple. "They gave us these," she says and opens her bag further to show us a beautiful dress and a coat.

Luba sadly strokes the coat and says, "I had a coat from home, all white and soft, but when we were leaving the orphanage I couldn't find it. Nurse said that it was packed away in a box somewhere."

Tiny asks, "What was it like there, at the orphanage?"

"Lots of English kids. Older girls looked after me, and I liked it when they asked me to play on the see-saw." Luba shakes her head and frowns. "But I didn't like climbing the stairs to the attic where I slept. They were so steep, I was afraid, but Nurse said I had to go and pushed me, so I had to go. I cried."

Johnnik, who has been listening to us girls talk, pipes up. "I didn't like those stairs either. The food was okay, though ... good soup ... though Petya worried there might be meat in it. He wouldn't eat it."

Tiny looks at the picture of her foster family again. "Mom and Dad asked if we could stay with them forever. They cried when we left."

Vera sadly adds, "We cried too."

I think, "Nadya stayed with a foster family too, but she has no picture or anything to remember them by. She looks ill and small. I wonder if she was well looked after."

Then, as we approach Grand Forks, we see a huge crowd gathered in front of the railway station. The friends I have lived with for

a year in the industrial school—Malasha, Tanya, Florence, Polly—
are met by relatives, and through the steamy train window it appears
a happy reunion. I also see awkward meetings where shy children are
introduced to their new foster families. Hrunya and Mary Nazaroff
cling to their older brother Sam as he prepares to get off the train to
stay with a distant uncle. The sisters are going to live with an aunt
in Castlegar.

As the train leaves Grand Forks, Luba and Johnnik impatiently
ask, "When will we be home?" Hours later we reach Castlegar and
then Brilliant, where more children are met by their host families.

Toward evening, we finally arrive in Thrums. Nineteen children, from babies to teenagers, tumble out of that train. Babushka
Hoodicoff and Tyota Polya receive the seven of us with hugs, tears
and prayers of thankfulness.

"*Slava Bohu, preeyekhalyee.* Thank God, you've arrived," says
Babushka. "We've been waiting every day for three days; we didn't
know when you'd be here."

Tyota Polya shakes her head. "Mr. Johnson told us that the train
tracks at the coast are flooded and no one knew when the train
would come in. Today we almost gave up and went home, but here
you are, *Hospadyee Bozhe.*"

Babushka greets Matron Westman. Babushka, short and dressed
in her traditional clothing—a fringed *platok* on her head, long-
sleeved dark blouse and skirt—is in contrast with the tall matron in
her white nurse's uniform. In the future I will recognize that they
are similar, these two women—kind in a no-nonsense way, both
doing what needs to be done, trying to make life better for those
around them. Matron Westman talks to Babushka for a few minutes, shakes hands with all of us and wishes us well. Then, she climbs
back aboard the train to deliver the remaining children to their
homes in Glade, Shoreacres, South Slocan, Crescent Valley, Taghum,
Winlaw and Perry Siding.

Babushka looks us over and shakes her head at the sight. Then
her practical nature takes over. She gathers us around her, and
with the help of Tyota Polya, we head off to her home carrying
our bags.

As we walk toward Babushka's rambling, one-storey, wood-
en-sided house, I breathe in the scent of home—the earthen path,

Upon their release, the Maloff and Popoff children were met by Babushka Masha Hoodicoff and Tyota Polya Konkin at the Thrums train station. Their parents came home a year later, but the long separation from their families troubled them for many years.

the smell of grass as we tread on it, the budding apple, plum and pear trees and the freshly dug garden. As dusk settles down on us, I hear frogs croaking in our ponds across the road. We see the long veranda at the front of Babushka's house and joyfully sprint toward our home-to-be. We enter the warm kitchen, with its big wood cooking stove and the smells of bread, herbs and onions.

Dedushka gives us a brusque hug, his whiskers scratching our cheeks. Our uncle Ivan and his wife, Polly, greet us. Their one-year-old son, Fred, who was born just before we were taken away, shyly glances at us from behind his mother's skirt. Uncle Bill, a tall, gangly teenage boy, strides in. We stand, say the Lord's Prayer and sit down to eat a milk and rice soup at the long wooden dining room table.

After supper, Babushka briskly organizes us. Vera and Tiny are to live with Tyota Polya and her family in our house across the road. Babushka's house has three bedrooms and two living rooms. Uncle Ivan, Aunt Polly and cousin Fred stay in one bedroom. Nadya will sleep in a little bed in Babushka and Dedushka's room, and Luba, Johnnik and I sleep in the third bedroom. Petya is to take a couch in one of the living rooms with Uncle Bill.

Early the next morning, we visit our old friends, the cows Betsy, Tyunkya and Dunya, and nuzzle their newborn calves. We feed some grass to Dan, the horse, and run to the chicken coop where a hundred chickens cluck noisily. Uncle Ivan is working in his blacksmith shed, and we hear metal being hammered and smell the hot burnt air. The hay barn is almost empty this early in the year, and even though Dedushka doesn't like it, we gleefully climb up and slide down the fragrant, loosely piled hay that is there. Familiar sounds and smells—we begin to feel we are home.

Babushka keeps us all busy. Petya fetches the cows and calves from pasture to the barn and feeds them their evening bran. Dedushka and I milk them. My hands get strong from milking Betsy. She stands peacefully chewing her cud while I butt my head against her soft brown flank and rhythmically pull her teats—squeeze, squirt, squeeze, squirt. Warm, foamy milk gushes out into the pail. Dedushka separates the milk from the cream, and I churn butter, up and down, up and down, for a long time. Babushka makes cottage cheese with the rest of the milk. Small banty chickens run around in the yard freely all day, and at night we gather them into the chicken coop with a handful of wheat and a call: "Teep, teep, teep." Babushka gives them a special treat, a bucket full of whey, that she says makes their eggs tasty. Luba and Johnnik collect the eggs, warm from under the hens. On Fridays, Petya and I accompany Babushka and Uncle Ivan, who drives the old Chevy truck to Trail to sell produce door to door.

We live with Babushka and Dedushka Hoodicoff for a year. They do their best for us, but it is crowded and I feel we are a burden. Dedushka grumbles about space and wanting peace and quiet. Uncle Ivan and Aunt Polly look for another house to move to. Being the oldest, I am expected to keep an eye on my siblings. I get sick and tired of hearing my name, as I am always being called. "Leeza, come help. Leeza, where are Johnnik and Peter? Leeza, look after Nadya." Thank goodness Luba is quiet and follows me around. It isn't Babushka's fault. It's just the way it is.

I often look longingly at our house across the road, and my thirteen-year-old self thinks, "We could live there by ourselves. I could look after everyone." Then I imagine all of us back in our warm house, gathered around our kitchen table, with Papa pulling buckwheat *kasha* out of the oven and Mama teaching us songs like she used to, and it only makes me sadder. Will Mama and Papa ever come back?

—*m*—

Lusha Maloff was allowed to return to be with her children after two years. Pete Maloff was also released in two years for good conduct.

Several generations of Doukhobor children were taken from their parents: in Mother's era, in 1932; then again in the 1950s and 1960s when police rounded up some of my classmates to live in New Denver, where the Japanese Canadians had been interned during the Second World War. In New Denver, for years the children could only see and hug their parents through a wire mesh fence. The lives of many Doukhobor families were disrupted for generations.

LAND

—∿∿—

It isn't a big piece: five acres in Thrums, sandwiched between High-way 3A and Mount Sentinel. There is some arable flat land, enough for a subsistence farm, but then the land steeply slopes up the mountain and becomes rocky and poor. There is a two-storey stucco-sided house built in 1918 where my brother lives, and the remnants of greenhouses, tool and tractor sheds and a *banya*, or bathhouse. Mother knows the trees, the herbs and flowers, the rocks, the places where she played as a child.

When you have lost and regained your home, it becomes cherished.

An old apple tree fell down last summer. Bears had climbed that tree for years, reaching for apples that grew on the very top, and finally the gnarled trunk could no longer support their weight. Mother saved the last apples, planning to start a tree from the seeds. She collected boxes of small, tasty apples.

"That tree was over a hundred years old, a Jonathan," she says. "Good for pies and applesauce. My great-aunt Fenya and her husband, Peter Vereschagin, planted that tree. All the trees on the property—Jonathan, Wagner, Northern Spy and King apples and Bartlett pears—came from CCUB[32] trees that were grown all over Ootischenia on community lands. Peter's sister and her husband were in charge of distributing trees to the communities, and they gave Fenya and Peter the apple, pear and plum saplings."

We look around at the few surviving trees in the tall grass. The orchard Mother can see with her long-ago eyes has gone wild with masses of water shoots sprouting out of the old branches, some of the branches supporting their weight only by resting on the ground. They still send up sap in the spring, the leaves still grow,

---

32.   Christian Community of Universal Brotherhood, the Doukhobor communal organization.

This small homestead supported the Maloff family in a market garden enterprise.

and the apples and pears they produce, though tough and scabby, still feed the bears.

As we walk around her garden planted with early lettuce, parsley and peas, Mother tells me the story of how the property came to belong to her parents.

"This land was owned by Great-Aunt Fenya. In about 1908, Sava Hoodicoff moved from the Saskatchewan prairies and bought a big chunk of land here in Thrums for himself, his brother William and sister Fenya. Fenya's husband, Peter, died on this land, and when she remarried, she moved down the road in Thrums." Mother gestures west, down Highway 3A, and recalls the memory of her great-aunt. "That second husband left her, and she lived alone for the rest of her days. She visited us often. Winter evenings she'd come by the light of a kerosene lantern. Everyone did that. Even after flashlights were invented, some people continued to use lanterns. The light was brighter.

"Aunt Fenya loved Mother best of all the grandchildren, and when Mother was marrying Papa, she said, 'I will sell it to no one but Lusha and Pete Maloff.' That is how Mama ended up living across the road from Babushka and Dedushka Hoodicoff and Great-Uncle Sava Hoodicoff and his large family."

I look at the old house standing back from the highway. It has a Spanish touch with an arch on the porch and pink-coloured stucco, reminiscent of California, where my *dedushka* Pete Maloff lived for periods of time between 1910 and 1927. Tall walnut and chestnut trees provide shade. In her mind's eye, Mother sees the house as it was—filled with the lives of her five younger siblings, two sisters, three brothers; her parents, my *babushka* Lusha and *dedushka* Pete; and friends that were always dropping in.

Mother continues, "Papa and Dedushka Nikolai built that house. They laid the basement foundation out of rocks collected from the mountain. It's a strong foundation. They built two stories on the house. Dedushka was known for his rock work.

"The living room was often full of visitors. The big window in the kitchen is where we started bedding plants in the spring. On the second floor, Papa had a room for his books and writing, and there was a bedroom I shared with my sisters. From the porch on the front of the house we watched the trains—short-distance ones departing to Nelson and Trail and the longer ones travelling to Vancouver."

With Mother leaning slightly on her walking sticks, we walk along the grassy path toward the mountain.

"The old hay barn was here. Papa scythed the hay, and then Mama and he collected it in a wagon that our old workhorse, Dan, pulled. He was such a quiet horse. We had a cow and a goat too, and they shared the animal barn."

The forest has reclaimed the old chicken coop, the hay and animal barns. Scrub trees grow in the centre of their foundations. There is a path up the slope of the mountain where Mother goes for a daily walk. We pass fallen fences and tall firs and climb up to the water source, a cistern cemented against the cliff.

"This mountain was our playground. Brother Petya and I climbed those rocks that look like caverns bears could hibernate in."

Mother bends down and picks a glacier lily close to a rocky outcrop. In the shady, wet areas under the trees, wood violets grow.

"In spring, we picked flowers for Mama. We'd sit at the edge of that cliff over there and look all around our property to see what Mama and Papa were doing. When we looked down between our feet, we could see where the spring bubbled out of the rocks at

Pete Maloff (left) and beekeeper, Yahor Abromivitch, inspect the hives Lusha kept. Lusha had a knack for working with bees and they rarely stung her.

the bottom. Sometimes, for fun, my brothers and I slid down tree branches all the way to the pool that Dedushka Nikolai had created to hold the cold, clear water. In the spring, it overflowed into a pond that was deep enough for us to wade in and find tadpoles and frogs. There was a chorus of croaking frogs from that pond. Such singing! You don't hear much frog song now."

I collect a handful of the yellow glacier lilies, and we wander back to the field gone to grass and weeds. Deer often graze in the meadow.

"We grew everything here," she says. "Mother would start early in the spring. She planted sunflowers, peas and asters just as the snow was melting, brushing it away from the rows. Tomatoes, peppers and cucumbers were started in the greenhouses. We seeded and weeded long rows of corn, carrots, beans and potatoes and had fields of strawberries and raspberries. There was enough to take to markets in Trail and Nelson.

"Papa tried to get other work. It would have been easier. When this highway was being paved, the foreman said he would hire him. He liked Papa and knew he was a good worker. Then he came back

This photo was taken on Elizabeth Maloff's 98th birthday. She turned 100 on July 4, 2020. She still finds beauty and joy in the land where she was born and has lived all her life. Photo Katya Maloff

and told Papa, 'I'm sorry, but they say you are a fanatic and if I hire you, everybody will be very angry. I don't know what they'll do to me.' Papa was disappointed, but he said that being a farmer and growing good food was an honourable way to make a living. Then, in 1932, we lost our land."

Mother sits down on a sun-warmed rock along the path and uses her walking stick to scratch in the dirt. Her face is downcast as she tries to explain why they lost this land.

"Papa believed in the Doukhobor ideals about land—land belongs to God and it should be shared for the benefit of all people. Morally, he felt he ought to live in the Christian Community of Universal Brotherhood, contribute his efforts to the group and share in the returns as the Community Doukhobors were attempting to do. It was a problem for him, because he also liked to be free to follow his own vision. He struggled with the whole land question. Our family lived independently, but then there were taxes. Along with many other Doukhobors, he attempted to have his taxes designated for peaceful projects. If necessary, he was willing to lose the land that Great-Aunt Fenya had passed on to Mama. Though she didn't like protesting and disrupting the family, Mama agreed with him.

"While Mama was in jail on Piers Island, Papa in the BC Penitentiary and all of us kids in foster care in the orphanage and industrial school, our land was sold for unpaid land taxes—one hundred dollars—to Mr. Bonderoff, a distant neighbour in Thrums. When we came back from Vancouver, we had no home."

The spring sun hides behind a cloud; the warmth is quickly gone. We walk back to Mother's house, set the table for tea and gather the flowers into a vase on her table. Mother starts to tell me about her *dedushka* Hoodicoff and how he got their land back. I remember him as a slight, stooped man, often wearing a plaid work shirt and cap. He was taciturn, not given to talking much, especially when we kids were around. In her story, he is a hero.

"Though Dedushka Hoodicoff was not a member of the CCUB, he respected the leader Peter Verigin, Chistiakov. Petushka,[33] as he called Chistiakov, often came to visit the Hoodicoffs. As soon as he arrived, word spread and Independent Doukhobors and Svobodniki alike from across Thrums gathered for prayers, singing and a meeting. There was standing room only at Babushka Hoodicoff's place. Chistiakov liked to meet the children too, and it became a tradition—Dedushka Hoodicoff would buy a box of oranges for Chistiakov to toss to the gathered children from the porch railing.

"Dedushka approached Chistiakov for advice about how to find a home for his son-in-law Pete Maloff's family. 'Petushka,

---

33.   An affectionate nickname for Peter.

many are returning from Piers Island to community land in Kresto-va and Gilpin. Maybe that is where Petro and his family could live.'

"Chistiakov's answer was 'Petro Maloff and his family need to come back to their homestead in Thrums. That's where they belong.'

"'Petushka, that can't be. It's been sold to Bonderoffs.'

"Petushka replied, 'They'll sell it back,' and he instructed Dedushka, 'Say a prayer and then go peacefully to ask Mr. Bonderoff if you can buy the land. Take a pen and paper for Mr. Bonderoff to sign the land over to you and make sure you have the hundred dollars ready for payment.'

"Dedushka was a temperamental man, not given to patience, and after a few visits to Bonderoff's he came back to Chistiakov, saying, 'Petushka, he won't even consider my offer. *Nyee pakaryaeetsa.*'

"But Chistiakov again advised him, 'Go every week or even more often. Ask civilly.'

"Well, Dedushka was desperate to find a home for our family; all five of us kids were living in his home at the time. He persisted in spite of the weekly embarrassment. After about six months of Dedushka's pleading, Mr. Bonderoff finally agreed, and Dedushka had his pen, paper and one hundred dollars ready. We were so thankful to have a home to come back to once Mama and Papa were released from prison."

—⁓—

Mother has often told us this vignette about how Dedushka Hoodicoff got their land back. She saw special significance in Chistiakov's assertion that Maloffs should live in Thrums. Over the last eighty years this land has been subdivided into smaller acreages. Mother got a section that was rocky and scrubby, but through years of pulling trees, moving rocks and adding compost and manure, she has developed a fertile garden. In her nineties, Mother carries on her stewardship of the land, seeing it as a precious heritage. And in her gentle way she insists that we continue looking after it as she has.

A Good Life:
My Prababushka

—⁓—

Thrums residents gathered to share their memories and say good-bye to Masha Hoodicoff, their eighty-six-year-old neighbour. After prayers and hymns were sung, quiet descended on the gathering as her son-in-law Pete Maloff spoke of her life.

"My dear *starushka* was born Masha Kasahova in a Caucasus mountain village in Georgia, Russia, in 1879. Her father died at a young age. Their Kasahov uncle and aunt, who already had four daughters and a son, provided a home for her mother and her four young children. In 1895, when Masha was sixteen, she was in charge of the young Doukhobor children as they huddled in a barn while the adults gathered in a field to burn their weapons. Through gaps in the barn walls they watched the Cossack horsemen round up their families.

"In 1899, along with over seven thousand Doukhobors, her family boarded a freighter and left Russia. Arriving in Canada, they were settled in Saskatchewan, where her uncle arranged a marriage with Vasil Hoodicoff, who was older than her by several years but who came from a good family of five brothers and one sister. They chose to live independently of the Doukhobor community, starting their own homestead in Blaine Lake, Saskatchewan.

"In the next seven years, three children—Lusha, Masha and Ivan—were born to Masha and Vasil, and their farm began to prosper. Then, in 1908, together with many other Doukhobors, they refused to take an oath of allegiance 'to defend the king.' Their homestead was repossessed and made available to new settlers. The family left the prairies, joining the trek of Doukhobors moving to British Columbia."

"Poor Masha, all the hardship she went through," a distant relative whispered to her neighbour.

This woman, well acquainted with Masha, quickly responded, "Masha was not poor. She knew how to live. She went everywhere, participated in everything and did what she wanted. She had a good life!"

⎯⎯⎯

I knew my *prababushka* when she was in her seventies and eighties. She was a small woman, but she had a presence and a lively air about her. She kept to the traditional Doukhobor clothing; long woollen skirts and long-sleeved blouses swathed her slim, wiry body. Her round, weathered, doll-like face peered out from beneath a flowered kerchief tied under her chin. She walked bent over with a cane, but walked with purpose. Masha and her husband, Vasil, had a market-garden farm across the road from us in Thrums, and the Maloff-Hoodicoff households were so connected that the worn path between them could still be found in the tall grass years after Prababushka died.

In the summer all of us cousins helped pick the long rows of strawberries and raspberries and wrap bunches of carrots, onions and beets to sell at the Nelson farmers' market, where Prababushka's table was next to ours. Afternoons, when business slowed down, were long, and Prababushka often gave us, her helpers, ten cents to buy an ice cream at the Shamrock Restaurant. We licked our double chocolate and strawberry cones in the shade of the restaurant awning and watched Prababushka cross the street and head through the Lord Nelson Hotel's Ladies and Escorts pub doors. "To use the washroom," she said, but we had a suspicion that it was for a cold beer.

Now that I am closer to my great-grandmother's age, I think of my *prababushka*. I live in the West Kootenay area of British Columbia, where access to shamanic healing is just as available as mainstream counselling. On the recommendation of a friend who suggested that Doukhobors had shamanic healers and "Why not go and see what it's about?" I went to see a shaman. The pretty young woman greeted me in her home, and after a chat and a cleansing with cedar boughs, we proceeded with the ritual. At the end of the session, she said, "Vera, you had a very powerful ancestor who is in your energy field." I immediately thought of my grandfather, who was influential in my life. "No, it's not a man. It's a woman who helped your family in the past." I scanned my list of relatives, and Masha Hoodicoff came to mind. A powerful woman? Yes, for her time, that was Prababushka.

My mother, Leeza, was Masha's first grandchild, and she was favoured. When I ask her about her Hoodicoff grandmother, she smiles and lovingly tells me about her early years with her *babushka*.

Leeza: She was always my champion. My grandparents watered their gardens from a creek on the Glade side of the Kootenay River. Dedushka Hoodicoff, my grandfather, and his brother had built a gravity-fed water system, erecting wooden towers on both sides of the river and then stringing a metal pipe attached to a cable to cross the river. On hot days, Babushka let me play under that spray of water. I loved spreading out my arms and dancing under that warm water as it flowed magically from the mountain stream on the other side of the river.

As a special treat, I'd go with Babushka to market by horse and a cart that Uncle Ivan built. Ivan drove, and when the noisy Model T roadsters passed us, Molly would rise up on her hind legs and paw the air frantically. She was a long-legged young horse and frisky! Ivan would chew on a long straw and sweat so that he'd have to mop his brow with his cap. "Whoa, Molly, whoa," he'd call. Babushka, her *platok* tied around her smiling face, sat peacefully gazing around her. I'd be in the back of the cart with the potatoes and cabbages, and I'd look around too, at the houses on the hillside of the South Slocan village, the Kootenay River far below the Beasley bluffs and the street lights of Nelson where we arrived in the evening.

The market was in the basement of a large wooden building on the corner of Vernon and Josephine Streets. We unloaded and went to a hotel across the street. While Uncle Ivan put Molly into a stable on the ground floor, we went upstairs. That hotel was pretty basic! The three of us slept in one room, on the wooden floor, wrapped up in our blankets.

The early-morning market was busy. The basement was like a cave, and it was packed: farmers selling, customers bargaining, everyone meeting and exchanging news. We set up next to the Leaf family. I loved their homemade cheese, especially the brown goat's whey cheese that was sweet and salty.

Babushka knew how to sell. In her broken English she'd call out, "*Hresh* eggs, one, two, three *dney* [days]." Austrian apples, which were beautiful to look at and smelled wonderful—but were sour— she would market as "make house smell nice." She had many loyal customers.

Babushka sold in Trail too. She didn't know much English, but with her outgoing nature she made friends with the Craigs, who owned a shoe store there. She would load her baskets, pay seventy-five cents to board the short-haul train to Trail and then stay overnight with the Craigs. The next day, Babushka sold her produce door to door and, in the evening, caught the train home. Craigs stayed at the Hoodicoffs' farm too, as Babushka often invited company for homemade bread and *borsh*.

When other grandchildren were born, Grandmother made Sundays special for all of us—the Maloff, Aseyev, Konkin and Hoodicoff cousins. Our large gang gathered together for breakfast after the Sunday prayer meetings.

—∿∿—

Mother's cousin Annie Konkin has kept many letters and memories of growing up with their grandmother Hoodicoff. Three of us meet in the Sidewinders coffee shop in Nelson on a winter morning. The sun is brilliant on the mounds of sparkling snow, but the streets are icy, and I give Mother my arm to negotiate the slippery path to the door. The aromas of coffee and fresh scones waft toward us as we enter and see Annie already there with a coffee and a newspaper spread out before her. She's an attractive woman, her sparkling eyes and vivacious manner belying the fact that she is in her mid-eighties. Mother, ten years older, joins Annie on the bench and they grasp hands. "Leeza," Annie says in greeting. I order tea from the counter and return to where they sit, still bundled up in warm jackets and woollen hats.

"Our *babushka* Masha Hoodicoff, that's a good place to start," Annie says. We lean toward each other to hear better in this noisy coffee shop where voices reverberate off the wooden benches, tables and walls. Drinks and noises are soon forgotten. Annie and Leeza are in a place of memories where they are young women and their grandmother is their favourite adult.

Annie laughs and says, "When my grandchildren come asking for money, I tell them about Babushka. She was generous, but we had to earn our money. She'd give us a *metyolka* made out of birch boughs to sweep the paths to the *banya* and to the dugout cellar that kept the cream and butter at just the right temperature. Then we'd wash the cat and dog dishes. 'Make sure they're very clean so the animals like them,' Babushka said. Our reward was five or ten cents to go to Johnson's store to buy candy.

"When we started school, we went Monday to Thursday until three o'clock. At three fifteen we'd be out weeding the potatoes, and on Friday we stayed home to prepare for market. Mother said, 'Fridays, you're just playing in school. There's work to be done at home.' But Sunday mornings were with Babushka. She baked big *peerahee* filled with *shchavel'* and homemade cheese, and we'd sit on benches around her long wooden table. First, she asked us to read a prayer, and then we'd devour those *peerahee*." Annie pauses, remembering those mornings, then adds, "She enjoyed being with us as much as we enjoyed being with her."

"*Shchavel'*, that spring green that grows wild by the creek?" I interrupt. "We use it in *borsh* to add a sour note. She used it for *peerahee*?"

"Babushka was creative," Annie replies.

Mother shakes her head. "I don't know how she did it. She had company all the time and she *always* had food to share. The widowers Sherstobitoff and Storshev, who had no place else to go, were invited to join us on Sunday. Babushka, she knew how to live without much money. Like her mother said of her, 'Masha could get by living on a rock.'"

"She'd wake at three in the morning, make her *borsh* and *peerahee* and then join in the prayer service. That's how she did it," Annie says and nods her head to emphasize her words. "We were a close-knit family. Babushka's house, the Maloffs' and the Aseyevs' houses were like ours. If our parents were busy, we'd go to the other homes and they'd be happy to see us. We were poor, but didn't know it. We didn't know a hungry day. Had clean clothes, clean beds, were never beaten, maybe grabbed by the ear and told, 'Listen and be good. God is watching.' The only bloodshed was when you cut your finger. And we were quiet, listened to our parents' conversations when everyone got together. There was no meat, no drink, no smoke."

Annie turns to Mother. "The only thing I don't understand, Leeza, is that in the 1930s when you kids were at the industrial school, the orphanage, Nadya in foster care and your parents in jail, we lived in your house—the Maloff house. Why was that?"

Mother frowns and says, "Dad wouldn't pay land taxes that supported the military. He said God was his authority rather than a government edict. So, we lost our house."

"We were living across the river from Nelson at the time, renting a stone house on the riverbank, you know, where the veterinarian Croxall lives now," Annie says. "The house is still there. My dad liked it, away from Doukhobor politics. But Grandmother asked my mother to move back to Thrums to live in your house; otherwise, she said, it would be taken away. If Babushka asked, you listened. We moved back."

"You lived at our place while your house was being built," Leeza answers.

"Tiny and Vera lived with us too," Annie says. "We even looked after your collie, Sport. She was a beautiful dog."

"Sport?" My eyes are wide at Annie's mention of the familiar, well-loved dog. "Is that the same dog who came to Grandfather in Blewett? He must have had a long life!"

"Fourteen or fifteen years," Mother says. "We got him as a puppy just before we were taken away."

Mother sighs. "When we got back, with the five of us at Babushka's place, we had to lend her a hand. Petya, at nine years old, myself, twelve, almost thirteen, and sometimes cousin Tiny went to Trail with her. Uncle Ivan drove the farm truck—Babushka had bought a truck by then, but its top speed was only thirty miles an hour. We piled in the back with the produce. In Trail, Ivan parked at the bottom of the Gulch hill, and Babushka sent us to climb the steep stairs to the Italian neighbourhood to ask for orders. Sometimes I'd protest, 'Babushka, they don't want to buy.' She quickly answered, 'They'll buy. Just say, "*Good* for you. *Hresh.* Just picked."'" She knew her customers from the years when she climbed those streets. As Tiny delivered a basket of vegetables, the woman asked how she knew it was for her. Tiny answered, 'I know. For lady with two big front teeth,' as Babushka had told her."

We chuckle at this memory.

Annie says, "I tell my grandkids Grandmother was a liberated woman. When the grandparents were finally able to buy a new farm truck, an International that cost $3,400, it proudly displayed 'William & Mary Hoodicoff & Son' in big two-inch letters on the door. She didn't drive, but she was part owner. Leeza, all the women, you, Aunt Mary and Mother, drove the trucks because the men couldn't get driver's licences—they hadn't registered."

I think of the war years in the 1940s when many Doukhobors, including Grandfather Maloff, refused to register under the National Resources Mobilization Act. They were barred from jobs and from obtaining licences. Grandfather was severely beaten, jailed for several terms of three months and eventually put under house arrest for several years.

The flow of conversation between Annie and Mother is quick, as if the memories have come to life and are pouring out of them. I scribble notes, their stories vivid before my eyes.

Annie says, "One day, Babushka took the bus to Nelson and didn't have the exact fare so she gave the driver ten dollars. In those days, drivers changed money. The bus was full, standing room only, but the driver said, 'I have no change; I'll give it to you in Nelson,' and started putting the bill in his pocket. Babushka quickly caught the man's hand, retrieved her money and said, '*I'll* give *you* change in Nelson.'"

Mother nods. "Babushka didn't get pushed around. One time in the Shamrock, a burly patron came up to her demanding to see her registration papers. Babushka had registered, but she didn't think it was his affair. 'Not your business. Policeman business,' she answered and carried on with her meal. Everyone in the restaurant chortled, and the man skulked out the door. 'Never show that you are scared of a bully. *Dela tahda prapala.* Then all would be lost,' she'd say."

"The Shamrock was one of her hangouts," I say.

Mother replies, "After market, she took her unsold produce there to trade for a meal. Sometimes she'd be so tired that she'd order her food, then lie down on the bench to have a power nap. The waitress would wake her when it was ready, and Grandmother, refreshed, would enjoy her dinner."

"I have to tell you this story about Babushka, even though

my mother and yours, Leeza, were mortified by what happened," Annie says. She clears her throat and we lean in closer. "You know how Babushka always liked to be *akuratnaya*, proper, and she'd remind us to be the same, to dress neatly, follow the rules, be polite. When she didn't have a driver for her truck, she asked the Thrums chauffeur, as we called him, to drive her truck to market. Paid him three dollars. One day she asked him to stop at the liquor store—it was where the toy store is now in Nelson—and pick up some beer. Dedushka enjoyed a beer once in a while and kept some on hand for visitors. It was hot, and at the end of the day, Babushka went to the truck to have a nap. She was thirsty; the beer was right there by her feet. She opened a bottle. And wouldn't you know it, just then a policeman showed up and gave her a ticket for drinking in public."

Our eyes widen. We laugh. Mother says, "Oh no! I didn't hear about that. Babushka drinking in public!"

"She had to go to court. But she really didn't know that having a beer in her truck was against the law. She told the judge, 'Mister, me not know. Very sorry. Me not know.' The judge fined her fifteen dollars and she walked out the door. 'Goodbye, Mister. Goodbye.'

"Usually Babushka was pretty level-headed," Annie continues. "When I separated from my husband and came back to my parents with my kids, she didn't scold. She wasn't the huggy, mushy type, but she reassured me, '*Slava Bohu*, thank God. It'll all work out.'"

"It's true, Babushka somehow always managed to make things work out." Mother nestles her cup in both hands and looks into it, perhaps seeing Masha in the tea leaves. "She paid her bills, bought her truck and even had extra money once in a while. She helped others, too. She'd add extra vegetables into a basket of a widow. One day at the Trail market one of her customers, a Mrs. Thompson, burst into tears at her stall. It appeared that she urgently needed a hundred dollars but just then she couldn't gather together that much money. To her astonishment, this poor farmer—Babushka—pulled out a hidden pocket in her skirt, unrolled a few bills and quietly said, 'Let me help.'"

Annie raises her eyebrows. "Did Babushka get the money back?"

"Oh, yes." Mother nods. "And Mrs. Thompson became a life-long friend."

Annie is an accomplished seamstress, and I ask her if she sewed for her *babushka*.

She chuckles. "One time I made a market apron for her out of flour sacks. Those sacks were used for everything. She told me the apron had to have deep pockets, and I embroidered a peacock on the apron and pansies on the pockets. One lady who came to market even wanted to buy it." Annie purses her lips. "When Grandmother died, she had her going-away clothes ready—a long burgundy skirt, a yellow lace shawl—but she didn't have a *zanaveska*, an apron, so I sewed one the night she passed away."

———

We gather on another morning in Mother's warm kitchen. The aroma of Mother's specialty—*peerahee* with squash, beet, cheese and sauerkraut—permeates the air as she takes them out of the oven. Annie and Mother sit in front of windows that look out onto a snowy yard. I enjoy this image of the two cousins: silver-haired, wearing fuchsia-coloured sweaters, resting their elbows on the table, intense in their conversation.

Annie brings out a box of letters and photographs her mother has saved. We spread them out. There is a black and white snapshot of Thrums before the Brilliant Dam flooded the fertile fields by the river. "That island of fir trees in the middle of all the fields and gardens is where we lived," says Annie. There was a picture of Masha and Vasil Hoodicoff in their yard, with blossoming fruit trees in the background. It showed Masha wearing a yellow-and-brown checked jacket, a long plaid checked skirt covered with an apron, and the ever-present kerchief on her head. Vasil's swarthy face featured a trim white beard, and a cloth cap covered his head. He was neatly dressed in a dark shirt buttoned to the neck and pants only slightly worn at the knees, held up by a dark belt with a silver buckle. In his hand, he was holding a metal pail. Annie says, "Dedushka always had a pail handy to take water or food to the chickens, cows or horses."

I place the *peerahee*, melted butter and sour cream on the table. We pull our chairs close to the table as Annie continues to talk, using her hands to emphasize her words.

"You know, Babushka had her portrait painted. Dr. Christie delivered all my babies. His wife—Joyce was her name—was an art teacher. She saw Grandmother at the Trail market and asked if she could paint her. 'Oh, I'm all wrinkled. You don't want that.' Mrs. Christie said, 'That's exactly what I would like to paint, your face and hands with all their beautiful wrinkles.' They arranged that Babushka would come on the bus to Trail on Sundays and sit for the portrait in Mrs. Christie's studio. After the sitting, Grandmother would have a rest and tea in the parlour and then take the bus back home."

A piece of a puzzle falls into place. In Grandfather's files I have found a 1950s *Trail Daily Times* newspaper clipping. The caption under the picture is "The chairman of the BC Registered Music Teachers Convention explains to the visitors a picture of local interest." It is a life-sized portrait of Great-Grandmother Masha Hoodicoff. She is wearing a dark fringed *platok* and a heavy woollen jacket. Her bright eyes look kindly at the artist, and her wrinkled face and hands tell her life story.

"That portrait was on sale for ninety dollars. Why didn't we buy it? We all could've chipped in," Annie says, shaking her head.

I tell Annie, "Even from the old newspaper clipping I could tell that it was a beautiful painting. Too bad the family didn't buy it. No extra money then, I guess. I wonder where it is now."

We pour melted butter over the *peerahee*, pick up our forks and eat. I sigh in enjoyment—our comfort food of childhood.

Annie tells us about the last trip she took with her grandmother. "In 1965 Babushka was diagnosed with stomach cancer. A neighbour had good results from laetrile injections at the Taylor Clinic in Dallas, Texas, and the family decided to send Grandmother for treatment there. I went with her.

"The clinic was in a private home, and we stayed three or four blocks away. Babushka got intravenous injections from nine to three, and at the end of the day a nurse asked for a payment of three hundred dollars. Babushka brought fifteen hundred dollars, which I had sewn into my bra. I was quite big chested at the start of the trip, and by the end … I was flat again." Annie grins. "By the third day, Babushka was feeling nauseous and irritable from the treatment. When the nurse came, Babushka told me in Russian to tell her, 'I will not give the *sabaka* a penny. I'm going home.'"

"That was Babushka. Didn't mince words," Mother says.

"She did get along well with the mostly Black staff in the

clinic cafeteria," Annie recalls. "She was polite and respectful, and on learning that we needed to go to the bank, the waiter even offered us his car.

"On the flight back to Spokane we sat across from two men, smartly dressed in suits. I had bought a lacy white dress in Dallas and I thought I looked pretty good. When they heard Babushka and me talking, they asked, 'Ladies, what language are you speaking?'

"'Russian,' I answered.

"'From Russia?'

"'No, Canada.'

"Babushka elbowed me. 'What do they want to know?'

"'Where we are from.'

"Babushka, with a twinkle in her blue eyes, looking straight at the men, said, 'Tell them that we're Russian spies.' After that the men did not ask any more questions. This was the time of the Cuban Missile Crisis, and such words were taken seriously, but Babushka had a sense of humour.

"Babushka died three, four months later, so I don't know if the laetrile injections worked, but she had no pain."

We are silent, remembering, grieving.

Mother says, "Do you remember, Annie, a spring ritual of Babushka's was to tour her children's families to make sure they had started their gardens? 'Aseyevs have their greenhouse going,' she would tell the Konkins. 'Konkins' tomatoes are up,' she would pass on to the Maloffs. 'Maloffs have already planted their sunflowers and peas,' she would announce to the Hoodicoffs."

"And she never said anything bad about anyone," Annie says.

"After she died I was telling your mother, 'Well, now that we don't have Babushka to get us going in the gardens, we'll have to do it ourselves.'"

——

Masha Hoodicoff died on September 10, 1965, her husband having passed away from Alzheimer's six years earlier. She was one of the last people buried in the small Thrums graveyard, in the forest just past the farm where she lived.

MARRIAGES

—✺—

Arranged marriages were a Doukhobor custom in Russia, and they continued in the first few years after Doukhobors immigrated to Canada. My great-grandparents Nikolai Maloff and Elizaveta Barisoff were introduced and married by their families in Georgia. My great-grandparents William Hoodicoff and Masha Kasahoff had an arranged marriage in Saskatchewan in the first few years of their arrival in Canada. However, their eldest daughter, Lusha, and Pete Maloff met through friends, and their second daughter, Masha, refused to accept an arranged marriage.

This story was inspired by a photograph of my mother and family relatives picking long rows of strawberries in the Aseyevs' field. Looking at the picture, I was moved by the women's happy faces with their wide, almost mischievous grins, as if they were revealing private stories and secrets. Mother shared one of these stories.

LEEZA: Babushka Hoodicoff told us this story as five of us—Babushka Hoodicoff; her daughter, Tyota Masha; her mother-in-law, Masha Aseyeva; my cousin Tiny and I—were picking strawberries in the Aseyevs' field. Long rows of the berry bushes continued to the mountainside. Heads covered with kerchiefs tied behind our necks, in long summer dresses, hands red with the juice of the strawberries and our backs warmed by the sun, we were bent like turtles, shuffling along the paths, staying close to each other for conversation.

"When Masha was sixteen—your age now, Leeza and Tanya—the Salikens asked us for a meeting to discuss a marriage with their son Vasil," Babushka began. "I prepared *borsh* and *plow* to welcome them hospitably. Vasil was twenty, a muscular man, dressed in his best suit that day. His father was tall and slim and his mother roly-poly, looking extra round in her layers of skirts. They sat on our living room couch while I went to tell Masha to come and meet them. Instead of greeting them politely, Masha refused to even come out of her room. The Salikens heard a loud conversation through the closed bedroom door.

"Masha shouting, 'No, I won't marry Vasil. I won't even see him.'

"Me trying to calm her down. 'Sh, sh. They're all in the next room. They can hear you.'

"'I don't care. You can't do that to me.'

"'Masha, he's from an excellent family. You'll be comfortable. They have money.'

"Tanya, your mother told me, 'There is no way. Tell them to go away.' So we had lunch, talked about the garden, the cows, the weather, not about wedding plans, and then Vasil and his parents walked back to their farm without meeting Masha.

"Masha was determined even then to marry your dad, George. The Aseyevs lived farther down the road in Thrums and were of old Svobodniki roots. They didn't believe in accumulating wealth, so they had nothing but a few acres of land they farmed. But your mother said, 'George is kind and has a good sense of humour.' Well, she had her way. And they did make a fine couple, both dark-haired and tall."

"Thank goodness I didn't marry Vasil," Tyota Masha said.

Babushka Hoodicoff turned to Tiny. "But your mama sure didn't have any smarts about her yet, shouting like that. *Eesho uma nyee nabralas'*."

Tiny broke into peals of laughter, dark head nodding, brown eyes glinting, as she digested this information about her mama.

"I know I was rude," Tyota Masha agreed. "But to marry Vasil— that would have been disastrous! He got my best friend pregnant and then he married someone else."

I was trying to imagine my *tyota*, Tiny's mama, as a young girl, adamant that she would be the one to decide whom she was going to marry. Now in her thirties, she was a robust, energetic woman with strong features, her thick straight hair escaping from a bun at the back of her neck. She was in charge of her husband and three children. Putting down her wooden bucket filled with strawberries, she turned to us.

"That Vasil was a crazy driver, always drove too fast. Remember, Mama, he was in that bad accident a few years ago. His car

In 1920, Masha Hoodicoff refused to accept an arranged marriage and wed her choice of husband, George Aseyev-Popoff.

went over the bank on the bluffs coming back from Nelson. The two fellows with him weren't hurt, but Vasil's back was broken. He couldn't walk and was in horrible pain for a whole year before he died. Left his wife with four young children."

I looked over at Tiny. How lucky her mother had been to escape such a husband.

"We have a good life with George," Tyota Masha continued, looking around at their farm. Around us were spreading fields of cabbage, potatoes, carrots, corn, strawberries and raspberries, destined for the local grocery stores and markets. There were cows and horses, tractors and trucks to help do the work. "We have everything we need, and George is a good man and father. I didn't have to worry about George having money."

Like many Independent Doukhobors, the Aseyevs lived as an extended family that was like a village. George's parents, Alyosha and Masha, and his uncles lived on the same property. Masha and her *starushka*, my great-aunt Masha Aseyeva, got along well. They were both straightforward, generous, helpful and welcoming to all who crossed their doorstep. My great-aunt Masha, whom we called Babushka Aseyeva, was an especially gentle, caring and devout woman. She was known for the large repertoire of Doukhobor psalms she sang and recited.

Babushka Aseyeva broke into the conversation. "*Dyevachkee*, girls, Leeza, Tanya," she said, looking at us, "you know nothing of marriages yet. Let me tell you about mine."

Our ears perked up. Babushka Aseyeva was a tall, sturdy woman in her sixties, with only her grey bangs—cut straight across—escaping from her *platok*. She always wore a traditional Doukhobor *platok*, a handwoven loose skirt, an apron and a baggy blouse hiding her generous bosom. To think of her as a young girl getting married took imagination.

"*Na Kawkaze*, in the Caucasus mountains, up on the high steppes, way back in the 1890s, before Doukhobors immigrated to Canada, I was married when I was twelve years old."

"Twelve!" we gasped, almost dropping our buckets. Tiny and I were in our teens, and marriage was not on our horizon.

"Twelve? Babushka, why so young?"

"My family, the Soukeroffs, were a poor family, and there were three daughters. I was the youngest. An opportunity came to marry me into a devoted Doukhobor family, the Fominovs, and my parents were afraid that if they didn't marry me then, they would lose the chance at a very good connection."

Tiny and I looked at each other—Fominov? Babushka Masha Aseyeva was married to George Aseyev's father, Alyosha.

"That was my first marriage." Babushka Aseyeva waved away

Aseyev-Popoff family: Vera, Masha, George, Tanya (Tiny) with Peter in the front. Peter Popoff was one of the first Thrums Doukhobors to attend the University of British Columbia in Vancouver.

our surprised look. "It was customary then to have an arranged marriage, and I met my husband, Ivan Akimovich—I called him Vanya—just before the wedding." She paused in her berry picking, her eyes focused on a faraway, long-ago picture as she told us about her first husband.

"The wedding was outside, in the summer, next to a small lake. Around us were the Caucasus hills of wild grasses and flowers. My sisters dressed me in a flowered *platok* I had embroidered, a ribboned vest and a long skirt covered with an apron. My mother led me to meet my husband-to-be. Coming toward him as he was standing with his family, I saw he was young too, slim, good-looking, I thought, with a Cossack hat covering his blond hair. Holding his sweating hand, I could feel he was nervous too, but we listened to our parents and carried on with the plans they had made."

"Babushka, in those days, in Russia, things were different," Tiny protested as she vigorously snipped berries. "Sure wouldn't happen to Leeza and me now!"

"Maybe not, Tanya, but the ceremonies are pretty much the same," Babushka Aseyeva explained. "Just like now, the engagement involved a blessing from the community. We stood in front of a prayer meeting, men on one side, women on the other. Everyone there blessed our marriage. They said that they would support and encourage us. We bowed down to the ground in front of them in thanks. This gave us courage, and we looked at each other a little more openly. Vanya's face was broad, with light blue eyes and a generous mouth. He wore a linen tunic tied around the waist with a long woven sash, and his pants were tucked into tall Cossack boots. I grinned at him and I guess Vanya liked me well enough; he squished my hand.

"We had a modest wedding," Babushka Aseyeva continued. "To show that our families were coming together in peace and friendship, our mothers brought a loaf of bread to share. A second time, we bowed down to the ground to our families and friends and to God in thankfulness. We had a meal, and then I packed my clothes, the wedding blanket and the rug that we had knelt on. My new husband hitched a cart behind the family horse, put me in it with my *sunduk*, and off I went to the Fominov household in the next village."

Babushka Masha Aseyev (on the left) was the beloved matriarch of her family. Masha sang from memory hundreds of Doukhobor psalms and hymns and passed them on to her musical family.

Ah, the wedding blanket. We could relate to that. Last winter, Tiny and I had been quilting our wool-filled blankets with our mothers to put away for our weddings. But to be married so young! How did Babushka Aseyeva manage?

Babushka carried on matter-of-factly, her hands busy picking the ripe strawberries. "Truthfully, it was a good family. My mother-in-law understood I was young. Often, after the chores were done, she'd say, 'Masha, go out and play with the girls.' I'd come home in time for supper. She was kind, like a mother to me. That was my best life. For a long time, my husband and I slept together like brother and sister, keeping each other warm."

Tiny and I grinned, raised our eyebrows and looked over at Babushka Aseyeva, but she continued shuffling along the row and telling us about her husband.

"We sort of grew up together, became friends, then lovers. But sood'ba, fate had a different path for us than a peaceful family life. As soon as Vanya came of age to be enlisted in the army, he, along with many of his Doukhobor friends, refused conscription. The Russian military court imprisoned them. Vanya was one of the prisoners sent to the Tatar villages in Azerbaijan to work as an indentured labourer. I didn't hear from him for months, and then we got word that he was sick. It was dangerous to travel in those days. There were abductions, and Doukhobors needed permits to leave their villages, still, I wanted to see Vanya.

"Vanya's parents tried to talk me out of this risky visit, but they shared my love for Vanya and after many pleas, helped me. Starooshka Polya created a disguise, a tattered kolpak to cover my hair, old pants and a long woollen Russian coat my body. She rubbed dirt over my face and hands, gave me a cane and told me to walk slowly, hunched over like an old man.

"It was dark when Stareechok Akimooshka and I left. We lived in the Doukhobor village of Terpeniye high in the Caucasus mountain steppes in the Kars area and the nights were cool, so we bundled up. As we walked down the mountain trails, it became warmer. Finally, getting rides in carts, hiding by the side of the road whenever any military or police rode by, staying in Doukhobor villages along the way, we came to the Azerbaijan oblast. As we got closer to the Tatar village where Vanya was held, it became hot and humid, the mosquitoes and flies were never-ending and I sweated under that great coat around me.

"Loud barking of the Tatar dogs announced us long before we entered the village and as we came closer a pack of them bared the way, snarling. Terrified, we shouted and waved our arms, but that only infuriated them. Luckily, a Tatar woman came out of the closest hut and after one look at us, led us to where the Doukhobor boys were. Other Doukhobor families had made this journey to bring whatever food and clothing they could.

"We found Vanya and another Doukhobor man in the house for exiles. They were both feverish, and so weak and thin! I don't know why they were sick. Maybe the water they were drinking was contaminated.

"Even though it was hot, my Vanya was cold. I covered him with that big old woollen coat I was wearing, gave him sips of water, sat by him and told him about the baby I was carrying. He smiled at the thought that he would have a child. Stareechok spoke to the officer in charge and even though it was against the rules, he let me stay with Vanya for a while. I cleaned his clothes, tried to get rid of the lice and fed him good soup but Vanya didn't get better. Before spring he died there in the Azerbaijan village. Stareechok built a coffin, the Tatar men helped dig a grave, and we buried Vanya.

"Stareechok Akimooshka and I returned to our village, getting rides when we could, walking when we couldn't, just putting one foot in front of another. My son, Petya was born shortly after."

Babushka Masha looked around at the strawberry field, at Tiny and me, and heaved a mighty sigh. "Such was our life," she said.

Pete Fominoff[34] and his family often came to visit the Aseyevs from Grand Forks. Now I realized why they seemed so close to Babushka Aseyeva. Pete was her son, born in the Caucasus.

We had been listening to Babushka Aseyeva in rapt attention, mesmerized by her story. Then, with my bucket and Babushka's full of strawberries, I ran to the shed to replace them with empty ones and returned to the conversation.

"Babushka, you were so brave. It's *so* sad that your husband Vanya died!" I wanted her to continue. "Babushka, how did you get married again?"

"I was happy raising my son and his family. He grew up, married and had three sons and a daughter here in Canada. But the Fominoffs thought I should get married. Alyosha Aseyev's wife died in childbirth, and they arranged that I marry him." Babushka Aseyeva sighed. "That's how it was in those days."

We knew that Babushka Aseyeva and her husband, Dedushka Alyosha Aseyev, were not a happy couple. Dedushka Alyosha believed in free love and had other partners. Babushka Aseyeva was often on her own. She raised her children, George and Ilya, and when the grandchildren came, she extended her abundant love to them.

Tiny and I looked at Babushka Aseyeva with new respect. Her story was fodder for our adolescent image of marriage. To have loved a husband in Russia, to have dared visit him in a Tatar *aul* and then to have lost him—that was a great love!

---

34.   The surname Fominov was changed to Fominoff in Canada.

Getting Uncle
Bill Married

———ᴡᴡ———

Tragic stories are plentiful in our family. One winter evening as I sit with Mother in her warm kitchen, a wood fire glowing in the stove, I ask her, "Mother did you ever have fun?" She wrinkles her brow, thinks awhile, then her face brightens, and she grins. "Let me tell you about Uncle Bill."

I remember Bill and his wife, Polya, as an odd couple. She was under five feet and, though not fat, of solid build; he was over six feet and gangly. Polya was talkative; Bill, quiet and undemonstrative. They lived in a two-bedroom bungalow overlooking the Kootenay River, next door to Babushka and Dedushka Hoodicoff and across the road from us in Thrums.

The story Mother begins to tell takes place in the Slocan Valley, when she was sixteen. The Slocan is a quiet neighbouring valley with the clear Slocan River running through it. In 1936, the lumber industry, small-scale farming and mining provided livelihoods for its residents. The eight or nine villages from South Slocan to Slocan City on Slocan Lake were connected by fifty-four kilometres of rail line and road. At the north end of the valley, a country road leads to the old Appledale schoolhouse, now converted into a daycare centre. The road, Berukoff Road, is where Bill met Polya on a March day in 1936. I like to think that the road is named in honour of Mrs. Berukoff, a Doukhobor matchmaker who arranged their meeting.

I pull my chair closer and lean in to hear Mother's quiet voice.

Leeza: A prodding hand shook me awake that early March morning. It was cold and still dark, but as my bleary eyes peeked over my warm wool-filled quilt, I clearly saw Dedushka Hoodicoff—short grizzled hair, wrinkled face, lips set into a determined line, dressed in his usual checkered red jacket.

"Leeza, get up. Hurry."

I didn't want to get up, but with Dedushka there was no talking back.

"We have to marry Bill and the bus comes soon, so be quick."

Who was he talking about? What did he want? Uncle Bill was my mama's youngest brother, ten years older than me. He was a tall, lanky man with large hands and feet, and painfully shy. What was I to do with getting him married?

I pulled on my long woollen socks, skirt and blouse, and as I ate a quickly prepared bowl of *kasha*, Dedushka told me, "You and Bill are taking the bus to Appledale. There is a matchmaker there, and she will know a girl Bill can marry."

And so there I was, when I would usually have been in our greenhouse seeding tomatoes and cucumbers and transplanting the first bedding plants, stuck with getting Uncle Bill married.

It was just getting light when Dedushka waved down the Greyhound bus in front of our house and Uncle Bill and I got on. I had dressed in my best coat and plaited my hair in braids (I had thick honey-coloured braids then). Uncle Bill was in a brown suit, with rubber boots on his feet.

The bus pulled away, and I began to think about the chore I was sent on. I didn't know Mrs. Berukoff or any family that she might introduce us to. Seeking advice, I turned to Uncle Bill, but he sat staring out the bus window, only his restless hands showing he might be nervous.

We changed buses at South Slocan and took an orange bus headed to Appledale. Mr. Cunningham, the owner of the Crescent Valley store, was the bus driver. Everyone knew him. He drove the valley bus a few days a week, looked after the store, had a herd of cattle and occasionally sold an assortment of silk embroidery thread and needles door to door. His three sons worked hard too. His daughter, Barbara, married Mr. Moran, who bought the general store in Thrums. She was always friendly to me.

We got off the bus by the side of the road and walked to the Appledale store. The storekeeper told us the Berukoffs lived a couple of miles down the road. As we walked, snow crunched under our feet and sparkled in the bright sunshine. I thought, "It's a fine day to find a wife for Bill."

In my mind, I still see the Berukoffs so clearly. Mrs. Berukoff, Nastya, was round, *zhirnaya*, with a plump face and body, dressed in layers of long skirts, blouses and a *platok* covering her brown hair. Her husband, Meetya, was tall and thin, a *delavoy muzhik*, hard-working and clever, who was involved in the local Doukhobor community. Their daughter, Tyunka, was a little younger than me.

Mrs. Berukoff quickly understood why we had come and made us feel welcome. She sat us down, brought us tea and, in the Doukhobor way, told us about her relations and asked about ours. Shkuratoff had been her family name, and she grew up on a farm in Alberta. She took a long look at Bill.

"Yes," she agreed, "Bill should be married."

"But how, Auntie?" I shrugged my shoulders.

"We just have to introduce him to the right person," Mrs. Berukoff replied and thought about where to send us.

After a couple of minutes, she nodded and said, "I know. The Popoff family has lots of children and several girls. The oldest is about your uncle's age."

The mother of this large family had married three times. When her first husband, Popoff, passed away, she remarried a Safonoff, but he died soon after, and then she married another Popoff. She had children with each husband. This family lived in the next village, and Tyunka walked us there. She was so chatty that we quickly became friends.

Mrs. Popoff answered our knock at the door. Her stern face and hefty body made me hesitate, but Tyunka spoke up. "Tyota, Mama sent us here." She pulled Bill forward and said, "Bill would like to meet Polya." Mrs. Popoff sat us down on a bench in the living room and called for Polya. The whole family (except for Mr. Popoff, who kept busy in his workshop), an older son Bill, Polya and her sister Fenya, three young sons and a younger daughter, showed up to see the visitors and crowded around us.

Mrs. Popoff asked about our family, and though I prodded Bill, he gave me a desperate look and tightened his lips. Whether I liked it or not, I had to do the talking. How else could I get him married? I told them that the Hoodicoffs had a farm in Thrums and they lived well. I said that Uncle Bill was a kind man and worked hard. He would like to marry, and Mrs. Berukoff thought Polya would be a good match for him.

Bill and Polya sat together after a while, glancing out of the corners of their eyes at each other. Then I was astonished as Bill leaned closer to Polya and quietly said, "We have a farm on the river in Thrums, and cows, horses, chickens. Would you like to live there?" At that point, Polya took a long look at Bill and nodded. Her sister Fenya took all this in, giggled, gave Polya a hug and jumped up to make tea.

We stayed over at the Berukoffs that night, and the next morning Uncle Bill and I returned to visit the Popoffs. Mrs. Popoff invited us in and simply said, "I know of the Hoodicoffs. They're a respectable, hard-working family."

She glanced over at Polya, who said, "I'll marry Bill."

I think they were glad to marry Polya off, and she wanted to get away from that family too. Her older stepbrother Bill was eyeing me, but I didn't like him at all. He was short, and *oy, Hospadyee*, I had to turn my back and ignore him.

We went home that day. The Hoodicoff family visited the Popoffs a couple of times in Appledale, but I never did go back, though I would have liked to have seen Mrs. Berukoff and Tyunka again.

There was a *zapoy*, an engagement party, and shortly after, Uncle Bill and Polya got married. They had a good wedding, with a dance and lots of food, *borsh, peerahee, plow*. It was nice to see them happy together.

They lived with Dedushka and Babushka Hoodicoff on the farm in Thrums. Polya helped Babushka prepare for market, and Babushka taught Polya how to be a good saleslady.

Eventually Polya and Bill got their own house. When the Brilliant Dam flooded the riverside land in Thrums, the neighbours chose to take money for their property. My grandparents wanted to stay in Thrums, so instead of money, they were given the neighbours' house and land that hadn't flooded. Uncle Bill and Polya moved next door, to what had been the Boolinoff house.

Polya was a good wife for him. They both got diabetes later on, but that was because they ate too much sugar. When Uncle Bill was young, Dedushka would let him have sugar, even in his soup and *borsh*. "Let the child have what he wants," he would tell Babushka.

Polya liked to talk a lot and told me many things. She made up for Uncle Bill's silence. She said that when her mother remarried

The traditional practice of arranging marriages through a matchmaker led to a happy marriage for Bill and Polya Hoodicoff. L-R Pete Kalmakoff, Elizabeth, Luba, Bill Popoff (Polly's brother), Bill Hoodicoff and Polly Sofonoff (the groom and bride), Tiny and Mike Fominoff. The woman kneeling is unidentified.

for the third time, she was left with her aunt in Ootischenia, and as an only child there, she was well treated. She liked to draw, colour and cook. Then her mother stole her back, to look after her babies. They were sort of an uneducated family. Polya would have been better off if she had stayed with her aunt. She could have gone to school.

Polya and Uncle Bill had a fine life. He respected her and they got on well enough. When Uncle Bill died, Polya gave him a decent funeral, with prayers, singing and a farewell meal. It was sad that Polya didn't have a funeral. They didn't have any children, so after Bill died, Polya moved in with her relatives. When she passed away, they said there wasn't enough money for a memorial service. That wasn't right. Polya deserved a proper send-off.

Conscientious
Objector

—–⁓—–

It was my grandfather Pete Maloff's fourth and final time in jail that broke him. When Vanya Perepolkin saw the shape he was in, he told Grandfather, "It's time you let *others* take the lead. Even horses take turns pulling the plow." His imprisonment in the Nelson provincial jail precipitated a three-year-long absence from the family home.

Growing up in the extended Maloff family in the 1950s and 1960s, I learned about what had happened to my grandfather in jail only through whispers between the aunts and Mother's comments. "What they did to him—no wonder he broke down," she once said. Years later, when I asked my mother for details, this is the story she told me.

LEEZA: During the war, in 1940 when the National Registration came into law, Father refused to register. The penalty for non-registration was three months in jail, but Father was sentenced to several terms of three months. He'd be out of jail for just a week or so when the police would pick him up again. The policemen came to know him well. Father was always courteous, and if the constables showed up during dinnertime, he'd invite them to a meal. Mother fed them *borsh* with thick slices of fresh bread, and they jokingly said, "Lusha, you should be running a restaurant here."

On one occasion, we had visitors: Dr. Jensen—a famous author and alternative-healing specialist befriended by my father—and his wife from California. As we were sitting at the dinner table there was a loud knock on our house door, and through the window in the door we could see a policeman's hat above a ruddy face. Father grimaced, sighed and went to answer the knock. When he opened the door, we saw that there were four uniformed policemen standing in our yard. The constable in charge handed Father a summons. "You know what this is about, Pete. Time you gave in."

Father usually threw a few things into a bag and left with them, but this time he pleaded, "Constable, I'll go with you, but could you delay my arrest? Just now I have dear friends visiting." My father turned and gestured to Dr. Jensen, who was dressed in a suit, white shirt and tie, and to his wife, who was wearing a smart dress and hat. Dr. Jensen came to the door, introduced himself and shook hands with the police officers.

The constable looked at the gathering around the table and stepped outside to talk with his fellow officers. To Dr. Jensen's astonishment, when the constable returned he said, "We'll be back in three days. But Pete, you are not to leave this property!"

Prison became a revolving door for Father. He wasn't even allowed to write or receive letters. But then we got worse news from our neighbour, Bill Ostoforoff. Bill was a handsome young man known for his beautiful singing voice and for frequenting bars in Nelson. It turned out that one of his drinking buddies was a guard in the Nelson jail, and it was he who told Bill to warn us about what was happening to Father.

—ᵚᵚ—

During warm summer nights our family often slept on the screened-in porch where it was cooler, and, especially with Dad in prison, the six of us found comfort there huddled close to one another on a couple of old beds. Through the fog of sleep, I heard loud banging on our screen door.

"Lusha! *Hde ti? Bistra ustavay!* Are you there? Get up!"

Already tense with worry, I bolted upright. Peering through the screen, I could make out the shadowy shape of our neighbour, Bill.

Bill kept pounding on the door and shouting, "Lusha, you've got to do something. Pete's in danger."

Mother wrapped herself in a blanket, opened the door and had Bill sit down on the bench outside. I stood beside her with an arm around her shoulders, and I felt her trembling as Bill gave us the news. Stumbling on his words and mopping his brow, Bill told us the guard instructed him to go directly to our house. He said that the warden, desperate to break Father of his refusal to register, had beaten him and threatened to either send him to the insane asylum or have him killed and make it look like suicide.

The guard had told Bill, "The warden means it. I've seen things happen here that no one should see. People get hurt—and worse. You've got to let someone know what's happening."

I was twenty at the time. Petya was sixteen, twins Luba and Johnnik thirteen, Nadya nine and Walter just five. How could we help?

Father had an amazing memory for names and addresses. He remembered a minister who assisted conscientious objectors in appealing their jail sentences in the States. On a scrap of paper the guard gave him, Father had written the name John Haynes Holmes and his New York City address. Bill gave the note to Mother, saying, "Pete said this man could help."

Mother's brother, Dyadya Ivan, was usually our backup driver, but just then he was fed up with what he saw as Father's useless protests against an intractable government. So Mother thought her sister's husband, George Aseyev, might take her to the telegram office. Asking me to look after everyone, she and Petya threw on some clothes and hurried along the railway track to the Aseyevs'. It was already dawn. Dyadya George was pulling on his overalls and heading toward the barn for the morning milking, but when he heard the news, he dropped his buckets and the three of them jumped into the farm truck. The closest telegraph station was in the hotel owned by the West Kootenay Power and Light Company in South Slocan, and by the time they arrived the doors were open. Dyadya George and Mother drafted this telegram to Reverend Holmes:

> Pete Maloff beaten in Nelson Provincial prison. Stop. Need help. Stop. Telegram Warden Macdonald. Stop.

When Mother returned, she slumped into a chair and said, "We need to pray that Mr. Holmes can help."

Months later the family learned that as soon as Reverend Holmes received the telegram, he sent one to Warden Macdonald:

> Pete Maloff is a conscientious objector. Stop. The American Civil Liberties Union will defend his right to freedom of speech. Stop. Any police misconduct in his case will be prosecuted to the full extent of the law. Stop.

The morning that Warden Macdonald received this telegram, the whole jail heard him pounding his fist on his desk. "Who found out? Who did this?"

Years later, when he was finally home, Father explained to us what had happened in the jail cell that night.

Warden Macdonald, inspector and commanding officer of the B Division of the provincial police, had offered to resettle our family on a farm in either the Fraser Valley or Alberta. The stipulation was that Father was not to have any contact with the Doukhobors. Warden Macdonald told him, "Pete, you could make a good living on a farm like that, and your children could have an education, even go to university." Father refused.

He never revealed the name of the guard who helped him.

—••—

I was astonished and shaken when Mother told me this story. This was life sounding like a bad cop movie. I set about to learn more. Searching Grandfather Pete Maloff's files, I found letters between Grandmother Lusha and Warden Macdonald. Lusha had appealed to the warden to let Pete receive correspondence. This produced a curt reply—Warden Macdonald allowed him to write and receive one letter.[35]

Lusha's reply was couched in a grateful manner but unequivocally stated that Pete was following his conscience in refusing to register. If thieves and murderers were allowed letters, why not Pete?[36]

The beatings happened later.

I searched the internet for information on the 1940 National Resources Mobilization Act and the National Registration and found the following:

> According to the 1940 legislation, everyone over the age of 16 was compelled to register with the federal government, giving their personal information and employment history, to provide an inventory of the available skills that might be mobilized for the war effort.[37]

---

35. See letter from Warden J. Macdonald to Mrs. Pete Maloff in the appendix.
36. See letter from Mrs. Pete Maloff to Warden J. Macdonald in the appendix.
37. "National Registration Comes to Canada," Wartime Canada, accessed April 15,

Many Doukhobors did not obey. Koozma Tarasoff, in *Plakun Trava*, his book on the history of the Doukhobors, wrote,

> 1943 December 12, Two majors in full military regalia try to persuade Doukhobors in Brilliant, B.C. to comply with national registration. 4,000 Doukhobors present petition saying, "No!" Early next morning, the jam factory complex worth $400,000 is destroyed by fire.[38]

Reading the papers of the time, I learned that refusal to participate in the National Registration was a major irritant to the legal system. A *Nelson Daily News* article described a Grand Forks demonstration in support of four Doukhobors who had been arrested for failing to register.

> Tear gas was used in one instance when 150 Doukhobors from the Ruckle Addition settlement attempted to march into Grand Forks. ... The Ruckle Addition demonstrators declared they too were unregistered and were ready to go to jail. Many carried suitcases filled with articles they might need if taken into custody.[39]

Magistrate Hodge, a judge in the Nelson provincial court who was hearing a case involving a Doukhobor man, stated,

> You and your gang are nothing but parasites. ... Registration is absolutely necessary and nobody with any reason but to conceal something against Canada could have any objection. I consider that you and your kind are a danger and a menace to the community at the present time and I am going to put you away for as long a time as the law allows.[40]

2020, http://wartimecanada.ca/document/world-war-ii/conscription/national-registration-comes-canada.

38. Tarasoff, *Plakun Trava*, p. 263.

39. "Doukhobors in Demonstration," *Nelson Daily News*, September 23, 1940.

40. "Crescent Valley Doukhobor Is Given Three Months for Refusing to Register," *Nelson Daily News*, September 25, 1940.

Others besides Doukhobors also refused to register, including Jehovah's Witnesses across Canada, and in Quebec, the mayor of Montreal and parliamentarian Camillien Houde were jailed for their protests.

Through an internet search I found that Reverend Holmes was a Unitarian minister who, in 1920, helped to found the American Civil Liberties Union to support freedom of speech and justice. Reverend Holmes was a pacifist whom Grandfather Pete had corresponded with and met in New York. Grandfather told Mother about a meeting they attended. He said that a man shouting at Holmes was so angry on account of his anti-war stance that his spit was spraying all over the reverend as he spoke. The reverend sat quietly, ignoring the vitriol. Later, when Pete asked him about his reaction, he simply said, "They know what I believe. I've said everything I need to." It was Reverend Holmes, with the support of the American Civil Liberties Union behind him, that Pete hoped would have the power to defend him.

The American Civil Liberties Union probably could not intervene to support a Canadian conscientious objector today, but in the 1940s perhaps the jurisdiction was not so firm. At any rate the telegram from Reverend Holmes to Warden Macdonald stopped the beatings and threats to Grandfather.

Wanting to find out more about Warden Macdonald and the provincial jail in Nelson, I approached the Nelson museum archives. An obliging archivist, Laura Fortier, located "The History of the Nelson Provincial Jail" by Wayne Lutz.[41] It included photographs taken just before the jail was closed in 1958. I opened the picture file to find a two-storey building with an attached tower that, from Ward Street, displayed generous windows and horizontal clapboard siding. Trees shaded the street side, and a lamp standard guided visitors to the double-door entrance. The warden's apartment consisted of a large kitchen, parlour, dining room, bedroom and pantry on the main floor, and there were three sleeping rooms and a bathroom for the guards in the adjoining tower.

The exterior facade camouflaged the grim purpose of the building; the rear view showed the barred windows and narrow jail

---

41.   Lutz, "The History of the Nelson Provincial Jail."

yard typical of a nineteenth-century penitentiary. Concrete walls and an overhead wire grid surrounded the yard. I read that three men had been hanged in this enclosure, the last in 1902. In 1896 officials and forty spectators watched as the hangman from Calgary sprang the trap to execute Samuel Wood, who had been convicted of murder. I wondered if the spectators watched from the street, looking through the wire grid.

This wire grid reminded me of photographs showing my eleven-year-old mother with her younger cousins, my grandmother and my great-aunt, standing behind the wire gate of this same prison in 1932. Soon after these pictures were taken, my relatives, including my mother, were sent to various institutions: the BC Girls' Industrial School, Alexandra Orphanage and Piers Island Penitentiary. That same wire grid had been in the background.

The photos of the warden's quarters showed a gas fireplace and a curved staircase with a wooden banister. The prisoners' cells contained no such comfort. Two tiers of cells, forty-seven in all, accommodated seventy-two male and twenty-two female prisoners. The cells were enclosed by steel bars, and double bunks without mattresses were attached to the wall by chains, one above the other in the minuscule rooms. I shuddered as I read about the dark cell in the basement for "refractory" prisoners.

With the archivist's help I continued my search. We found an obituary and death certificate for John Macdonald. He was born in Scotland; his occupation was entered as "Inspector of BC Police." He retired in 1945 and passed away in 1953 from a cerebral hemorrhage in the Athlone Hospital in Vancouver. He was survived by his wife.

I was left with many questions. Did Warden Macdonald and his wife live in the warden's apartment at the provincial jail in Nelson? Was Macdonald at peace when he walked up the concrete stairs of the jail and closed the heavy wooden door separating the jail from his office and living quarters?

The jail history notes that Thomas Camm, who had been a guard and then in 1939 became deputy warden at the Nelson provincial jail, was transferred to Oakalla in 1942. Was he the man who had passed on information about Pete Maloff's beatings? Was this why he was transferred? Some histories are unspoken and unheard.

My research into Grandfather's past in the Nelson jail unearthed painful memories for my mother. But as I read a draft of this story to her, she sat quietly, nodding occasionally. She survived those years and is satisfied that others would finally hear these stories.

Grandfather had collapsed after this episode in the Nelson provincial jail. It took many years for him to regain his health. But throughout his life, he did not dwell on this past, nor did he identify with being a prisoner. We knew him for his love of books and classical music, for the many friends and correspondents who visited and wrote to him. He brought to us a world outside our narrow BC valley, the world of those who strove after the same values and who thought of the world they wanted to create—one of equality and fraternity. Grandfather defined himself not as a victim of the jail experience, but as a worker for peace.

Second Gear

The 1940s. With the Second World War raging in Europe and Asia, Canada geared up to support the war effort. Doukhobors as pacifists were considered unpatriotic and even traitors by the government and other Canadians, many of whom had family members fighting overseas. The tension in the Doukhobor community was tremendous. When many Doukhobors refused to comply with the National Registration, legionnaires suggested that they be stripped of Canadian citizenship and interned for the duration of the war.[42] The jam factory in Brilliant was destroyed by fire in 1943. I could not find much information regarding this event, but everything pointed to arson. Doukhobor workers, many of them employed in fruit picking and canning, were banned from working in the industry.

In the Maloff family the anxiety was multiplied. With Pete Maloff having been beaten in jail, the family was worried for his life. My mother told me there was nowhere to turn to for help. They felt ostracized from both Doukhobor communities—the Union of Spiritual Communities of Christ (USCC) and the Sons of Freedom, or Svobodniki. The former Christian Community of Universal Brotherhood had been forced into bankruptcy and was reorganized into the USCC. Their spiritual leader Peter P. Verigin (Chistiakov) had died in a Saskatchewan hospital in 1939, and his grandson Ivan Ivanovich (John J. Sr.) Verigin, who had been groomed to be the leader, was still in his teens. At that time the Maloff family did not belong to the USCC; furthermore, they were looked down upon for Grandfather's association with the Svobodniki. The Svobodniki were angry because Pete spoke out against those who increasingly turned to violence—burning and bombing of USCC and government properties. The Maloff home also became a target.

Leeza had to step into her father's shoes and support her mother, Lusha, and the younger children. She was twenty and had just

42. Tarasoff, *Plakun Trava*, p. 263.

returned home after a disastrous marriage. When I ask her about this time, she purses her lips, frowns and tells me, "It was difficult. We had no money. We lived off the garden and hand-me-downs." She does not mention the emotional strain she and the family were living with.

They had a car but no driver, so her practical mother made getting Leeza's driver's licence the first order of events. Then they had to get help. Here is Leeza's story of that time.

LEEZA: When the Second World War started, Father gathered with other Thrums men at Uncle Ivan Hoodicoff's in the evenings to listen to the six o'clock news. They pulled their chairs close around Uncle's big round cherry-wood radio set while Lorne Greene announced the evening news. We followed the war through the headlines that Father shared with us when he returned. "Russia and Finland are at war!" "Convoy ships are bombed!" "London is Burning!" Visions of dead women and children, soldiers killing, planes bombing cities, fires burning and people starving crowded into our brains.

Father continued to protest against the war, refusing to participate in the National Registration. Uncle Ivan disapproved of Dad's dissent, badgering him. "Why aren't you registered? You have to think of your six children! How will they survive?" He wouldn't accept Dad's response: "I won't compromise. If Doukhobors don't protest, who will make a stand against war?"

When Dad was arrested for non-compliance with the National Registration, Uncle Ivan growled at him, "Why do you do this to yourself? You won't win against the government." He wanted to wash his hands of us.

With Father in jail and Uncle Ivan reluctant to help, we needed a driver. I was the oldest, and my mother firmly told me, "Leeza, you must take that driver's test."

I groaned and my stomach knotted. It wasn't that I was unprepared; I had driven many times with Father. The problem was that the driver examiner's office was next door to the Nelson provincial jail where Father was imprisoned, and I had tremors just glimpsing the barbed wire fence around the compound. I had known that place as a child of eleven when my family was held there in 1932, before I was sent away to the BC Girls' Industrial School. I did not have to imagine the cramped concrete cells, the bars on the windows and the overhead wire grid in the yard.

It was a rainy spring day, slippery on the steep streets of Nelson. The driver examiner, a robust middle-aged man, inspected me in my neat blue-grey dress and sweater, my hair waved from the rollers I had slept in the night before. The way he frowned when he looked at me made me suspect that he knew about my dad, but then he nodded and said, "You're Elizabeth Maloff? You're next." We stepped outside the office and he turned his gaze toward the dark blue 1925 Chevy I had cleaned and polished. "This your car?" Dad had bought the Chevy for a few hundred dollars from an orchardist he had worked for in the Okanagan. I loved that car as I could feel all four wheels as I drove it, but I couldn't hide that it was old. The examiner walked around the car, looked at the spoked wheels, the running board and the roll-down windows and scratched his head, but it passed his cursory inspection, for he shrugged and said, "Okay. Let's go."

He opened the door and stepped up on the running board to sit in the passenger seat. I followed suit, turned the key and mechanically went through the motions of starting the car that I had rehearsed so many times. Put the car into neutral, pull the emergency brake on, set the spark advance lever, go around to the front to turn the crank to starting position and give it a turn. So far, so good: the engine fired up.

As we drove away from the motor vehicle licensing office, I noticed my uncle Ivan and his buddies standing on the corner of Vernon and Ward Streets, scrutinizing my driving. I cringed and tried to ignore them. Like all cars of the time, the Chevy had a manual transmission with three gears, and as I drove past my uncle, I shifted jerkily from first to second gear and the whole car shuddered. In the rear-view mirror, I could see my uncle's gang turn to follow our jolting progress down Vernon Street. I had practised faithfully, knew how to give hand signals, to parallel park, to stop on steep hillsides, to check for traffic at stop signs and in the blind spot before proceeding, and I did all of this perfectly—but I didn't trust my shifting again and I did it all in second gear.

The well-loved 1925 Chevy Elizabeth drove for her driver's licence test.

My palms were soaked with sweat; the steering wheel was slip-pery and I was shaking by the time I finished that test. I turned to the driver examiner for the verdict.

He raised his eyebrows, leaned back in the passenger seat and looked out the window and then back at me, slowly considering. "Are you always going to drive in second gear?" he asked.

I'm sure my face was red and I thought I was done for as I stut-tered, "No." He must have understood how nervous I was, for he made a generous decision to give me my licence. As I left the ex-amining office triumphantly clutching my precious card, I inwardly rejoiced. Uncle Ivan be darned; I passed!

——ᴡᴡ——

It was when Dad finally returned from jail that we found out Warden Macdonald had received a telegram from Reverend John Haynes Holmes stating that the American Civil Liberties Union would prosecute any police misconduct regarding Pete Maloff. The warden had stopped the beatings, but he continued to harass Father. We had to find a way to have him released from jail. Mother was desperate. She sought support everywhere.

Vanya Perepolkin, Father's friend, often came to talk to her, repeating what he'd said to Pete directly. "Pete has pulled the plow for long enough," he said of Father's protests. "Even horses take turns being in the lead. It's time for Pete to rest. He's done his share."

Others wanted Father to continue to dissent, to defy the law even while he was in jail. But when Mother went to see these so-called friends, she came home after her long walk, head bowed, feet dragging, and broke down crying. "They laughed at me. They just joked, 'You're looking for a man? No man at home?'"

When Vanya heard about this response he said, "Go see Ivan Ivanovich Verigin. No one else."

"But he's so young," Mother responded.

"Never mind. He'll know what to do. His grandfather taught him well."

So Mother sent me to Brilliant, where Ivan Ivanovich lived with his grandmother. Why she didn't come with me I don't know. But there I was, driving past the Brilliant bluffs on my first road trip in the Chevy.

Ivan Ivanovich Verigin, at seventeen, had become the interim leader of the USCC after his grandfather's death. He lived with his grandmother in one of the large Doukhobor houses next to the ball field in Brilliant, and in the evenings he was often found there. When I went to see him he was nineteen, a year younger than I, but he had been his grandfather Chistiakov's personal assistant, interpreter and office clerk for several years, so despite his youth, Ivan Ivanovich Verigin was accepted by the USCC Doukhobor community as their "secretary." (In 1961, at the age of forty, he was unanimously declared honorary chairman of the USCC.)

You have to understand that we were Independent Doukhobors, not members of the USCC. Father supported the cause of the USCC and often had discussions with the former leader Chistiakov, but he hadn't lived in the community. Additionally, USCC members had registered as directed under the National Resources Mobilization Act after they were given assurance that as conscientious objectors they would be exempt from military service. USCC members had served as registrars. This, Father refused to do, believing registration was the first step to military indoctrination. He followed the Doukhobor doctrine "Render unto Caesar that which is Caesar's, but first obey God," which he understood as: Be obedient to Canadian laws if they did not conflict with his conscience.

Brilliant, at the confluence of the Kootenay and Columbia Rivers, was a burgeoning USCC centre in those days. There was a busy train station, the productive Brilliant jam factory that shipped jam everywhere in Canada and donated cases to Canadian soldiers in Europe and their dependent families at home,[43] a fruit packing house, a co-op store that stocked everything one needed for farm life, the USCC *kantora* or office, a sizable brick hall for prayer meetings and the sports field, all surrounded by orchards.

I drove up to the ball field and sat in the car, watching the players throw a softball around, warming up for a game. As I wondered how to approach Ivan Ivanovich, I saw him throw the ball to a teammate, rub his hands clean on his ball pants and head my way.

He jogged over to the car and opened the passenger door as if he expected me. "Leeza, you've come to see me? About your dad?"

As I nodded I could feel tears start to well up. Maybe he could help.

He slipped into the passenger seat and turned to me. "Tell me what's happening."

Though he had heard about Father's imprisonment, I haltingly explained the details: how through one of the jail guards, we learned that the warden was threatening to have him put in an insane asylum or have him killed and make it look like suicide if he continued to refuse to register, how Father had become very ill. My voice just a thin thread, I added, "We're afraid for Father. We don't know what to do. Maybe he should accept the registration."

Ivan Ivanovich looked at me and put an arm on my shaking shoulders. "You and I both know he's not going to do that, Leeza."

"*Bokh pamahnyee nam*, God help us! He will not last long in jail."

As we sat side by side in the blue Chevy at the edge of the ball field on that bright spring afternoon, Ivan Ivanovich Verigin in his ball uniform and me in my second-best dress, the orchards sur-

---

43.   In May 1938, the receiver for the National Trust Company Limited foreclosed upon the Brilliant jam factory and other properties, but production continued for a time. Jonathan Kalmakoff, "Doukhobor jam factories stood at Nelson, Brilliant, Grand Forks," *West Kootenay Advertiser*, April 30, 2020.

rounding us in full bloom and swallows flitting above us, I felt my shoulders begin to lighten.

His teammates glanced over toward the car once in a while but he ignored them, listened and asked questions as we discussed possible ways to help Father. Finally, he suggested, "Go talk to the warden, and pray before you go." Then he looked at me sternly and said, "Above all, do not get angry."

"Ivan Ivanovich, the warden is furious with Father."

"Go with peace in your heart, *s dabrom*. Tell him that that you will arrange that your father will live in a remote area. He will have no contact with anyone but the family." He gave my shoulders a squeeze. "Tell the warden that six children rely on him."

Mother and I travelled the road to Nelson many times to get a meeting with Warden Macdonald. We sat in the waiting room for days, it seemed, before the warden would see us, but finally he agreed to house arrest after Father's current three-month jail term was up.

EXILE IN BLEWETT

———

We are sitting around a table drinking mint tea and enjoying slices of birthday cake. It is Luba's eighty-eighth birthday and her daughter Elaine, Mother and I have called in to Talarico Place in Castlegar to celebrate. As we sit and talk, I ask her to tell us the story about how she visited her father in Blewett when he was under house arrest in 1941. Luba sometimes forgets the day-to-day things happening in the nursing home, but this story is vivid in her mind. As she talks, it's as though she is on that riverbank.

I imagine her as a young girl. It's 1941, fall. A Canadian Pacific Railway day train winds its way along Kootenay River toward Nelson; then, just past the Corra Linn Dam, the whistle blows and it stops in a puff of steam. A young girl, slim and lithe, steps out, pulls a couple of bulky sacks from the train carriage onto the siding and places a small brown suitcase next to them. She frees her hands, lifts back her long dark hair and waves to the conductor. He pauses on the carriage platform, a wry look on his face, and shouts, "Be careful, Luba," then shrugs and waves back.

She looks around. There's the old Queen Bess Mine shack, and behind it, through the fir trees, is a short, steep trail to the river. Across from her, closer to the Blewett side of the river, is a small island with three fir trees, and the crows that have made them their home flood the sky. Above their raucous caws she hears the distant roar of water gushing through the dam gates. The fall afternoon is sunny, but the churned water that has sluiced through the gates creates a mist that hovers over the dam. The picture is crystal clear in my mind as Luba begins her story.

LUBA: I was only thirteen. I might have died on that river, but somehow I made it across. Papa had been in jail in Nelson for protesting against the national mobilization. Everyone over sixteen had to register, just like for war, but Papa wouldn't. Warden Macdonald was furious with him. Mother and Leeza drove into Nelson to talk to the warden almost every second day to try to get him freed. Finally, he agreed to release Papa. He'd have to live far from the Doukhobor community, and only the family could visit.

Dyadya, Uncle Ivan Hoodicoff, found an old cabin up on the mountainside close to Fortynine Creek in Blewett. In those days hardly anyone lived there. He helped us put a little bit of money down on the property—it wasn't worth much, just trees and rocks. Papa came home for a few days to make arrangements to move there, and the family decided I would be the best person to visit and take him food. Peter, my older brother, was needed on the farm. Nadya and Walter, they were too young. And Johnnik, well, he was too *besheniy*, wild. Leeza had her troubles at that time. So it was up to me.

Papa and I agreed on the time and place to meet. I'd take the train from Thrums to Beasley, where there was a whistle stop. He'd row across the river, meet me there and row us back to the Blewett side where the cabin was. Simple, right?

But, first, the train conductor didn't want to let me off in Beasley. He told me, "There's no one here. Come to Nelson. You could stay the night and get a ride back in the morning."

"I don't know anyone in Nelson," I told the conductor. "Papa said he would be here."

But he wasn't. So I dragged those sacks down the hill, slipping and sliding all the way, and when I got to the water, I could see Papa waving at me from the other side of the river.

"Lubochka," he shouted. "*Ya tut*. I'm here!"

I was glad to see him but shouted, "Papa, why aren't you over here?" And then I saw the boat, pulled up onto the shore just where there was a little sandy beach on my side of the river.

"Lubochka, don't worry. I'll find another boat and row across to you," Papa shouted back.

We were yelling back and forth so loudly I could hear the echo of our voices. An old man and two old women who lived on the farm by the water on the Blewett side heard the commotion and came over to Papa.

"Oh yes, the boat. That happens," the man told him.

"People row it across, then they stay in town and we're stuck," explained one of the women. "I don't think you'll find another.

Everyone uses this boat to catch the train."

All three shook their heads.

So it was up to me, but I got into a fluster just thinking about rowing—I hadn't even *been* in a boat before—and I couldn't swim. But those old people, they encouraged me. "We row across all the time. You can do it."

In those days that's how it was. I did what I had to do. I loaded my bags into the boat, waded into the water—it was cold—and then slowly clambered over the side and sat down on the old wooden bench. The boat tilted and wobbled, my hands were shaking, and everyone started giving me directions.

"Okay, push off. Now, pick up the oars and slowly pull—both together."

At first I just got sprayed with water and rowed in circles, but then I dug the oars into the water and the boat started to move out toward the middle. Everyone may have used that boat to cross the river, but I doubt if anyone looked after it because water started seeping through the floorboards. I panicked and yelled, "It leaks! What do I do?"

From across the river the man and women shouted, "You need to bail or you'll sink! Use the bucket!"

The water in the boat kept getting higher and higher. I scrambled for the bucket.

Papa shouted, "If you're scared, I'll swim out to you."

That didn't help. The dark water looked calm, but toward the middle of the river the current began to pick up. I saw eddies and whirlpools. With Papa in poor health, I was afraid he'd drown. "No, no. I can do it," I shouted. I looked at the riverbank I'd left, then at the side Papa was on—they both seemed far away. The island was getting closer, though, so I breathed a prayer and began to sway backward and forward, pushing the oars, my whole body moving like I remember Papa's did when he rowed the gophers from our farm in Thrums to their new home on the other side of the river.

I bailed and rowed for my life and then bailed and rowed some more. I was so scared my heart was pounding. Once, I almost lost an oar. I reached out into the water and the boat began to tilt, but somehow I managed to grab the oar just in time. And all the time everyone was shouting. "You're almost here. Keep rowing, dig deep with both oars. Slowly now. That's it." And finally, "You've made it. You don't need to be afraid now."

When I reached the other side, I needed more than anything that hug Papa gave me. I shivered and he hugged me so hard until finally my legs felt as if they could hold me up again. Everything I brought was soaked, and so was I, but I had rowed across the river for the first time in my life!

I lived with Papa for a couple of weeks at a time and then I'd go home, get supplies and visit my friends. Thank God, I never had to row across the river again. Dyadya Ivan drove me, but those logging roads weren't much better. I hung on to the door when the truck rounded the sharp corners around Fortynine Creek and the gears ground as we churned up the mountain.

Papa's cabin was up a steep path above the creek. There were a couple of farms down the road toward Nelson and a cedar mill, but mostly it was a cedar and fir forest. In fall the few golden birch trees, like a splash of sunlight in the dark forest, helped to cheer me up.

That first day, when I was so wet and cold from paddling and it was almost dark when I finally saw the cabin, I thought of the Russian stories that Mama read to us as kids: about the Baba Yaga, a wild witch who flew in a mortar holding a pestle and trapped children in a hut deep in the forest.

"Don't think like that, Luba," Papa told me. "We bought this place from the man who logged the trees and built this little house. He tried to homestead here, but the land is poor and it's far from anywhere. No one has lived here for a while. It's perfect for us right now."

It still felt spooky to me. Shingles were missing off the roof, and caulking had fallen out from between the logs. When Papa opened the door, I smelled the musty smell of a pack rat.

The cabin had two rooms. There was a pot-bellied stove against one wall, but it wasn't very good—you could see the fire through the cracks in the thin metal and it burned out at night. On the other wall, against the window, stood a wooden table and two chairs. I looked at the way Papa organized everything. He had two pots, two bowls, a knife and two spoons all arranged in an apple box he used for a shelf. Buckwheat cereal, oatmeal, rice, salt and flour were in olive oil cans. I told him, "Papa, you are living here just like a Russian bear in the forest, and I'm like Masha, come to help you."

"I'm so happy you are here, Lubochka."

"But remember, Masha tricked that bear and found a way home!" I teased him.

And then he laughed. But, although I loved Papa, I did feel trapped. At night, as the wind rattled the window and blew through the walls, I dreamt the Baba Yaga was knocking at the door. She snatched me from my bed where I huddled, and we flew into the sky, past stars, and then I glimpsed my home. Leeza, Nadya and Johnnik were gathered around a warm fire in the kitchen, chatting. Mama was stirring something in a pot on the stove. Walter was looking out the window at the stars. I waved and called, "Hello, I'm here." Could he hear me? In the morning I found myself back in the cabin, curled up under my blanket until Papa lit the stove.

At first I spent my days stuffing moss, clay, newspaper, whatever we had, between the logs. Papa was busy chopping firewood and he'd say, "Luba, grab that bucket. We need water for dinner." I thought of the pile of bear poop I had seen by the creek and walked slowly, peering into the gloom under the trees, flinching at every branch that cracked. It was a rushing, noisy creek full of big boulders. I lowered the bucket between the rocks, and water filled it quickly. Glancing up the hillside, just as if my eyes had suddenly become "mushroom eyes," I noticed mushrooms pushing up from under the thick layer of needles—big and small, white, brown, orange and even with purple caps and sponges or gills underneath, and some that were like cauliflower, but I gathered just the *abcheennyeekee* that grew in bunches at the bottom of old trees.

"Look what I found!" I showed Papa my sweater full of the brown *abcheennyeekee*.

"Luba, you're a dear. Mushrooms and potatoes for supper!" he said as he swung the axe. I stacked the wood against the house wall and then went in to fry mushrooms.

I never saw so many animals as at that place in Blewett. There was a raven that watched us from a branch way up in a tall fir tree. It would croak, caw, caw—and swoop down to grab *pishkee*, a pan bread I made, right out of my hand. Deer peeked out from the forest and nibbled on the bushes at the edge of the clearing. I would hear rustling and a sound like people singing far away, and then a family of wild turkeys waddled out, one after another in a long row. Papa gave them our leftovers and they began to show up any time he came outside with a pot in his hand. In the evening, when I heard them calling from their roosts high up in the trees around the cabin, I almost felt I was among friends. We could count on a coyote symphony about the same time every night. They would start yipping and chattering, one after another, their high-pitched voices answering calls from across the valley. It gave me goosebumps to hear them, and I would dream of coyotes howling.

One morning I opened the door and a cougar was right there, not afraid at all, looking at me with its big yellow eyes. For a moment, I wasn't afraid either. I admired his beautiful shiny fur, his long tail, until I realized, "It's a cougar!" and slammed the door.

"Don't be afraid," Papa told me. "It's hunting the turkeys and deer. That's its nature."

After a while we got to know the neighbours. John Gorkoff, a logger who worked in the forest above us, was the closest. His sister came to visit him sometimes. "Come up and get water from our well here," he invited us. "In winter, that creek freezes solid." Polly and John Chernenkoff and their children lived a couple of miles away, and once in a while, when he'd been drinking, John would drive up and play the harmonica for us. I didn't feel comfortable having him hang around, but it turned out that we were lucky he visited. Then there were the Soloveoffs, who had a dairy farm on the road toward Nelson. But mostly Papa lived alone, like that bear, hibernating in the cabin.

Cooking? Well, of course we had our buckwheat, and Papa or I made soup on that pot-bellied stove—oatmeal, carrots, potatoes, some cabbage. In the evenings, we'd sit by the flickering coal oil lantern, sip our soup and munch on sunflower seeds from the shell.

Dad did some writing, I darned his socks and mended his clothes, and we took turns reading *The Adventures of Tom Sawyer* and *Adventures of Huckleberry Finn*. That was the best time for us. Tom and Huck were never afraid of rowing down the Mississippi River or living in the forest. And then we talked, but Mama said to tell Papa only the good things about how we were doing at home. She was right, Papa wasn't very strong. The way that warden treated him! I could tell he was nervous by the way his hands trembled.

Often he didn't sleep all night. I'd wake up in the dark to find him pacing the cabin.

—⁓—

Luba looks around her room at Talarico Place, at Leeza sitting across from her, at her bed where Elaine and I are perched, and past us into the cemented courtyard. Even now, seventy-five years later, a tear trickles down her cheek. She wipes it away, and Leeza takes her hand and gently massages it. "I tried to be brave but I was worried about Dad all the time. I was only thirteen and I missed my friends."

"I heard that Father's friends hiked up there in the winter. Everyone ran and hid when the police made a surprise inspection," Mother says.

Luba shakes her head. "I didn't see anyone, though one day, Sport arrived in Blewett. He was a small, fluffy dog, always by Papa's side at home, but when he found us his fur was matted and he was so skinny we hardly recognized him. Papa was ecstatic. 'Sport, how did you find us? How did you know where to go?' We shared our food with him and gave him a warm place by the fire, and he did get better. When Dyadya Ivan came to pick me up, Papa hugged me and then bent down to pet Sport. 'Sport will keep me good company,' he reassured me."

"We all loved Sport. It was almost like he understood the difficult time we were going through," Mother says.

"We could always tell our troubles to Sport," Luba says, smiling.

We settle in again as Luba becomes immersed in telling her story.

LUBA: Papa was in Blewett for three years. I especially remember the winter of 1942 when I thought he might die. It had been snowing for days, and it was a couple of weeks before I was able to get a ride to Blewett. Dyadya Ivan drove me to Blewett Road above Fortynine Creek, but the side road was blocked with snow. "Don't worry, Dyadya," I said as I pulled on my mittens and tied my woollen kerchief tightly under my chin. "It's only a mile or so. I'll walk from here."

I tied my packages onto our wooden sled and trudged off, pulling it through the knee-high snow. At the bottom of the hill, where the log bridge crossed the creek, I stopped for a breather. The usually noisy creek was now a series of frozen waterfalls that draped over boulders and moss, and I heard only a tinkle of water. The driveway leading into the trees on the left of the bridge was the last sign of a home—John Gorkoff's—before the wild forest began. I had been there to fetch water when the creek had frozen and to visit Florence, John's sister. John was in his forties and had separated from his wife, so Florence, twenty-four and still single, came to help her brother cook, mend his clothes and knit his socks. I decided to let them know I was back.

The dogs John kept for chasing coyotes barked as I approached the house, and John came out, pulling a wool cap over his short brown hair. "Luba, *usyo kharasho*? Everything fine with you?"

"Oh yes," I answered. "Back to stay with Papa."

"Come and warm up before you head up the mountain," John said. "Florence is here."

"I'd like to make it to the cabin before it gets dark, but I'll visit soon."

"Say hello to your Papa. Hope he's well. There's a flu going around," John told me.

I crossed the bridge and tramped up the road on the other side of the creek until I came to the trail on the left—Bird Road, they call it now, but back then it was just a rough path that was used by prospectors. Tall fir and cedar trees, giant snow sentinels, leaned in on either side. As I walked, I imagined the welcome Papa and Sport would give me: warm hugs, conversation, sharing the soup I had brought from home.

I turned up the path to the cabin. No smoke from the chimney. No footprints in the snow, either, but I heard barking. I pushed the last few feet through the snow and shoved the door open.

Sport dashed toward me and jumped up and down, doing a frantic welcome dance. I petted the furry head. "Sport, I'm glad to see you, too. Where's Papa?"

The sour smell of sickness and the thin figure under the tangled quilts on the bed told me all was not well. Papa was scrunched up into a ball and, though every blanket that was available was on top of him, I could see he was shivering. Hurriedly, I threw off my coat and boots and knelt by his side. His forehead, when I felt it, was burning, but his hands were cold.

Papa opened his eyes, grimaced, swallowed and said, "Masha, it's you."

Masha? Masha Hoodicoff was Grandmother! "Papa, it's me, Luba," I answered him. "I've just come back. I've brought fresh barley soup that Mama made, and Leeza baked bread just like Babushka used to make."

But Papa was looking past me and mumbling something I couldn't understand. I busied myself: I lit the stove, put the soup on to warm and kept up a banter, more to ease my worry than to talk to Papa. He had closed his eyes.

"Good news, Papa. Warden Macdonald said that you may come home for a few days. No visitors, but we'll be so happy to have you home." Sport wagged his tail too when he heard "home."

There was no water left in the kettle. Papa had been ill for a while. Going outside, I scooped a bucket of snow and saw that the short winter day was ending. The snowbanks were purple shadows, the path I had walked up, a thin ribbon of grey, and above the mountain ridge a moon was rising.

I walked back into the cabin, emptied the snow into a kettle on top of the stove and turned to look at Papa's sallow, sunken face. When I tried to spoon soup into his mouth, he shook his head. It was no use. I didn't want to think what might happen in the night. It had to be now.

Papa's old wool pants and jacket were hanging on a nail next to the stove, and I pulled them on top of my coat and long stockings and tied a scarf around my face. Sport whined, wanting to go, but I let him out to do his business and then told him, "Stay with Papa. Those Gorkoff dogs will eat you alive." Sport seemed to understand and burrowed in the quilts next to Papa and licked his face. Papa muttered something but didn't respond when I told him, "Papa, I'm going to the Gorkoffs. Florence is there. She may have something to help you."

In the growing dark, I let my feet retrace the path I had walked an hour ago. The snow crunched, the shadows were deep under the trees, the forest was still. I was alone. I shivered but I kept my feet moving forward as I recited every psalm I knew to keep me safe. *Dom nash blahadatniy* ... God be with me in my journey. *Ukrepee menya Hospadyee* ... Lord, quieten me quieter than the trickling of water, strengthen me stronger than a rock.

I heard the howl of the Gorkoffs' dogs long before I saw their house. As I stumbled up their driveway, frost in my hair and eyelashes and looking more snowman than human, John came out. "What're you mutts barking at?" he yelled at the dogs. Then he spied me. "Luba, is that you? Where's your Papa? *Eedyee, eedyee!* Come inside."

He opened the door wide and a rush of warm air embraced me. I stumbled inside, my feet feeling like logs, my hands tingling as if they were on fire. John latched the door and turned to Florence, who was sitting by the stove, a ball of wool in her lap, her hands busy, her needles clicking.

Florence smiled. "Look who's back!"

"Papa's sick," I blurted. "I don't know what to do. He's so hot and babbling to someone I don't see. And shaking." I burst into tears.

Florence brushed the balls of yarn off her lap, pushed her ponytail back and came to give me a hug. "Lubochka, *sadyees'*, sit here, put your feet on the rug, here next to the stove. Your hands. They're icicles. You walked all the way in the dark? Lubochka, don't cry. We'll think of something."

They covered my shoulders with a blanket, rubbed my hands until they weren't so painful and gave me hot tea.

"Now, what have you given your dad?" Florence asked.

"Just sips of water. He won't take anything else."

"Let me look. I'll see what we have."

She came back from the kitchen carrying—would you believe—half a lemon!

"Lubochka," she said, "that's all I have for now. Make hot tea with the lemon, add some honey if you have it and give it to your papa."

Florence, holding a lantern in one hand, the other linked with mine, walked back with me across the creek and up to Bird Road. I held the half lemon tightly in Papa's old jacket pocket. At the trailhead, she held her lantern up high until she couldn't see me anymore, then shouted, "Lubochka, I'll come tomorrow to see your dad."

The moon, higher in the sky now, shone brighter, and after a while, thank God, I heard Sport's welcoming bark.

"It's lemon tea with honey," I told Papa. "Florence said it'll help. She'll come to see you tomorrow."

Papa opened his eyes. The glazed look was still there, but then he patted my arm. "You're a good girl, Luba. Thank you."

That was enough. Papa had called my name; he had thanked me. It was enough, for now. I put my head down on the table, Sport nuzzled up to me and I fell asleep right there, Sport keeping my feet warm. In the morning, Papa sat up for the first time in days.

I wasn't always there for Papa. There was the day that he broke his arm falling off the roof as he tried to patch it with cedar shingles. Fortunately, John Chernenkoff made one of his sporadic visits and found him leaning against the house wall, his arm hanging loose by his side. John took him to the Doukhobor *kastapraw*, Vasil Bloodoff, a gifted bone-setter. Vasil gingerly felt the bones, then wrapped the arm tightly with old flour sacks and said, "You're lucky. It's been broken for a while, but it's healing in place."

—⁓—

Luba has the Maloff family album on her table, and as I flip the pages I find a photograph that has "1943" stamped in the corner. Luba tells me that it was taken when Grandfather Pete left the cabin, still under house arrest but allowed to go home. He's white-haired and thin, his arm is in a sling and he looks older than his forty-three years. Grandfather is sitting on a stump, and to his right stand his sons Peter, tall and handsome at twenty, and eight-year-old Walter, just up to his father's shoulder, his pants held up by suspenders. Grandmother Lusha is there with Ivan Hoodicoff. "I'm not in the picture," says Luba. "But I think I did my share of looking after Papa. I tried my best."

When Grandfather Pete Maloff stood up for his beliefs against the law of the government, the entire family suffered. Grandmother Lusha was left as a single mother of six, with little income to support them. My mother, Elizabeth, became a co-parent and throughout her life she has felt responsible for the well-being of her younger siblings. Petya, serious and intense, became more so at sixteen as the oldest male of the Maloff household. Luba looked after her ill father at thirteen, a time when other young girls would have been visiting friends, thinking about boys. Her twin, Johnnik, nine-year-old Nadya and Walter, just five, all needed a father's guidance.

In my grandfather's papers I find a letter written by G.A. Butling of Nelson to the Honourable St. Laurent, minister of justice, Ottawa, Ontario. The date is January 18, 1946. This letter is an appeal for the release of Doukhobor war resisters. Butling writes, "The last phase of the war ended on Jan. 1st. Therefore, could not some appropriate day be speedily found on which to declare amnesty in favour of war resisters, especially the Doukhobors of this province; the severity of whose sentence seemed to us to partake of vengeance rather than of justice."[44]

Mother does not know the exact date her father was released from house arrest, but I wonder if this letter, though it doesn't mention Pete Maloff's name, refers to his continued confinement. Mother tells me that for a long time, if anyone came to visit them, her father would take his jacket, which was always hanging on a hook by the door, and say, "Good to see you, but I must go." And he'd head to his walk by the mountain or to the barn to be with the animals.

---

44.   See letter from G.A. Butling to the Honourable St. Laurent in the appendix.

SAINT VOLODYA

—〰—

When I was young, an old man, Volodya Meeralyubov, lived in a cabin through the thicket behind our house. It was dark under the cedar trees as we—my sister, my brother and I—walked in a tree-lined tunnel toward the light on the other side. An oasis of Jonathan apple trees and grapevines grew there in a sunny corner, and behind them my *dedushka* Pete Maloff and his friend Vasil Koochin built a one-room dwelling for Volodya.

This cabin was a curiosity for us. Tall walnut trees and hazel-nut bushes framed it, and with its cedar siding it seemed to have grown right along with the forest and into the mountain behind it. The hut consisted of a narrow vestibule opening onto a room large enough for a bed, a cupboard containing cooking supplies, two chairs and a chest full of books. In front of the one window stood a table stacked with Russian magazines. In the middle sat a black pot-bellied stove.

We accepted Volodya as part of our family; for us he had al-ways been there behind the cedar thicket. In the summer we saw him stooped over, weeding and watering his small mossy garden of flowers: fragrant white lilies, blue forget-me-nots, climbing pink roses trained on a trellis. He grew herbs, parsley and caraway he said his mother loved, and beets and potatoes. His white hair was neat-ly tied in a ponytail; a trim moustache, a white beard and deep-set eyes adorned his broad Slavic face. He wore homespun linen: loose, baggy pants and a long shirt in the Russian style, tied with a rope belt as he did not wear leather. In winter we'd see him early in the morning, dressed in layers of woollen clothing with a knitted *kalpak* on his head, piling the snow in high banks alongside the paths be-tween our houses.

Volodya settled into this hidden recess as if he had sprung up from the soil, and indeed, we seldom saw him elsewhere. Dedushka would shop for the few supplies he required—salt, olive oil, pea-nut butter—otherwise, he was self-sufficient. Dedushka invited him

Volodya Meeralyubov (left) arrived in Canada as a refugee from Eastern Europe. Seeking freedom from strife, he became part of the extended Maloff family and helped Nick and Hannah clear land for their farm in Castlegar.

fora weekly *banya* in the bathhouse, so we would see Volodya on Saturdays, walking the path to the *banya*, a stick in his hand, towel slung over his shoulder.

We understood that Volodya came from Russia, as our ancestors had, but he had arrived in Canada more recently, in the early 1920s, and his Russian was cultured, unlike our peasant dialect that absorbed words from the countries Doukhobors had travelled through and lived in for a time: Ukraine, Georgia and now Canada. We never heard him speak English, and living among the Doukhobors in Canada, he got by with Russian.

Volodya had few visitors. Alexander Zuckerberg, a fellow immigrant and Russian teacher who had arrived in Canada about the same time as Volodya, visited monthly, riding the fifteen kilometres from Castlegar on a black bicycle. Alexander and Volodya, together with Grandfather, shared a love of Tolstoy's literature and philosophy. A daily routine of Volodya's was to read and write out passages from Tolstoy's *Krug chteniya* (A Circle of Reading). Years later, among my uncle Walter's papers, I found verses written out in his large loopy handwriting. An internet search of Leo Tolstoy's quotes provided me a translation of one that he had written in Russian.

> I believe that order is better than chaos, creation better than destruction. I prefer gentleness to violence, forgiveness to vendetta. On the whole I think knowledge is preferable to violence, and I am sure human sympathy is more valuable than ideology.

> Leo Tolstoy

A bachelor neighbour, Vasil Chernoff, would include Volodya in his round of visiting. Vasil liked to express himself by spewing out a string of oaths, but Volodya did not like harsh language and arguments. He would quietly say, "Vasil, it's not good to talk like that." For the most part, he appeared to enjoy his solitude, rising with the sun and retiring at dusk.

Volodya helped my grandparents on the farm, and his nature was evident in the way he worked with the animals. When the cow, Tyunya, got out of the pasture, as she often did, he would quietly lead her back, saying, "What a well-behaved cow Tyunya is. I just call her and she peacefully walks back." He chuckled as he told us about the pecking order in the barnyard. "The goat picks out the best hay, then Tyunya and finally Dan, the horse, has his fill. Even though the horse is the biggest!"

In Volodya's later years, Mother would cook him a meal and we would deliver it to him. He'd answer our knock, shuffle over to lift the handle, thank us profusely and sit down to eat in front of the window. One day he was gone, and the only reminder of him was the cabin, which became a home for our greenhouse trays and pots as it gradually sank into the ground.

Years later, I became curious about the people who inhabited my childhood and asked Mother about our reclusive Volodya Meeralyubov. She told me what she knew of Volodya, that he was born into a well-to-do Russian army family. When he was young, his father was killed in one of the border skirmishes that Russia was always involved in, and Volodya's uncle, a general, became the honorary head of the family. When he came of age, Volodya joined the army and fought in the First World War on the Russian-Austrian-German front.

She shook her head. "Incredible! Out of seven thousand soldiers, three thousand survived. What carnage! Volodya told me that somehow he managed to live through that massacre. But he lost his mind, and his body was no good either."

At the end of the First World War, with the political chaos in Russia, his family did not know if he was alive or dead, and not hearing otherwise, they assumed he had died. Volodya had become one of the many homeless, wandering the land, searching for a way to go home. Eventually, he returned to his village only to learn that his wife had married his best friend and that his young sister had passed away. There seemed to be little left for him.

The soldiers who had survived the massacre of their regiment were given the privilege of being further trained as captains in the army. Volodya's uncle advised him to immigrate to the Americas instead. Volodya wanted to go to the United States, but since there was a long waiting list, he immigrated to Canada, where he was able to gain entry as a refugee in 1922.

Volodya did not know anyone in Canada and found it was difficult to communicate, as he did not speak English. But as he travelled across the country, he met the Russian-speaking Doukhobors in Saskatchewan. They suggested he continue on to the Kootenay region in British Columbia, where he would be sure to encounter other Doukhobors. Following their advice, he arrived in Nelson.

Alighting at the Nelson train station, he heard Russian voices. As he sat on a station bench and wondered where to go next, he soaked in the sounds of a language he understood. As they waited for the short-haul train to their villages, the gathered Doukhobor men were in lively conversation, emphasizing their words with energetic waving of their arms and nodding heads. Pete Maloff, my *dedushka*, glanced over at the stranger dressed in white linen gazing at the group and nodding back. He approached him. "You're new here. You're Russian? *Preevet!*"

That is how Volodya became part of our family. As the two men sat side by side on the wooden train station bench talking, my grandfather sensed a connection with Volodya's quiet soul and invited him to stay with his parents in Shoreacres. He came to live with my great-grandparents Nikolai and Elizaveta at first, and then, when they lost their home in 1926, he moved to their son Nick Maloff's farm in Castlegar. When Nick's family moved to

Langley, Volodya joined them on their hazelnut farm there. After a time, homesick for the Kootenays, he resettled in Krestova with the Kooznetsoff family. In the 1930s the Sons of Freedom, whose stronghold was Krestova, were demonstrating against taxes that supported the military and requirements that their children be sent to government schools. Their use of nudity and fire in protests troubled Volodya. He packed his few belongings and asked a friend to take him to the Maloffs in Thrums. Thereafter, the hut against the mountain became his home.

With Grandfather refusing to register under the National Resources Mobilization Act, the Maloff home was a turbulent place in the 1940s. People came for advice and assistance at all hours. Pete Maloff served as a translator and a scribe in writing letters. Young Uncle Walter, five at the time, became attracted to the quiet at Volodya's cabin next door, and his hut became a refuge. When Walter was fourteen, he and his friends built a one-room cabin across the creek from Volodya's. They used this as their gang hideaway, and Walter eventually moved into the cabin to live. Many years later I found pictures of Volodya in family photo albums. Underneath a photograph of Volodya, Walter printed in large letters "Volodya, THE SAINT." Many of the family photographs from the 1950s include Volodya standing behind or slightly to the side of Grandfather, dressed in his loose white linen shirt and trousers.

—⁓—

As children, we accepted Volodya for who he was, helpful to our grandparents, gentle, kind and reclusive. We knew him by the last name Meeralyubov and did not realize that the name, translated as "lover of peace," was one he chose. I was to discover that Volodya had another identity, different from the one we knew.

The only memento from Volodya's previous life was a picture of an attractive young woman. Grandfather Pete had surreptitiously pulled this photograph from a bonfire Volodya had started. As he fed old letters, pictures and documents into the flames, he said to Grandfather, "My past life is finished. I don't need anything."

Years later, as Grandmother Lusha was sorting through pictures at her kitchen table, Volodya walked in. Seeing this photograph, he cried out, "Why do you have this? She is my beloved." The story of his marriage and subsequent loss came tumbling out.

Volodya lived with the Maloffs for over forty years. Volodya (left) with his adopted family, Tanya, Elizaveta, Lusha and Pete Maloff in the back row. Nick and Hannah Maloff in the front.

He told Babushka, "Now I live as a monk, but a *free* monk."

There was more to Volodya's life. My mother told me that Grandfather Pete knew of his background as he had applied for old age security for him, but she could not remember the details. She suggested that I contact Andrej, a family friend, who had worked with Volodya on our grandparents' farm for a few summers in the 1950s.

Andrej was a fellow refugee from the wars in Europe, though he had lived through the Second World War. Andrej recalled those summers: "Afternoons we'd sit on logs in Volodya's clearing. He'd be chopping clippings from fruit trees into kindling. I'd talk about my boyhood in Yugoslavia while he listened, his head cocked to the side, nodding. Interestingly, he never once invited me into his cabin. We'd walk as far as the doorstep, and then Volodya would turn and wish me *dobriy dyen'*. Wasn't much of a conversationalist! He did come to where I had set up my tent behind your *dedushka*'s barn."

In the evenings, the whole family gathered in the pasture behind the barn, forming a close circle around Andrej while he played the zither. As the sounds of the day quietened and the shadows became long, European alpine music drifted over the farm like a blessing.

Andrej said, "He'd listen to my music, then as darkness descended, he'd wave, say, '*Dobriy vechir*, good night,' and set off homeward."

Eventually, Andrej bought some land on the river in Thrums. "Volodya used to visit me," he said. "I'd be building my cabin or digging terraces for the garden on that rocky outcrop. He'd sit on a bench, lean on his walking stick and talk. Seemed he needed to tell somebody his story."

In a conversation over the phone, Andrej tells me what he recalled. Feeling like I am uncovering a long-held secret, I hold the phone in one hand, and with the other I scribble into my notebook: "Volodya's past life."

> Birth name: Vladimir Mol.
> Ancestry: Czech and German.
> Birthplace: Volynia, now in the Ukraine.
> Languages spoken: Czech, Ukrainian, Russian.

I thank Andrej profusely and sit down at my computer to unearth more information. According to Wikipedia, Volynia, a region in eastern Europe, had been a battleground for centuries. Lutsk, a major city of Volynia, was an ancient Slavic town founded on a bend of the Styr River by the Rurik dynasty. Over the next eight hundred years the population struggled to survive as numerous empires—Tatar, Lithuania, Poland, Russia, Austria, Germany—conquered it and were in turn subjugated. The multicultural mix was evident in the languages spoken: Polish, Czech, German, Austrian, Ukrainian, Russian, Yiddish and Hebrew.

In 1915, during the First World War, the Hapsburg army of Austria-Hungary seized Lutsk. In June 1916, the Russian army reconquered the city in the brutal Battle of Lutsk that resulted in the death of 130,000 Austro-Hungarian soldiers in two days. By the end of July there had been little progress in this war, and the Russian army also had been decimated. Subsequently, Germany took over the area, and then, after the First World War, it was ceded back to Poland and eventually the Ukraine.

I imagine the threads of Vladimir's life. Russia controlled the area during his youth, such that he learned Russian in school. His mother tongue was Czech; Ukrainian was his street language. In 1915 the Austro-Hungarian Empire was in power and Vladimir was of age to be recruited into the Austro-Hungarian Army. According to Andrej, he was drafted into an elite military regiment and his detachment fought the Russians. Though badly injured, Vladimir survived to be sent to detention camps in Siberia.

I delve into *Travels in Siberia*, a history book by Ian Frazier. At the end of the First World War, civil war continued as White Russian imperialists and the Russian Bolshevik Red Army fought for control of the country. English, Czech, American and Japanese forces, alarmed by the Communist Bolshevik revolution, were all active in Siberia supporting the White Russians. According to Frazier, during the First World War, fifty thousand Czech soldiers were Allied prisoners of war in Siberia. Then, in 1918, in a turn of events, the Czech prisoners, armed and supported by the English, took control of sections of the Trans-Siberian rail line.[45]

These are the cold facts. Volodya Meeralyubov, born Vladimir Mol, survived decades of war and deprivation from these seemingly endless conflicts.

Safe in Canada, I have not experienced war, but films of the First World War come to mind—seeing and hearing thousands of dead and dying humans and horses in the mud and blood. As evident by the scars on his legs even years later, Vladimir was severely wounded, then transported thousands of kilometres to Siberia.

Siberia. The name evokes a collective memory—mournful songs and tragic stories of Doukhobor martyrs. Resisters against the czars' wars are plentiful in the Doukhobor saga: prisoners chained together, shuffling to exile in a remote, inhospitable land, suffering extreme cold, heat, hordes of mosquitoes and blackflies, hunger. The conditions for Vladimir as a prisoner of war would have been as horrendous. Many in Russia at that time were starving and dying.

Vladimir survived by a twist of fate. As the Bolsheviks were marching east to take over the Trans-Siberian rail line, Vladimir, with the former Czech prisoners, also fled east to Vladivostok and then boarded an English ship leaving Russia.

In the First World War, Japan was an ally of Britain, and after, during the Russian Revolution, it established a buffer zone against the Bolshevik regime. Vladimir's ship docked in Japan for repairs, and he went ashore. The routines of ordinary life were nourishment for his war-ravaged eyes. Andrej said Vladimir greatly admired how

45.   Frazier, *Travels in Siberia*, p. 143.

Volodya arriving in Canada in the 1920s.

the Japanese women dressed their long hair, how they served tea. The ship travelled through the British-dominated Suez Canal, and in 1920 Vladimir disembarked in Dubrovnik, a city that had become part of a new country, in the future to be named Yugoslavia. Years after he fought for Austria in the First World War, Vladimir was finally able to return to his homeland, but little remained of his former life. The Christian Baptist Church offered assistance with immigration, and Vladimir took the opportunity to come to Canada.

—ᴡᴡ—

Strange as it may seem, both of Volodya/Vladimir's stories could be true. With the shifting of boundaries and allegiances, it is possible that Volodya's father and uncle were in the Russian Imperial Army when Russia was in power in Volynia. A short time later, Austria-Hungary took possession of the area, and Vladimir was enlisted in the Austro-Hungarian Army to fight former Russian comrades. Losing health, marriage and family, being a pawn of governments as they battled each other—I understood his desire to leave the country where he was born, extinguish his past and settle in a hidden corner of Thrums with a group of pacifists.

Late in his life, Volodya developed dementia, and my grandparents looked after him as best they could until he was admitted to the Castlegar hospital before his death. They visited him there daily until he passed away in the late 1960s. My grandparents gave Volodya a Doukhobor funeral: a day and night vigil by his open casket, accompanied by the singing of psalms and prayers and a farewell meal attended by friends and guests. Volodya Meeralyubov, Lover of Peace, was buried in an unmarked grave in Shoreacres, where he first found a home with the Doukhobors.

I visit the quiet Shoreacres graveyard where my mother said Volodya was buried, "just across from cousin Nick." Birds sing in the cedar trees that surround the cemetery; the grass is neatly clipped, and I hear the murmur of the Kootenay River as it flows past. A fitting place for Volodya. I think of mounting a plaque on his gravesite. Would he have wanted that? Or would he prefer to become one with the earth?

GRANDFATHER'S
FRIENDSHIP WITH
DR. BERNARD JENSEN

—⁓—

For all sixty-five years of my life Mother has been our family's healer, and she still relishes that role. When I walk through the doorway to her home she says, "Vera, so nice to see you. I'll make you some juice." Today she's made wheat-grass juice in her blender. Other days the drink is made from herbs and greens she collects in the garden—dandelions, parsley, nettle, plantain—or in winter, it's carrot, beet and celery juice.

As we sit down at her Formica table and sip the wheat-grass drinks, I tell her, "I just got a coupon for five dollars off on frozen wheat-grass pucks at Save-On-Foods."

She laughs and wipes her face with her large hand. "We've been growing wheat grass ever since Dr. Jensen recommended it back in the thirties." She shakes her head. "He did say he was fifty years ahead of his time."

I lean back in my chair and think about Dr. Jensen, a natural-healing physician who introduced us to a plethora of healthy practices: vegetable juices, nut and seed drinks, fasting, iridology. This was way back when Cheez Whiz and white bread were popular. "Those chia-seed drinks you made us swallow, now they are the latest superfood," I tell Mother.

Mother nods and says, "I was fourteen when the family first met Dr. Jensen. It was just after Grandfather came back from the penitentiary. That day Dr. Jensen came to our house is so vivid, it's like a movie in my head."

I sit back and listen as she tells me about Dr. Jensen's first meeting with her family.

LEEZA: It was spring, the season for early mushrooms. The previous year's forest fire on the mountain across the river from Thrums and recent rains had enticed morels, *smorchkee*, to proliferate. Whole families were hunting for those dark brown fungi, so desirable for cooking, pickling or drying. Father, Petya, Uncle George and I joined the search. We rowed across the river in the morning and were returning, carrying full canvas rucksacks on our backs—at least Father and Petya were. I had fallen over a tree; my knee was skinned, my ankle ached and I was limping. Our hands, faces and clothing were streaked with charcoal from the burnt stumps and fallen trees. I saw twigs stuck in Father's hair, and we smelled not only of the *smorchkee* but of ashes and sweat. Petya was tramping on ahead, most likely thinking of the delicious mushroom soup Mother would make. I watched him wave goodbye to Dyadya George and turn into our driveway, where Mother met him.

"Petya, please hurry to heat the *banya*," I could hear Mother say. "We've got company!"

A *banya* would be wonderful after our long day on the mountain and for the visitors too, but what must we look like! Father rolled down his sleeves, ran his fingers through his hair and gazed in astonishment at the tall, bearded man striding toward us. They greeted each other with a bear hug.

When Father recovered from his surprise, he grasped his friend by the shoulders. "Welcome! Good to see you! You've come to the Doukhobors to find a like-minded community?" he joked. Then he turned to me. "Leeza, remember Dr. Zigmeister from California? You were a little girl when we last saw him."

"Yes, and now, grown up." Dr. Zigmeister looked at me, smiled and then noticed that I winced in pain as he enthusiastically shook my hand. Even though I protested that I was okay, Dr. Zigmeister insisted, "You're hurt! Here, let me help you." He and Papa constructed a sling with their hands clasped and carried me over to a bench.

"I've brought special visitors," Dr. Zigmeister said to Father as he waved to a well-dressed, slim man and an attractive woman who were in the garden. "Bernard, come meet my good friend, Pete Maloff." A baby at their knees was grasping the early lettuces, parsley and dandelions and chewing on greens and soil alike. They gently brushed the dirt from the baby's face and hands, picked him up and joined Father and Dr. Zigmeister.

"Pete and I spent months together in California visiting other idealists who might like to join the community we were dreaming of," Dr. Zigmeister said in introducing Father. Then he turned to us. "Dr. Jensen here has just graduated from the West Coast Chiropractic College. This is his lovely wife, Grace, and"—he patted the baby on the head—"David."

Father rubbed his hands on his overalls and shook hands with the Jensens. Petya followed suit and then grinned at baby David, who looked to be about five months old.

"Dr. Jensen said he'd heard about the Doukhobors, so I told him about you. He asked me to drive up from California with him and I decided to bring my travelling companions with me." Two young women, who had been checking out the gardens and the resident goat, cow and chickens, came over to be introduced. Then they all turned to look at me still sitting on the bench against the wall of the house.

"What happened, Leeza?" Mother looked at my bruised and bleeding leg and said, "Petya, bring some water and a towel."

Dr. Jensen knelt down and cleaned my knee with the wet towel. "Let's look at you."

Then, to my surprise, he put his forefinger around my eyebrow, lightly rested his thumb on my cheek and gazed into my eyes. After a minute he patted my knee and said, "You'll be okay, my dear. Just a sprain."

Dr. Zigmeister explained, "Dr. Jensen has studied iridology. He's become an expert at reading the iris of the eye to diagnose medical conditions."

"One can learn much from examining the eyes," Dr. Jensen told us. Then he looked at Mother. "Lusha, I've also been studying nutrition. I've heard many Doukhobors are vegetarian."

"We *were* vegan, but since the birth of the twins we've added eggs, milk, honey." Mother shrugged. "It's cold here in winter, and though we don't like to use animals, well ..."

"Maybe I could share some ideas to help with your diet."

"That would be wonderful, Dr. Jensen."

Then Mother reminded Petya, "Now, Petya, the *banya*."

"Marvellous!" Dr. Jensen said. "I do enjoy a good steam bath." Mother smiled. "You know about banyas?"

"The best kind of bath. The sweat cleans your pores right out!"

"Every Doukhobor family has one." Mother pointed to a shed next to our outhouse. "Ours is over there. We use it for bathing and washing. There's no running water in the house yet." She shrugged. "I'm sorry, you'll have to use that outdoor toilet next to the *banya*."

"Not a problem. In many places in the world, toilets are just a hole in the ground. You don't get constipated when you squat!"

Father took the guests over to the *banya* and showed them the rooms, one to change in and the other a steam room. The wood stove was in the first room along with a stack of wood, a bench and pegs on the wall for clothing and towels. As he opened the door to the second room, we breathed the scent of cedar, pine and heated wood. Inside, the rest of the barrel-shaped stove was encased by rock. Two benches, one above the other, were built against the wall.

Having lit the fire and now carrying a bucket of water, Petya squeezed past the guests and began to pour it into the big metal tub on top of the stove. He then returned to fill the cold-water barrel in the corner.

Dr. Jensen picked up bundles of birch twigs hanging on the wall. "What are these for?"

Feeling better, I had followed the group to the *banya* and answered Dr. Jensen's question. "*Venyeek*. My *babushka* Hoodicoff likes the *banya* very hot. When she gets sweaty, she asks me to slap her back with the wet *venyeek*."

"What a way to get the circulation going!" Dr. Jensen enthused.

Dr. Zigmeister insisted that the Jensen family take the first bath. He privately told Father, "Look after Dr. Jensen. Give his family the best. We three will sleep in the hay barn. It'll be an experience for us city folk. Just give us some of those warm, wool-filled quilts."

Mother arranged for the Jensens to sleep across the road at my Hoodicoff grandparents' home, where they had a guest bedroom. In the morning, relatives and friends came to listen to Dr. Jensen give the first of his many lectures on nutrition. The guests stayed for several days, and Mother's sisters helped with the meals.

Dr. Zigmeister (tall dark bearded man second from the right) brought Dr. Jensen and his family to meet the Maloff family. Dr. Jensen is the photographer. Mrs. Jensen is sitting with baby David on her lap. Elizabeth is on her right, Lusha on her left.

Father and Dr. Jensen spent time together walking in the forest behind the gardens. They were different, those two. Father, dressed in neatly mended working clothes, was tall with broad shoulders, deep-set eyes and large, callused hands. Dr. Jensen, in a white shirt and sports jacket, was shorter with a long torso, refined hands and eyes that seemed to penetrate into one's heart when he was looking at you. Father was born in 1900, in January, on the Saskatchewan prairie in an outbuilding kept warm by the horses stabled there. Their sod home was shared with another Doukhobor family. Dr. Jensen, eight years younger, was born in California to a family in which the father was a chiropractor.

Nevertheless, even from a distance I could sense their connection and absorption in conversation. Father would wave his arms when he talked, and Dr. Jensen responded by calmly nodding his head. I could almost see the sparks of energy dancing between them as they discussed their shared interests: philosophy, natural healing methods, vegetarianism and pacifism.

I was used to looking after my sisters and brothers and enjoyed playing with baby David. Seeing the fun we had together,

Mrs. Jensen mentioned to her husband, "It would be so good to have Leeza come stay with us. She could help with David when you are away or when we are travelling."

Imagine what I could have learned from Dr. Jensen if I could have lived with them! Eight years had passed since we lived in California. I had freedom then. But ... I glanced at Father, who was shaking his head, and then at Luba, Nadya, Petya and Johnnik crowded around us. It wasn't to be.

Mrs. Jensen looked at my disappointed face and gave me a long hug. "Perhaps another time. Your mother needs you now."

—⁓—

For a moment Mother is lost back in those days when she was young. Then she looks at me and out the window at the tall cedar trees framing her house. I stand to refill our glasses and think about Dr. Jensen's influence on our family. His natural-health practices weren't always accepted by conventional health-care practitioners, but my family has always believed in them and found them beneficial. I return with the drinks and tell Mother, "It's a good thing we learned from Dr. Jensen. I remember how you cared for us when we were sick. We never went to doctors. And the trips we took to California to Jensen's health ranch—they were the best holidays."

Mother sips her juice and says, "For several years in the 1940s, Father and Dr. Jensen didn't see each other, but they wrote. I could always tell when Dad got a letter from Dr. Jensen. He'd be reading it as he walked home from the post office. Sometimes he'd have a wide smile; other times tears would be running down his cheeks. Those years were difficult for Dr. Jensen and for us. His wife, Grace, had been in a car accident and died shortly after. Dr. Jensen was devastated!" Mother sighs. "And during that time Father was often in jail for resisting the war registration."

I look at Mother's creased face, her hunched shoulders, and marvel at her resiliency. She lived through difficult years, yet her positive outlook has survived. Now she recalls again the time the police came to arrest her father when Dr. Jensen was visiting, and they agreed not to interfere with the dinner that was underway. I had heard it before but was happy to hear the story again.

"They didn't detain him?"

"Oh, they came back in a few days and then took him away.

Finally, when Father was allowed to travel to the United States, we visited Dr. Jensen in California."

"The United States government allowed Grandfather into the country even though he had a criminal record?" I shake my head in disbelief. "He sure wouldn't get in now!"

"Sometimes you never know where help comes from."

I reflect on how true that was in my mother's life. Many times help arrived when the family needed it most, and other times ...

"Inspector Cruikshank gave Father a letter of recommendation. He wrote that Pete Maloff was the most trustworthy and honest person he had met. Imagine! He said this after Father had spent so many years in prison. For nothing!" Mother bangs her glass down on the table and scrubs away the imaginary spill.

While searching the newspapers I learned that Inspector Cruikshank had supervised Grandfather Pete Maloff's arrest at an unauthorized peace march in 1929 in Nelson. The inspector was also in charge of the apprehension of over a hundred Doukhobor men and women at a gathering in Crescent Valley where my great-grandfather Nikolai was arrested, and he oversaw the Porto Rico detainment camp where Mother's family had been interned. Yet he had written the letter of recommendation.

Mother doesn't dwell on that difficult time but instead proceeds to tell me more about Dr. Jensen.

"When you were three years old, Vera, I left you with your dad and went with Luba and Tiny to visit the health ranch Dr. Jensen had just bought. I hated to leave you, but Luba needed me. After she had the babies, she became so anemic and weak—doctors here couldn't help her."

"How did Dr. Jensen help with the anemia?" I ask. Because we are vegetarians, anemia tends to run in our family.

"He told us the food on our plates should be a rainbow of colours, including dark leafy greens, and he taught us about fasting to cleanse our bodies. Luba and Tiny fasted for a week, and I for eighteen days on water and four days on juices. I had a sore knee and foot, and after the fast, for three days my leg gave me horrible pain." Mother rubs her leg and then continues. "Dr. Jensen said it was a 'healing crisis.' Then the pain went away, and that knee didn't bother me for years. That's how I looked after myself—fasting twice a year, in the spring and fall."

Lusha and Pete Maloff found a second home with Dr. Jensen (centre) at his Hidden Valley Health Ranch in California.

Even now, in her nineties, Mother continues her fasts, and though I worry about her getting weak, she insists it helps her.

"In the evening after his patient appointments, Dr. Jensen gave lectures on nutrition, water therapy and spiritual topics. That was the best education! Tiny and I came home after a month, but Luba stayed on for three months."

Mother has a framed photograph hanging on her kitchen wall of my grandparents with Dr. Jensen. They are standing in front of a large branching oak tree and under a sign that reads "Hidden Valley Health Ranch Dining Room—Patio, Outdoor Lectures." Everyone is smiling. I open the family photo album on Mother's table and find pictures of Dr. Jensen and Grandfather Pete Maloff that span six decades. In the early years, the two men have a young, excited demeanour as they pose with their wives and children in front of the Thrums house. In later years, in California, Pete and Lusha stand together with a Doukhobor work crew before an almost-finished addition to the ranch cafeteria. In another photo they have returned to Thrums, and Dr. Jensen is sitting on a flowered couch with his new wife, Marie. There are many grandchildren who stand behind that couch and great-grandchildren who sit on the laps of Marie Jensen and Grandmother Lusha.

As Mother and I flip through the pages we find pictures of people and foreign places: India, Russia, Turkey. She tells me, "In the 1960s, Father and Dr. Jensen travelled together. Father only had to mention 'I'm planning a trip to see my correspondents in Russia and India,' and Dr. Jensen would respond with 'I'm coming with you.'" I see pages of pictures of vigorous-looking older men and women. Mother says, "This is Armenia, where some of the oldest people lived. Father said that one man they interviewed was 135 years old."

———

I was a teenager when Grandfather Pete Maloff went on those journeys to the East. On his return I looked forward to the family gatherings in my grandparents' living room. Uncles, aunts and parents would sit on chairs, cousins on the floor with our knees pulled close and our hands on chins, as we crowded together.

As Grandfather talked, images of India emerged in my mind. He said members of the Ghandi community had met them at the train station. We roared with laughter while Grandfather told us about how his false teeth fell down a drain hole in the train just before he disembarked. The whole welcoming group said that it was meant to be—they were destined to walk the rail line to find the false teeth. Seven kilometres down the track they did find them, and luckily a dentist in the group fixed my grandfather's teeth good as new. I felt the crush of the crowds when, among thousands of devotees, they visited the ashram of the spiritual teacher Sathya Sai Baba, and I listened in awe as Grandfather talked about his meeting with Sai Baba and the miracles that he performed. He brought sacred ash, *vibhuti*, and a poster of Sai Baba that hangs on Mother's bedroom wall today. Grandfather took a rickshaw, and halfway through the trip he insisted on trading places with the runner as he felt uncomfortable having someone pull him.

From India, Dr. Jensen and Grandfather Maloff flew to Turkey, landing in Istanbul in late summer. Istanbul's many markets attracted their interest. The Grand Bazaar was noisy and opulent with goods from everywhere in the Middle East, but Grandfather said the smaller street markets were similar to those back home in the Trail hockey arena where we and many of our neighbours set up wooden tables to sell our harvest. Overflowing bins of colourful fruits and vegetables and sacks of nuts were displayed on tables and on benches. Conical pyramids of yellow, orange and red herbs and spices perfumed the air. Shoppers were adding large bunches of cilantro to their baskets. "Cilantro is the best food for vitamin K. Builds strong bones," Dr. Jensen told Grandfather.

And then, what a find! An elderly man in a Turkish prayer cap was selling fresh figs—soft purple on the outside with pink juicy interiors that crunched when they bit into them. They couldn't wait to return to their hotel room and began to devour the succulent figs as they walked, and then bought more to fill their bags. But what a price to pay for their overindulgence! That night they were unable to leave their hotel room, running to the toilet every few minutes.

"This is the same as being on a thirty-day fast. What a great cleanse!" Dr. Jensen remarked.

After a couple of days trapped between bed and toilet they asked the hotel clerk to send up a doctor. The physician who arrived—

a woman—immediately diagnosed their problem and the solution: an enema. Hands on her hips, she scolded them in Russian on their reticence to undergo this treatment. "Why are you embarrassed? I'm a doctor. This is what we do here."

Grandfather said, "Dr. Jensen and I looked at each other, grimaced and realized we didn't have much of a choice." We all laughed as Grandfather made a face and said, "We gave in to her treatment. What a bonding experience that was!"

Working through the Turkish, Armenian and Soviet governments of the time, Dr. Jensen and Grandfather were able to travel to Armenia, Dagestan and Azerbaijan. It was the Cold War era, but even in the Russian Kremlin offices they were given full co-operation. In Armenia they were greeted by Mr. Vahan Ghazarian. With his help, Dr. Jensen, with Pete Maloff by his side, met some of the country's centenarians.

Once he returned home, Grandfather told us, "All these old people still work in their gardens and help their families. They're revered and are involved with the whole community."

Dr. Jensen added, "They stay active, walk the hillsides and are limber." Their diet, as Dr. Jensen observed, contained seeds, nuts, berries, garlic, kefir, olives and little meat and sugar. Many belonged to the Muslim faith and did not drink alcohol. Beside each plate at every meal there was a large helping of cilantro greens.

On their return to Turkey, Uncle Walter picked them up in Istanbul and drove them through eastern Europe to Bulgaria, where again Dr. Jensen studied the diet and lifestyle of the aged. I find a photograph of them posing in front of Walter's white Volkswagen van. In the 1960s such vans were often occupied by long-haired hippies seeking Shangri-La. Grandfather Maloff and Dr. Jensen, then in their sixties, were dressed in suits, white shirts and ties, and their shoes were polished. Dr. Jensen *was* searching for a kind of Shangri-La. He would later write a book titled *World Keys to Health and Long Life*.

After a couple of weeks of driving through Bulgaria and sleeping in the van, Walter left Grandfather and Dr. Jensen at the Sofia Airport, and they flew on to Russia. In Moscow, they were given access to a hospital that specialized in fasting cures. Dr. Jensen and Grandfather Maloff donned white lab coats while the resident doctor gave them a tour around the clinic and introduced them to

Dr. Jensen's and Pete Maloff's visits to centenarians in Eastern Europe became the basis for Dr. Jensen's book *World Keys to Health and Long Life.*

staff and patients. Dr. Jensen was delighted to be able to compare his experience with the patients who had fasted at the health ranch in California to those of the Russian doctor.

As Dr. Jensen was scheduled to speak at a conference in Finland, they took an overnight express train north. At the Russian-Finnish border they were stopped by the Russian border police and told to produce their money and account for their spending. Any American in Russia in the aftermath of the Cuban Missile Crisis would have been nervous to be questioned by the Russian police, and Dr. Jensen couldn't account for all of his cash. He didn't have a receipt for some jewellery he purchased for his wife. Smuggling money into or out of Russia was considered a serious offence, and the Russian border guards had a reputation for harshness.

Grandfather said, "I couldn't let Dr. Jensen go to jail. He didn't speak Russian, and I thought, 'Well, I've been in jails before.' So I told him, 'I'll give you the money that you spent. If need be, I'll go to jail.' Then I remembered the letter of recommendation."

Grandfather's belief in the importance of having economic equality and opportunity for all people had led him to investigate communism. He corresponded with Nigel Morgan, the leader of the Communist Party of British Columbia at the time, who was respected by many as an honourable man concerned with improving the lives of working people. They became friends, and Nigel Morgan visited Grandfather several times. When Grandfather was planning a trip to Russia, Nigel Morgan wrote him a letter of recommendation. This is what saved them.

Grandfather said, "The guards looked at the letter and passed it on to their *vazhniy*, their boss. We were finally able to breathe when the captain in charge came to shake our hands, wish us well and give us safe passage across the border."

But to take the chance of being incarcerated in a Russian jail! We shook our heads at Grandfather's foolishness.

—⁓—

I have a shelf of books written by Dr. Bernard Jensen, and as I peruse them I find *World Keys to Health and Long Life*. To my joy, the first few pages of the book contain photographs of Grandfather Pete Maloff with Mr. Vahan Ghazarian, taken in front of the Hotel Erevan in Armenia, and of Dr. Jensen and Grandfather posing beside the Volkswagen van they had travelled in. The book, published in 1975, three years after Grandfather's death, is dedicated to two people. Dr. Jensen wrote,

> The first man, Mr. Pete Maloff, was a man of peace, a man of deep convictions and one who had a deeply earnest motivation to bring about the survival of mankind by ending war and helping others to live a higher and better life. He was a vegetarian of three generations and a Doukhobor.
>
> The second man, Mr. Vahan Ghazarian [of Armenia], made it possible for me to be in touch with those who had to consider survival a necessity. I am indebted to the country to which he introduced me, a country that has gone through much strife, mental oppression and the hatreds of war. Yet, in spite of it, this country demonstrated more love and generosity to me on my visit than any other.[46]

---

46.   Jensen, *World Keys*, p. ii.

In 1972 Dedushka Pete Maloff was the master of ceremonies for my wedding. A few days later, he and Babushka Lusha travelled, by Greyhound bus, to visit Dr. Bernard Jensen in California. They never reached the Hidden Valley Health Ranch. Halfway there Dedushka Pete suffered a severe heart attack and died.

We were all shaken and deeply saddened. Dr. Jensen, who had been looking forward to his friend arriving, was stunned to learn of his passing. I do not have the eulogy that Dr. Jensen wrote then, but I do have one he wrote for his twenty-year memorial.

In Memory of Pete Maloff

While we feel that Pete Maloff has been gone here some 20 years, he is uppermost in my mind when I think of bringing peace and harmony to this world. … The greatest memory that I have of Pete Maloff is the fact that he cared for human beings. … [He] has been a great friend of mine for many years.[47]

Dedushka Pete Maloff and Dr. Bernard Jensen had the gift of a deep and enduring friendship. When Mother told Dr. Jensen that it was wonderful they had been introduced to one other, Dr. Jensen said, "We would have met anyway. We were spiritual brethren."

---

47.   Jensen, "In Memory of Pete Maloff."

MARKET GARDENING

In late winter and early spring, when I visit Mother, I often find her at her kitchen table that is covered with Stokes, William Dam and West Coast Seeds catalogues. She has spent hours examining them, checking to see if the seeds of old favourites are available and selecting new varieties to experiment with. She laughs and says, "When I start looking at seed catalogues, I forget about everything." In her large handwriting she's written her order for the vegetables and flowers she plans to start in her greenhouse and garden.

Not one to record the selections she has planted, she keeps a record in her memory of the strains that grow successfully in the Kootenay region, where frost may come in early September, the corn and tomato varieties that are sweet, and her favourite, the heritage beans that she saves. The top of a cupboard next to the table is covered with bowls containing seeds labelled "Italian," "Nastya Shkuratoff's green pole beans" and "Isabelle's mother's yellow pole beans." And she is on the lookout for varieties she has not grown before, telling us when we travel to see if we can find aster seeds her mother used to grow in Oregon where there are seed farms, or a special herb we should be able to find in Italy.

This passion of hers started at a young age, in 1932, when she and her siblings lived with her grandmother Masha Hoodicoff and, at twelve and nine years of age, respectively, Leeza and her brother Petya sold vegetables door to door in Trail.

She says, "It was such a relief when in the late 1930s the Friday market opened in the summers in the Trail rink, located in what everyone called the 'Doukhobor block.' We didn't have to tramp up those steep hillsides anymore." I have a photograph of Mother at the market from the *Trail Daily Times* newspaper. The date is missing, but on the back it is stamped "Photo by Howard Hebig."

"Howard came at the end of the market day. Our table had only a box of potatoes and a bunch of gladiolas left, but he insisted on taking a picture of me in front of our stand even though I told him, 'I went to bed late preparing. Got up at four o'clock to come here. I don't look so good.' Seeing his camera out, other farmers, John Kinakin, Hannah Demoskoff and Auntie Masha Popoff, shouted from the other end of the market, 'Take a picture of us,' but he wanted one of me. In an hour—market finished at four in the afternoon—he came back with the photograph and said, 'Here you are. You don't look bad at all!'"

In the photo Mother, looked tired but is smiling as if it was a good market day. Her hair was swept back in a French roll, and she was wearing a flowered apron with pockets where she kept change. I am reminded what an attractive mother I have, and how hard she worked to earn a living.

The market-garden farm in Thrums was, at the most, five acres in area, a portion along the Kootenay River and a piece across the highway and butting up against the mountain. The rich land along the river had been in my Hoodicoff great-grandparents' family since 1908, and when they were making their will, the eldest daughter, Lusha, was not included as a beneficiary. In farming families of that era, land tended to be passed down to the men in the family, and when Lusha was going to be left out of the will, Mother protested to her grandparents, "We've been farming this land for years now. We need it to make a living. The men, Uncle John and Uncle Bill, got their piece; so should Mother." So, thanks to Leeza, her mother, Lusha, inherited a couple of acres of the fertile land along the river where they grew berries, apple and plum trees, vegetables and hay. On the piece they bought, between the highway and the mountain, my grandparents built their house, greenhouses for starting bedding plants and barns for the animals.

Farming needed to be a family affair to succeed. My grandparents' family of three sons and three daughters worked in the gardens and hayfields when they were young. But as the sons grew, they became carpenters and labourers working away from the farm. Daughters Luba and Nadya had their own families, though they continued to live close by and assist with harvesting. Mother—Leeza—was the daughter who carried on market gardening, helping her parents and earning a livelihood for our family.

In the growing season, it was a dawn-to-dusk job. An early memory of mine was waking up alone and realizing Mother was gone. I learned I could find her either in the garden, watering in

When Pete Maloff was black-listed from many jobs because of his pacifist activities he decided farming was an honourable way to make a living. Lusha and Pete worked the farm, side by side all their lives.

the early morning, or in the barn, where she'd be milking the goats. My sister, brother and I grew up in the garden patch, weeding, pulling carrots and beets, knowing by touch when corn was ripe and that we couldn't pick beans in the morning—the plants were damp with dew and were susceptible to rust. When I started school I would get a ride into Nelson after class, with a teacher who lived there, to help Mother with the sale of bedding plants, and on the weekends I woke early to travel to the farmers' market with her.

In the summers when school was out, Grandmother would round up all of us grandchildren and pay us ten cents a bucket to pick the long rows of raspberries, strawberries, blackcurrants and gooseberries. The berries were plentiful, hanging on burdened branches, almost falling into the metal buckets tied around our waists. Grandmother set herself up in the shade of a large spreading old Royal Anne cherry tree, and after we filled our buckets we brought them to her. She arranged wooden flats on top of boards and sawhorses, and there she checked our berries. "Good job, Vera," she'd say. "You picked just the ripe ones." Or she'd admonish, "Don't swing your bucket like that; the raspberries get crushed." Then her red-stained, gnarled hands gently distributed the fruit into baskets, twelve to a crate, and she handed the bucket back to me.

I could see Grandfather through the berry bushes, a crushed straw hat on his head, his shirt sleeves rolled up to the elbow and his baggy tan pants held up with a rope. He had two buckets, one tied on his back and one in front. His hands moved quickly, and after he filled one container, he shifted it to his back.

My aunts Luba and Nadya often helped, and as they picked, they swapped stories with Mother. The tall bushes and rustling of branches lent us a certain anonymity, and our young ears perked up to hear the adult conversations from both sides of the row. I do not so much remember the stories as the feelings of working together as a family, of comradeship and community.

Dew would be on the berries if we started too early, so we picked into the heat of the day. "Finish your row, help others finish theirs and then you can go swimming," Grandmother said. The riverbank and the shallows were reedy and the bottom silty since the Brilliant Dam had flooded the land by the river and slowed the water flow. Nevertheless, a memory I cherish today is the feeling of cool water on my sun-baked body as I leapt into the Kootenay River from the rickety old dock Uncle Walter had built to launch his kayak.

Or I might be asked to help Great-Grandmother Hoodicoff with her rows of heritage strawberries—not my favourite job because I had to crouch to pick the flavourful but teeny berries, and there was no shade in the strawberry patch. Then I'd look longingly at the river and rush through the rows, leaving some strawberries for the birds.

The night before market, everyone gathered in my grandparents' yard to wash and bunch beets, carrots, radishes and onions, which sold for twenty-five cents. "Don't forget the flowers!" Grandfather would say. Our stall was decorated with buckets of flowers, starting with fragrant sweet williams early in the season, followed by sweet peas, asters, gladiolas and, in the fall, burgundy, white and yellow chrysanthemums, all twenty-five cents a bunch.

On market day my mother would be up for hours before she woke my sister and me to drive to market. Sometimes cousin

At the market, Pete Maloff would be surrounded not only by customers buying vegetables, but also by those who wanted to discuss politics and philosophy with him.

Sharon came along. We were country kids in the city—hands dirty
from digging out bedding plants and wrapping bunches of carrots
in newspaper. In the afternoons we got to go to the movies. Mother
gave us thirty-five cents for the movie and ten cents for popcorn, and
we escaped into the cool, dark Civic Theatre to watch John Wayne
westerns and Elvis Presley musicals. Afterward, if we were lucky,
Great-Grandmother would give us a dime to buy ice cream from
the Shamrock Restaurant on the corner of Vernon and Hall Streets.

Now, many years later, as we look through the catalogues on
Mother's kitchen table and add to the seed orders, I ask Mother for
her market-gardening memories. She has a favourite anecdote that
I never tire of hearing, even though I sat next to her in that Fargo
truck that stalled on the main thoroughfare in Nelson. She settles
in to tell me again.

Leeza: In spring, during the week, I sold bedding plants from the
parking lot of the SuperValu store in downtown Trail. Young Willie
Garnett had a table next to me. He had good plants too. He went
on to start the Columbia Valley Greenhouses in Trail, which is still
in business. I moved to the Safeway lot in Nelson, paying them ten

percent of my earnings. Plants sold well there too. When the garden came in, I'd go to the regular market in Trail on Fridays and Nelson on Saturdays.

I drove Father's blue 1956 three-quarter-ton Fargo truck, but the trouble was it had a habit of stalling at stop signs. In case this happened, Father gave me a nail and hammer to whack the battery connections with. One morning in Nelson the truck stalled on Vernon Street across from the courthouse and just past where Downtown Automotive is now. It was fall. I had a load piled high in crates tied together with ropes in the back of the truck. Traffic stopped behind me. A couple of policemen

Lusha and Pete had dedicated customers and friends at the Trail and Nelson markets.

approached, and the mechanic from the service station came out to the street to see what the problem was. Sitting there with cars honking around me and the police coming toward me, I broke out in a cold sweat. There was no money for a ticket or a repair bill, so I took a deep breath and fished out the nail and hammer. Opening the hood of the truck, I stood on my tiptoes to hit the battery connections as Father had shown me, lowered the hood and hopped back in the truck. Thank goodness the engine revved, and I breathed a huge sigh of relief as the truck rumbled down the hill to the market on Lake Street. I arrived late, and wouldn't you know it, Grandmother Hoodicoff looked at me crosswise and muttered, "*Shto ti?* What's with you? Slept till noon?" I was worried about the police giving me a fine for the heavy load. They followed the truck to the market and stood watching me, but I was so busy unloading, organizing and selling that when I finally looked up, they were gone.

I had the corner stall; Grandmother Hoodicoff was next to it, and then Aunt Popoff and the Konkins. The Ostoforoffs, Rebalkins, Demoskoffs and Sherstobitoffs also had tables. We sold many varieties of vegetables, fruit and flowers. There was cheese, cream and butter behind the counter, out of sight of nosy inspectors. Mr. Pratt sold meat. All the produce was grown on small, five-acre family farms, most of them our neighbours in Thrums. Everything sold quickly that day—Golden Bantam and Chief corn at seventy-five cents a dozen, tomatoes, cucumbers, cabbage.

I didn't have to get help from the mechanic that day, but he supported me another time. One spring day I was surrounded by customers asking questions about varieties of plants, when a *preekly-opka* (nuisance) came. She had bought a tomato plant from me and apparently it was not doing well. In front of the whole crowd she started loudly complaining about this plant. The mechanic—he was a big, burly man—happened to be there. He turned to this woman and, towering over her, shook his finger and growled at her in his deep voice, "This lady has the best plants. She is trustworthy!" He wasn't even a customer, but he must have had a dispute with that woman previously and decided to put her in her place. The way that mechanic glared at her, she slowly, slowly backed away and left. Later, when I thanked the mechanic, I told him, "You work so hard. I see you morning and night at the garage." He shook his head and boomed back at me, "Lady, you found someone who works harder than you!" When I mentioned this incident to Father, he laughed and laughed.

Our farm also supplied local grocery stores, but in the 1960s the manager of Safeway reluctantly told Father that their policy had changed. "I'm sorry, Pete. Your vegetables are clean and fresh. But the company insists that all produce must be sprayed so that customers don't find worms in their cabbage." Though we kept on gardening organically, other local farmers started spraying with insecticides. But by then most stores ordered large quantities from the Fraser Valley and California.

Markets continued into the early 1970s and then closed. It wasn't because people stopped buying from farmers. I'd see customers on the streets, and they'd ask, "When are you coming back to market? We miss it." But the farmers were getting old; some died. The sons and daughters went away, got educated or got easier jobs. I got a job in a Castlegar hotel restaurant washing dishes. The staff was welcoming and hard-working, but the job was not for me. I need to feel the earth under my feet and in my fingers. I love working with plants. I'd ask cousin Tiny for the saddest begonia and hydrangea plants she was going to throw out anyway. I planted, watered and fertilized them, and they grew beautiful flowers. When Tiny saw them again, she'd ask, "Where did you get those?" She couldn't believe it when I said, "From you!"

⸺⸙⸺

My memories of family working to make a living on the small acre farm are tinged with nostalgia. Now, farmers' markets have been revitalized in the local towns and there are a growing number of young farmers. As Mother and I walk through their colourful displays on Baker Street in Nelson, she reminisces about her days of growing, harvesting and selling. She talks to the farmers, sharing knowledge and acknowledging the effort it takes to grow the produce.

My daughter and her friends consider starting farms. Land that has been lying fallow for a generation must be cleared of weeds, bushes and trees. Fields that have been subdivided into smaller plots must be fenced. I wonder how I can support her. Back then, it took a large family and a neighbourhood. Have the times changed so much?

Doukhobor Footsteps
in Oregon

—w—

In Oregon nature itself uplifts and strengthens toward a better life. The whole atmosphere seems tire-
less, fresh and always alive. The trees are enormous,
the air invigorating, and the rustle of the leaves of
oak, maple and ash as well as other varieties of southern trees give intimations of inexplicable mystery.

P.N. Maloff

September 15, 2016

The ocean with its booming voice is left behind as we turn our
1998 Chevy truck and Bigfoot camper east to follow the gentle
Umpqua River toward the Willamette Valley of Oregon. We've
walked the Oregon coast's long sandy beaches, hugged tall Sitka
spruce trees, climbed lighthouses and camped in rustic camp-
grounds, where we fell asleep to waves crashing onto beaches and a
wild wind rocking our camper. Small coastal towns have been just
as the guidebooks said, "charming," and the food, beer and wine
satisfying. We've watched whales feeding and diving in the tumul-
tuous Pacific, and my husband, Steve, and I have shared the feeling
of wonder that such creatures exist.

However, we've come on this journey not only to experience the pleasures of the coast but to find the land where my
great-grandparents, together with forty Doukhobor families, established the Svoboda Colony of Freedom from 1913 to 1917 in this
central valley of Oregon. Our Kooznetsoff friends, who also had
ancestors living in Oregon, drove this route the previous year and
gave us survey maps and recent aerial photographs of the land. I have
brought my grandfather Pete Maloff's manuscript, *Doukhobors, Their*

History, Life and Struggle, a chapter of which describes his family's life in Oregon, and a copy of the 1917 Supreme Court of Oregon's document on the investigation of fraud charges in the sale of the land to the Society of Independent Doukhobors.

The Kooznetsoffs told us about the location of eight hundred acres of land that Doukhobor leader Peter Vasilevich Verigin (Haspodnyeey, or "Lordly") purchased in 1923. Back then he envisioned a united community of Doukhobors and Molokans living here and called the land Druzhelyubaya Dolina, "Friend-Loving Valley." This is our first destination.

Eileen Kooznetsoff's directions were: "East of Eugene, on a hill close to the village of Crow, there's a road named Dukhobar Road. That's where the two Doukhobor families started preparing the land in 1923, for others to come later."

The day is warm, though it cools slightly as we leave the landscape of small farms and wineries and travel higher into a forest of oak and pine, where a sign warns that logging trucks share this narrow road. The road dips and winds along rolling hills, and after a couple of hours we feel we may be lost.

"There doesn't seem to be any such sign. Should we give up?" I say, and just as I repeat this, we see Dukhobar Road. The signpost also holds the notice Dead End. In 1924 Peter "Lordly" Verigin was killed; the Oregon land was sold in 1928, and the idea of a common Doukhobor-Molokan community abandoned. We take pictures of the surrounding countryside; cattle graze on the dry hillsides and the grapevines are yellowing. A warm wind blows and we feel empty—only the could-have-beens flowing through our minds.

We drive north toward Peoria and Svoboda Colony. Along Peoria Road, the dividing line between Benton and Linn Counties, the farmland becomes flatter and is plowed and seeded with a fall crop. Small dust devils spin in the distance. At a bend in the river, we find the blueberry farm that the Kooznetsoffs told us would be across from the original colony land, and in an excited flourish we jump out of the truck and take numerous pictures of the farmland and the riverbank with its grove of aspen trees. Mother has told me that when Great-Grandmother moved into her house in the colony, she planted pink Livingstone daisies and yellow dandelions, and all the neighbours praised their beauty. But we find no pink daisies

and no ruins of a village or rusty plows, no evidence at all of the
Doukhobor colonists. These large tracts of land, we are told later,
are now farmed by Mennonite farmers, and we find no one who
remembers a Doukhobor settlement.

A sign, Welcome to Peoria, is a few minutes down the road.
Peoria is a cluster of houses along two streets, and about a hundred
people live here. The small county park between the road and the
river has picnic tables, a boat launch and pit toilets.

That night we locate an RV site in the Benton County Fair-
grounds, a half-hour drive from Peoria and in the outskirts of Corvallis. There is room for one night only as all campsites are booked
the next night for the football game: the local Oregon State Beavers
are playing their rivals, the Idaho State Bengals. Football fever is high.

We curl up in the camper next to enormous RVs, and I scan
my grandfather's book for what he has written about his family's sojourn in this valley. He writes that a group of Doukhobors
founded the Svoboda Colony of Freedom, where "each had the full
right to tell the truth and fear no one," in response to their feelings
that the community established by Peter V. Verigin in Canada cur-
tailed individual freedom. His parents, Nikolai and Elizaveta Maloff, moved from their Saskatchewan farm to this colony when Pete
was thirteen.

> We reached Oregon in the winter. In comparison
> with Saskatchewan this was heaven on earth. It was
> warm and green and the rivers shouted merrily. We
> were met by a delegation which had already settled.
> From the station we went by horse and wagon. Vasil
> V. Vereshchagin fluently set forth the advantage of
> this land over cold Canada.
>
> We were soon settled and entered the new cir-
> cumstances in a smooth and orderly way. We brought
> with us money so we suffered no undue hardship.
> Thanks to the help of the colonization carpenter,
> Alyosha Bloodoff, our home was soon ready for oc-
> cupancy.
>
> Life passed so pleasantly here that for several years
> I lost sight of the Doukhobor horizon. Our colonists
> bought 1,000 acres of land which they subdivided.

We were not far from the town of Peoria, in the valley of the Willamette River.[48]

Grandfather Pete finished high school here and worked for a surveyor who offered to lend him money to go to university in Portland. The community had many visitors—Doukhobors from Saskatchewan, Molokans from California—and the neighbouring farmers appreciated their hard work ethic. They seemed to be thriving. Why did they leave? I read further:

> Life in Oregon passed quietly for about four years, and then it was suddenly cut short. There appeared to be serious shortcomings in the documents dealing with the buying of the land. There were forty owners for one thousand acres. The documents were drawn up inadequately: if any one of the settlers failed to pay his share the rest must lose their land too. Quite the commotion was created over this matter.[49]

The commotion, I find out through an internet search, was raised particularly because this land deal was reminiscent of fraudulent land schemes in Oregon a decade earlier in which many people were indicted.[50] The *Oregonian* sent a prominent journalist, Mrs. Osborne, to follow the trial, and she became a close friend of the Doukhobors and championed their cause. Grandfather included a picture of her with his mother in his book, both strong, good-looking women in turn-of-the-century fashionable clothing.

I search through the court documents: *Society of Independent Doukhobors v. Hecker* (Supreme Court of Oregon, January 30, 1917). They confirm that the seller, Mr. Hecker, would not deal with individual Doukhobor buyers but wished to sell the thousand acres to a corporation (thus the Society of Independent Doukhobors), which later subdivided the land into individual plots. Charges of

---

48.   Maloff, *Doukhobors*, pt. 2, chap. 5.
49.   Maloff, *Doukhobors*, pt. 2, chap. 5.
50.   *The Oregon Encyclopedia*, s.v. "Oregon Land Fraud Trials (1904–1910)," last updated March 17, 2018, https://oregonencyclopedia.org/articles/oregon_land_fraud_trials_1904_1910_/.

bribery and fraud were made against the person who acted as the interpreter between the corporation and Mr. Hecker. Furthermore, the plaintiffs claim the seller's statement that "the land would pay for itself in the course of two or three years" was false. An island of ninety acres that was said to be a desirable place to build on flooded each year, and forty-five acres were in the bed of the river. Though the first decree was in the colonists' favour, in an appeal to a higher court the decision was reversed. The colonists lost their initial payments and the land. Grandfather wrote, "The decision shook the colony and for a long time it could not recover. Little by little the colonists began to leave."[51]

This Oregon migration has become a family myth—a promised land that was lost, we were never sure why. It is recalled during family gatherings, often at the end of winter when we are ready for the warmth of spring and freedom from heavy winter coats. "Oh yes," we sigh, "Grandfather lived in Oregon. He went to school there." We'd gaze at a framed picture of the family that was taken in a Corvallis photography studio. The men—Great-Grandfather Nikolai, eighteen-year-old Nick, and Pete, thirteen—are dressed in suits and ties, Great-Grandmother Elizaveta in a light embroidered blouse and long skirt, and four-year-old daughter Tanya, sitting on her father's knee, is wearing a lacy white dress with big bow ties in her hair. They look distinguished and proud, except for Pete, who looks a little uncomfortable in the unaccustomed clothing.

I look at the surveyor's map of the Svoboda Colony dated May 26, 1913, and notice an island in the river where the land is subdivided into just over forty small parcels of land, building lots for a village, and farther away from the river there are large rectangles of land for farming. The building lots are in two long rows, parallel and facing each other, reminiscent of the Doukhobor villages in Saskatchewan and the Doukhobor villages we visited in Russia, where the houses faced a street that was planted with trees and kitchen gardens grew in the backyards. Was this where Great-Grandmother Elizaveta planted her flowers? Where, as she told my mother, they gathered to pray, make *borsh*, sew quilts and hold meetings? Grandfather mentions that Anton Savelievich Popoff, who was one of the

---

51.　Maloff, *Doukhobors*, pt. 2, chap. 5.

Nikolai and Elizaveta joined a democratic Doukhobor cooperative in Oregon. Their sons finished their high school education there and, if not for American conscription in World War I, they may have become part of the American "melting pot."

instigators of the migration, frequently had talks on how to dry out the land. Did they build dikes to barricade the houses from flood waters each spring?

Later, at home, I will search the internet for more information. I will find that the fourteen-kilometre stretch of river between Peoria and Corvallis is a popular canoeing and kayaking destination. There are pictures of the Willamette Riverkeepers carrying bags to pick up garbage, planting shrubs and trees, floating down the river in life jackets and camping on the sandbars. Upstream of Peoria, they have purchased a ninety-acre island that had been farmland, and they are replanting it with native trees and shrubs to create a campsite. Could this island be the village site? It's a possibility, but searching Google Maps, I find the colony settlement seems to be farther downstream on an old oxbow that has dried up.

SEPTEMBER 16, 2016

The following morning, we bike into the Bald Hill Natural Area behind the fairground, where trails lead us through a mixture of oak savannah, old farm homesteads and country estates. When we ask for directions from a woman walking along the path, she tells us that this area has been preserved by land donations to a conservancy and about the extensive network of trails established to connect four county parks. We walk together, and Steve, interested in the political situation in the United States, starts discussing politics. Her comment is chilling. She is afraid that because of the recent murders of black people, there will be a "race war" in the United States. Despite her words, she is not afraid to walk these trails alone and is friendly to us, strangers from a different land.

We stop in Corvallis to have lunch at one of the ubiquitous local brew pubs and walk along the Willamette River. A group of young people, wearing green T-shirts and carrying shovels and rakes, chat vivaciously as they pass us by, and behind them is their supervisor, a young woman. The Americans we have met are usually genial and pleasant, so we ask her about the group and she explains that they are volunteers helping to look after parks in Corvallis.

After a visit to a tea shop we travel north toward our next destination, Portland, which Grandfather, as a young man, visited several times a year. He wrote that he enjoyed the river, the parks with their roses and the theatre where he saw Anna Pavlova, Caruso and Kreisler, among others.

SEPTEMBER 17, 2016

The weather has become rainy and cool. "Welcome to Portland," locals tell us. "This is what the weather is like nine months of the year." We park our truck and camper on the outskirts of the city and take a bus into town. An all-day transit pass is $5.00 or $2.50 for seniors, and we find that the buses, trains and streetcars are frequent and uncongested. It is dorm-moving day at Portland State University, where we get off. Everyone is rushing toward a lineup—we think for the farmers' market—but we find the students and faculty are in line to pick up trolleys for their move. The huge Saturday farmers' market is in a park next door, and, despite the rain, it is crowded. We buy mocha cappuccinos and croissants before taking pictures of the overflowing booths with their attractively arranged organic produce, baked goods and flowers. Then, following Grandfather's footsteps, we visit the extensive rose garden and the Chinese and Japanese gardens. We walk along the Willamette, snack from the food trucks and wander into the Pearl District to visit art galleries. Yes, aside from the rain, Portland is an agreeable city to live in. But such was not Grandfather Pete's experience.

—⁓—

After they left the Oregon colony, Nikolai and Elizaveta Maloff bought farmland in Yuba City in the Sacramento Valley of California. Pete moved to San Francisco, where his father arranged an apprenticeship with a Russian editor of the journal *Veleekiy Okean*.

In the next few years, with the entry of the United States into the First World War, Nikolai decided to relocate his family back to Canada, where Doukhobors had conscientious-objector status. True to his principles of not profiting from land, he sold the farm to the Dobrinins, a Molokan family who had just immigrated from Russia, for the same price he had bought it, though land prices had escalated. Nikolai felt that they had "wandered from the right path" when they separated from the Doukhobor leader in Canada. He wanted to return to community life, and in a Christian Community of Universal Brotherhood (CCUB) meeting, he asked if he would be allowed to become a member again. The spiritual leader, Peter V. Verigin, turned to the congregation and asked, "Shall we welcome Nikolai back?" "Yes!" was the resounding answer. Mother tells me that the congregation sang a Doukhobor song, "There Is Room for Everyone," and Nikolai and Elizaveta settled on community land in Shoreacres. To his sons' chagrin, Nikolai donated most of the money from the sale of the California land to the CCUB.

Pete Maloff met and married Lusha Hoodicoff and developed a small farm next to her parents in Thrums. Six generations have now made the small collection of houses along Highway 3A in Thrums their home.

—⁓—

Do I have a yearning to live in the Willamette Valley of Oregon? There are vineyards on the hillsides—which in my mind means good weather—and Corvallis is an attractive university town. I'm impressed by the level of volunteerism in beautifying and protecting the land and the rivers. But just now the politics in the United States is charged, and the frequent news reports of the random killing of schoolchildren, students, colleagues and black people shock me. The *How To* supplement of the *Cottage Grove Sentinel* (Cottage Grove is a city close to Corvallis) has an article titled "How to Choose a Handgun" and provides a phone number to call for firearms training. Would the Doukhobors, had they stayed in Oregon, assimilate into this society? Some of Doukhobor ancestry who had lived in Oregon longer had urged the Svoboda colonists to accept American naturalization.

Except for the times at the end of a long winter, when I impatiently look out my window and measure the slowly shrinking snowbanks, I am grateful to be living in Canada. Perhaps here, as Doukhobor peace seekers, we have contributed toward our communities. Pete Maloff strove to make a difference.

A PASSION FOR
TRUTH AND JUSTICE

—⁓—

Though my grandfather Pete Maloff passed away almost fifty years ago, it is only now, through his writing, that I am discovering his thoughts, passions and disappointments. His written legacy is stacked on a table next to my desk: his book, *Doukhobors, Their History, Life and Struggle*, printed in Russian, the pages highlighted with sticky notes. Next to it sits a box containing loose papers, carbon copies of the English translation of the same book. Grandfather edited these pages, crossing out phrases, adding comments and punctuation. This translation is also on my computer, easy to access, and a challenge to have it published as he wished.

In a file folder I find three of his works: the 1954 Russian Doukhobor literary magazine for which he served as editor; a chapbook, *In Quest of a Solution: Three Reports on Doukhobor Problem*, second edition, 1957; and *Maloff's Research Library, an Anti-Militarism and Vegetarian Idealism Newsletter*, published in 1967. Yellowed pages containing an essay on his visit to Hiroshima in 1961, several copies of lectures he prepared for the International Peace Garden meeting in September 1966 and an address to the Trail Rotary Club in 1968 are tucked in beside the booklets.

Somewhere in dusty cupboards there is more: articles that he submitted to *Iskra* magazine and letters to friends and correspondents.

As I read, the intensity and passion of the writing informs me that Grandfather poured his soul into the pages. To me his writings are a precious legacy. I knew Grandfather Pete Maloff in his outward appearance, a thoughtful, caring and generous man. As I read his words, I feel I am able to look into his inner spirit. He wrote about Doukhobors, vegetarianism, pacifism and spirituality. I find that, as well as his love for Canada and the Doukhobor community he was born into, he had dark moments when he was disappointed with his people and the Canadian legal system.

It is gardening season here in the Kootenays, and I struggle to find minutes for reading and writing. I ask Mother how Grandfather had time to write and still do his farming chores. She wrinkles her brow, clasps her hands and looks off to the distance as she tells me about his writing.

LEEZA: Though Father was strong and hard-working, he was labelled a radical and wasn't able to obtain work off the farm, so the family started a market-gardening business. "Growing good food is an honourable occupation," he told me, and he worked hard at cultivating the plot of land Mother had inherited. But his true love was philosophy and writing. As he dug in the garden, I would see him stop, take out a small notebook and pencil from his overalls pocket and scribble something. Later, when he'd look at his notes, he would shake his head, trying to decipher what he wrote. Mother was always chiding him, "Petrunya, pay attention to your work. Your head is in the clouds." Especially when he was driving, she would remind him, "Think about the road. Get out of your thoughts."

At the market, Father would be surrounded not only by customers buying vegetables, but also by those who wanted to discuss politics and philosophy. Others would come to him for advice on their personal lives. People were attracted to him, but sometimes he would be exhausted by their demands. Even the warden of the BC Penitentiary, where Father was incarcerated in 1932, noticed that there was always a circle of men around Father. He told him, "Pete, you need to stay away from people. They will eat you up." He sent him to work on the penitentiary farm, and that was lucky because while he was away there was a riot in the prison.

When he was home, in the early morning and late in the night after finishing his farm work, Father would be up in the attic library at his desk, reading and writing. Our Doukhobor leader, Chistiakov, told him, "Someday you and I, we'll write a book together." Chistiakov died in 1939, but Father did write his book. His research led him to archives on Doukhobors in Russia, the United States and Canada. Vasil Koochin helped him with Russian grammar. My brother Pete typed the pages using carbon paper to make triplicates, and Father self-published it in Russian in 1948. Then he worked on the English translation, sending it away to professor friends to edit.

Pete Maloff speaking at the International Peace Garden on the border of Manitoba and North Dakota in 1966. Photo Koozma Tarasoff.

At the end of his life Father was hoping to escape the constant pressure to make a living and to write a second book, about his time with Chistiakov. In 1971, while he and Mother were travelling on a Greyhound bus to California, headed to Dr. Jensen's ranch where he planned to focus on his writing, he passed away.

—*—

Mother finishes her story by saying, "It does not hurt so much now when I think of him. It *has* been almost forty-eight years." Then she sighs and adds, "But I should have helped him more."

I return to Grandfather's writing I have spread out on my table.

In 1949 the government of British Columbia appointed a commission to look into possible solutions to the "Doukhobor problem" as violence toward and within the Doukhobor community escalated. Commissioner Colonel F.J. Mead requested that Pete Maloff give an opinion. In the preface to his report, Pete wrote that at first it was not his intention to speak before the commission. After his house arrest in the 1940s he had continued to live in seclusion. On seeing the seriousness of the situation, he could not stand idly by. In the preface to his report, *In Quest of a Solution*, Grandfather wrote a short account of his life. He saw himself as an outsider who took a historical view of Doukhobors.

> I proceed with a brief account of the experiences that have gone towards forming my character as a man, and as a student of history; my love of truth regardless of the consequences.
>
> My first contact with the Doukhobors was in 1928 when the Doukhobor community staged a spiritual revival and displayed a unique example of idealistic aspirations worthy of high consideration. This religious revival attracted my whole being and I sympathized with all three movements in the community, and in particular with the Sons of Freedom who represented at the time the strength of spiritual and moral power. Their unceasing struggle against war and causes of war attracted my whole attention; and to find such a movement among my own people was certainly a joy.[52]

Grandfather had high ideals and a strict code of conduct: vegetarianism, abstention from intoxicating substances, and living a simple life. From his research into Doukhobor history he grew to believe that in faithfully following the teachings of Christ, they made a tremendous contribution to religious life and thought. Grandfather became disillusioned when he saw the Doukhobor religious foundation crumble.

> My ten years of close contact with the Doukhobors from 1928 to 1938 have faced me with some bitter experiences and revealed to me some unusual glimpses into their strange faith. For the last seven to eight years I have led more or less a secluded life, and for the last four years I have entirely severed my connections with the Doukhobors, Sons of Freedom and, as much as possible, all society. I did this for certain reasons. In my dealings with human

---

52. Maloff, *In Quest of a Solution*, p. 3.

nature, Doukhobors, and the civilized society as a
whole, I have suffered two big surprises, disappointments, and terrific stunning blows.[53]

I read this report to the commission with an awareness that, in the
1940s, as a condition of his release from jail, Pete Maloff was not
allowed to communicate with any outside his family. Perhaps he
is cautious when he mentions that he had severed all connections
with the Doukhobors.

His disappointments were first with the Doukhobor community. He saw that the basic Christian concept of equality of all humanity, the sense of brotherhood, embracing every race and creed,
no longer bridged the split between Doukhobor factions. He said
it was nonsense that many of the Community Doukhobors were
trying to prove that the Sons of Freedom had no connections with
the rest of the Doukhobors. He said that the Sons of Freedom
movement was a legitimate child of all Doukhobors. They spoke
out against government encroachment on Doukhobor principles,
against swearing an oath of allegiance to the state and against accepting private ownership of land, when others in the Doukhobor
society would not. Still, their resorting to arson, setting houses on
fire and bombing railroads was criminal, no matter what intentions
drove them. He said that they were deluding themselves if they
thought they could achieve a good end by these acts. Furthermore,
rather than thinking for themselves, he saw that the Sons of Freedom became dependent on leaders. This exposed them to the danger that any adventurer could penetrate into their midst, mislead
them and create dissention and chaos in their lives.

He chastised many Doukhobors for reverting to eating meat and
using tobacco and intoxicating liquors that they had rejected in Russia.
Furthermore, in their hunger for material possessions, many gave little thought to the means of acquiring them. And more crushingly he
wrote, "Many Doukhobors have lost sight of their historical mission
and, not only this, but their morality is decaying."[54]

His words were harsh, and in his determination to speak the
truth as he saw it, the whole family became alienated.

Mother says, "The Community Doukhobors believed he was

---

53. Maloff, *In Quest of a Solution*, p. 4.
54. Maloff, *In Quest of a Solution*, p. 4.

a fanatic. The Sons of Freedom were angry that he wouldn't join them. Many respected Father for his honesty in speaking out, but mostly they shunned him. It was not until the 1960s, when Doukhobor leader John J. Verigin asked Father to become a member of the Union of Spiritual Communities of Christ, saying, 'We need you,' that Father rejoined the Doukhobor community."

In his pamphlet, *In Quest of a Solution*, Grandfather Pete Maloff also wrote about his harrowing experience with Warden Macdonald in the Nelson provincial jail. He did not name him and did not write about the beatings he received, but his account becomes intensely real when I read these paragraphs:

> I was imprisoned in Nelson on three different occasions for violating the National Registration Act. During my last confinement there, I was confronted with an ultimatum, that unless I registered, I should be transferred to the Essondale Insane Asylum for the duration of the war and perhaps for the rest of my days. The only cause for this threat was my alleged stubborn resistance to registration on conscientious objection to war, which according to the representatives of this democratic civilized society, was an influence on others to follow my example.
>
> I had a serious fight on my hands to keep myself out of the bughouse, and if it had not been for the help of my family and a few friends here and there, I may not have been here today.[55]

Further, he believed that the harsh response of the government to Doukhobor transgressions of the law had much to do with creating the Doukhobor problem.

> This problem has originated from the mutual misunderstanding between Canada and the Doukhobors when they first came to Canada.
> The Doukhobors came to Canada with firmly established ideologies and principles which they

---

55. Maloff, *In Quest of a Solution*, p. 5.

considered to be infallible and they had no intention to abandon them. It was the ultimate meaning of their life.

The Government of Canada failed to take into consideration these factors and treated the Doukhobors as ordinary immigrants. It proceeded to subjugate the Doukhobors under its control and the first failures did not discourage the Government. As years went by, the Government pursued its relentless onslaught upon the Doukhobors, so that many bitter conflicts have taken place since. The Doukhobors suffered tremendous losses, both of property and lives. ...

All these persecutions and oppressions upon the Doukhobors were presumably committed with the intention of assimilating them into the Canadian way of life. ... It seems to me that this policy of assimilation, especially when done by violence, coercion and intimidation is one of the chief causes of Doukhobor unrest. Such a policy may also be said to be highly unjust from a humanitarian viewpoint.[56]

Pete Maloff spoke out not only in this report to Commissioner Colonel Mead, but also through a Russian-language magazine he edited, *Rassvet: A Russian Doukhobor Literary Magazine, the Voice of Free Thinkers*, which aimed at an international Russian audience. The November/December 1954 and January/February 1955 editions contained a variety of literature—essays, poems, a short story and a book review contributed by his correspondents.

The opening essay, written by Nikolai Demedov Sherman of Switzerland, was titled "Spiritual Crisis: An Exploration of Religion and God." Four pages of poetry follow, with varied titles such as "Those Who Go to War" by Margaret Lalet, "Prayer" by P. Gordon and "My Family, All of God's Creation" by Fanny Spencer. The Los Angeles author Rodion Berezov's short story "Storm on the Volga" and a review of his new book were included. Finally, there was an in

---

56.   Maloff, *In Quest of a Solution*, p. 10.

memoriam to the Swiss writer Nikolai Alexander Rebalkin, which included his personal letters to Pete Maloff. Pete Maloff also wrote the editorial on how the Cold War and weapons of mass destruction were pushing the earth toward catastrophe.

Grandfather's 1955 editorial was a torrent against the government for removing Svobodniki children from their families. He described an incident where forty policemen entered Glade with the purpose of taking the children from their families, although on that day they were unsuccessful, as the children had been hidden. In their anger the police broke locks and doors and carried out other "hooligan acts." In the next few weeks the Sons of Freedom village in Krestova was raided and many children snatched from their families. Pete wrote that internationally, people were amazed that in a democratic country such acts were tolerated and that the surrounding population did not speak out.

Mother does not recall how long Grandfather published this magazine. Though it gave him a platform to voice his concerns, funds were scarce, and he was not able to maintain the journal for long.

At the end of the magazine I read numerous congratulatory letters from friends and correspondents in various countries including Germany, Switzerland, Finland and the United States. Their names trigger a memory of walking to the Thrums post office to pick up stacks of mail from Grandfather's large mailbox.

And I am reminded of a 1960 travel itinerary I found in Grandfather's files. That year airlines offered a special deal on international travel. Pete Maloff was sixty years old, and this sale motivated him to pursue a long-held dream to visit his friends and correspondents throughout the world. Vipond Travel Agencies in Trail organized a tour for him to fly from October 4 to December 19. Over seventy-seven days he landed in twenty-seven countries in Europe, the Middle East and the Far East—including Egypt, Israel, Iran, Afghanistan, India, Sri Lanka, Thailand and Japan. I am further astonished when I find a receipt dated January 22, 1961, scarcely a month later, for his stay in the Marunochi Hotel in Tokyo. He visited Hiroshima and wrote of his impressions as he stood at the site of the atomic bomb blast.

Pete Maloff created a worldwide network of like-minded correspondents connected through the regular postal service. His passion

fuelled his energy, but after that exhausting tour, Grandfather was ill
for a lengthy period.

—∾—

As I read the speech Grandfather Pete Maloff made to the Rotary Club in Trail in 1968, I hear his voice calling out for justice and
peace. He spoke about the tremendous scientific advances of the
space age and of the unresolved realities of wars, assassinations, fam-
ine, race riots and fraudulence in society.

Four peace activists: Anna Markova, mother of Doukhobor leader John
Verigin Sr.; Eli Popoff; Doukhobor historian; Abraham Johannes Muste,
clergyman and leader in the American peace movement; Pete Maloff.

Mr. Chairman, distinguished guests, and all members of Rotary:

I thank one and all of you for this privileged occasion of being here once more and addressing you. I understand that the International Rotary Organization is a group which feels concern for the interests of others and thus commits itself to a general principle of mutual understanding of one another, and even more, always being alert about the sad happenings in the whole world.

Now if I have a correct definition of this organization, then I can say that this is a significant factor in Rotary's achievements. Because without understanding of one another, without knowing the basic background of different people, their cultures and customs, we shall never restore the true status of man in all his human dignity. ...

Certainly, man of the twentieth century has made astounding discoveries, and many of them we must recognize are good and worthwhile achievements. Our so-called high standard of living has really made our life in many ways easier and happier. But nevertheless, these great technical developments have not solved the main crucial problems of our age.

Now in my half-century of soul-searching for a more comprehensive truth about the whole man, I came to the conclusion that these four points are most important to contemplate on.

1. How shall we care for our bodies so that we won't need to be worrying about the transplanting of our hearts or dying prematurely from dozens of other maladies that are devouring man every day?

2. How shall we live with our fellow man so each and all would freely unlock the dormant reservoirs of human generosity, kindness and nobility of man?

3. How shall we hear our children and youth so that they will not be slaves to dissipation and delinquencies, ending in riots and immoral behaviour?

4. How shall we build peaceful and harmonious relationship with our neighbours and nation with nation?

I am not asking anyone to believe as I do, but I want to share some of my findings and experiences with those who are interested in seeing life more deeply, to realize that our life on this planet has an immense significance. For life indeed is incomparable and every human being is nothing less than God's miracle.

Grandfather finished his address to the club with his reaction to his recent visit to the death camp of Auschwitz:

So staggering was my experience in this death house, that at first, I was unable to grasp the full meaning of it. ... The longer I stood by the crematoriums the more I felt and heard the undying heartbreaking echoes of those millions who perished there crying for justice, justice and justice. What a tremendous call and claim! But there was no answer but only the dead silence. While there I really was ashamed for Man, supposed to be the most glorious creation of Almighty God. I was ashamed for all religious denominations and their pulpits, including the brilliant preachers who are so intensely waiting for the second emergence of the master. I was ashamed for our cultural heritage and our political world. Because this barbaric mass murder in Auschwitz revealed to me a horrifying symptom of Man's soul disease, or is it the embodiment of Satan's terrific cry: "Evil be thou my God."

... What are we going to do about it? Do we think to overcome this worldwide crisis by using the same old outworn methods: bigger armies, navies, air force, hydrogen bombs, poison gases and all our other confused values. I myself doubt it. I stand for creative intelligence which is distinctly distilled in the unchanging truth of that one cosmic law: "Thou Shalt Not Kill."[57]

In 1966 Grandfather sold his collection of rare pamphlets and books to the University of British Columbia Library's Special Collections department. Mr. Robert Hamilton, assistant librarian of the Special Collections department, came to Thrums to sort and catalogue the material, and Grandfather became friends with him. A few years ago, when I accompanied my daughter to the University of British Columbia (UBC), I visited the library to investigate the materials UBC had purchased from Grandfather. I was not able to do so, but in an underground vault, I found the Doukhobor research collection. At the double glass doors to the Rare Books and Special Collections library, I was told to leave my belongings outside in a locker, and if I wanted to take notes, I would be given a notepad and pencil. I signed a register, and in the quiet, where the only sounds were the hushed voices of six librarians investigating manuscripts next door, I proceeded to browse through boxes of files.

After an hour, I discovered file 135–36, labelled "Pete Maloff, Thrums, B.C." My hands trembled as I opened it to find that Robert Hamilton had kept all of his correspondence with my grandfather. To my surprise it included a letter Grandfather had written to introduce me to Mr. Hamilton when I was looking into UBC as a possible university to attend. In another letter, Grandfather wrote of his plans to travel to Turkey, Bulgaria and the USSR with Dr. Bernard Jensen. He added that his archives and notes were intact, and though he had no time to dig into their contents at the moment, he planned to deal with them eventually and assured Mr. Hamilton that UBC would be the recipient. He wrote, "I hope to break the tyranny of the greenhouse business that is so demanding. I want to start writing about my time with the Doukhobor leader, Chistiakov."[58] The last letter in the file was one I had written to Mr. Hamilton in 1971 informing him of the unexpected passing of my grandfather Pete Maloff.

---

57. Maloff, "P.N. Maloff's Address before the Rotary Club."
58. Pete Maloff to Robert Hamilton, file 135–36, Doukhobor Research Collection, Rare Books and Special Collections, University of British Columbia Library.

—ᴧᴧ—

Farmer, peace activist, researcher, writer, thinker—Pete Maloff was all these things. Mother said he was driven in his pursuit of peace and justice. "He could not help himself." When I ask her about the effect on the family of his passionate drive, she says, "We did not really understand him."

In a file of Grandfather's clippings, I find a quote by André Maurois: "Here we are on this earth with only a few more decades to live, and we lose many irreplaceable hours brooding over grievances that, in a year's time, will be forgotten by us and by everybody. No, let us devote our life to worthwhile actions and feelings, to great thoughts, real affections and enduring undertakings. For life is too short to be little."

LET THEM GO THEIR WAY

——*w*——

This rainy March evening I've driven the winding road to Nelson to hear Professor Kathleen Rodgers launch her new book, *Welcome to Resisterville: American Dissidents in British Columbia*. Others have braved the downpour, and the public library is noisy with folk greeting each other with hand clasps and hugs. It is mostly an older Kootenay crowd, several women wearing woollen shawls, men in checkered shirts. Many are draft resisters who have come to hear how Dr. Rodgers has told their stories. I see fellow Doukhobors and recognize Quaker friends. The scents of musty damp clothing, wood-burning fires and coffee fill the air.

Rodgers's treatise on the influence of American war resisters on British Columbia is not an outsider's view. She grew up in the Slocan Valley, where her father was a teacher in the local high school and where many draft dodgers settled. They were her neighbours and parents of her friends. She chuckles as she says that it was not unusual for her to look over her backyard fence and see the neighbours gardening and building in the nude. As we watch a slide show of pictures donated by people she has interviewed, we laugh at the long hair, bell-bottoms, idealistic communal living and "toking up of weed."

"Yep, that was us," many in the crowd say.

Rodgers nods to the handful of Doukhobor and Quaker folk in the audience and says their support to the war resisters was invaluable. Many families provided shelter, food, employment and comfort for fellow pacifists. I purchase her book and, at home, scan the pages to see if Rodgers mentions my grandparents Pete and Lusha Maloff. In the chapter "Brokering Friends and Allies," Pat Forsythe, an American expat, says,

> In Vancouver in the circle of draft dodger friends there was a man who had gotten his master's degree working with Doukhobors in the Slocan Valley. ...

He arranged with them that they would look after us, and so we were sent to the Maloff household in Thrums, and those people had it all sorted out— where we were going to live and who was going to feed us.[59]

Further, on the next page, Rodgers quotes a resident Doukhobor:

The Maloff family was heavily connected with the draft movement and would have incredible exchange on the social level and the cultural level with the Americans.[60]

I think back to my grandparents' market-garden farm in Thrums in the 1960s. When the young Americans started to arrive, Pete and Lusha Maloff welcomed them as kindred spirits in the fight against militarism. For me, a teenager at the time, this stream of refugees arriving on our doorstep was exciting; I felt connected to the anti–Vietnam War protest movement. Draft dodgers often pulled up to my grandparents' farmhouse, their possessions tied to the rooftop and back of a vehicle. They looked weary, in need of a bath, rest and food. Grandfather stoked up the *banya*, and Mother and Grandmother put on a pot of soup, potatoes or whatever was available. The stories they shared around the kitchen table were intriguing and distressing: receiving induction letters for the draft, their turmoil in deciding to leave their homes, fear of the FBI and their escape across the border into Canada. Some stayed for a month or two; others found shelter with Doukhobor families in the Slocan Valley or with Quaker friends in Argenta.

The morning after the book launch I drive to Mother's. As I enter her kitchen, the aroma of baking bread fills my nostrils. Although it's early, seven loaves are in the oven, and mother is shaping the second batch. She beams a smile and, with her hand sticky with dough, waves me over to her counter. Mother learned to make bread from her grandmother Elizaveta Maloff and, even though she is in her nineties, once a month she still gets up at three o'clock in

---

59. Rodgers, *Welcome to Resisterville*, p. 79.
60. Rodgers, *Welcome to Resisterville*, p. 81.

the morning to make bread for the family.

As she divides the dough I tell her about the book launch. She says, "Grandfather felt those draft dodgers were the conscience of America. And when they showed up here, well, he did all he could to help them." She slaps the dough into the bread pans. "I wish I could remember the names of that couple who stayed with us one summer. Didn't know a thing, but wanted to learn. They helped in the greenhouse, canned tomatoes, made sauerkraut. Even helped me make a wool-filled quilt."

Mother places the loaves by the oven to rise. We sit down, and I mention that Ross Klatte, an American expat, described *Living the Good Life* by Helen and Scott Nearing as his bible. Mother says, "Your grandfather corresponded with Scott Nearing. He and his wife visited us here in Thrums. The Nearings lived a simple life, and his ideas and your grandfather's were alike." She laughs. "They ate a sack of sunflower seeds as they sat talking on our porch. There was a huge heap of shells beside their bench, and Scott Nearing insisted the shells go into the garden for compost."

The first loaves come out of the oven, and Mother places the second batch in. I slice the hot crusty bread and slather it with butter. "Remember Len Walker?" I ask as I munch. He arrived on a motorcycle, his blond hair tousled, his face tanned, speaking with a Southern Californian accent. I'd spent many Saturday afternoons after market in the Nelson Civic Theatre, and he was like a figure out of the beach party movies I'd watched.

My grandparents gave him a home in Walter's cabin behind our house. Grandmother and Mother fed him; Grandfather counselled him. He stayed for four months, helping with the winter wood supply and working in the garden. He cooked for himself, but whenever Mother or Grandmother made bread, *borsh* or soup, I'd take him some. He'd come to the door and give me a wide smile and a thank you, and my fourteen-year-old self would grin and blush. He left before winter but came back the next spring looking more ragged, his hair longer, with fellow draft resisters and a series of girlfriends.

"When he showed up with his first girlfriend, Grandparents welcomed her, didn't they?"

"Yes, but by the second or third girlfriend, your grandfather

Draft resister Len Walker finds common pacifistic ideals in Pete Maloff and the Doukhobor community. Len and a friend (middle), with Pete (far right), Lusha (third from left) and others, 1964.

had a talk with him. There were many good things about those draft dodgers, but Grandfather was not happy with their free-love lifestyle."

In this, Grandfather was a traditional family man. But that lifestyle echoed the beliefs of some Doukhobors. I remembered Mother's story about Vanya Perepolkin, who lived in a community that experimented with free love. They believed wives and husbands shouldn't own each other.

"Len was handsome." I glance at Mother. "Even I had a crush on him."

Mother grins. "Len had his eyes on you too. Told me you were very good-looking. Took a picture of you by that old apple tree."

Len was twentysomething, a *nyee nash*. Mother would not have encouraged any connection there. But when my uncle Walter, mother's youngest brother, came back to Thrums, he and Len developed a friendship. They travelled to California, where they visited Len's parents. The meeting did not go well.

In her book, Rodgers describes how American draft resisters

in the sixties came from various backgrounds. Some had parents who were supportive of their choices; others did not. Len's father was a colonel in the US Army, and his first reaction to Len's refusal to serve in the Vietnam War was condemnation; his son was a coward for running away from his duty. Len was distraught about this denunciation and torn about leaving his home in America.

Walter introduced Len to Dr. Jensen, and Jensen's Hidden Valley Health Ranch became a haven for Len. For a time, he worked and hid from the US military in the hills surrounding Escondido.

Len used our Thrums address for his mail, and Grandfather began to correspond with his parents. After learning that our family was making a trip to Southern California, the Walkers invited us to visit their home in San Diego.

In the fall of 1966 my grandparents, mother, brother and sister and I piled into the blue Mercedes that Walter had imported when he returned from Germany. After a three-day drive through the western states, we reached the suburbs of San Diego and turned into a gated community. Homes behind pebbled courtyards planted with cacti climbed the dry hillside. The Walkers were waiting by their front door and welcomed us with handshakes. We shook off our long drive and traipsed into their home. In the entrance vestibule, Colonel Walker showed us his prize collection of samurai armour. Low Japanese sofas and tables furnished the living room. Everything was gleaming. Mrs. Walker served tea while my grandfather, a fervent pacifist, and Colonel Walker, a career warrior, seemed to get along splendidly, talking animatedly about Len and about Asia. We kids sat on the edge of the sofas and gawked at the elegance of their home.

When I ask my mother about that visit, she says, "The Walkers were hospitable, but nervous. Our car had Canadian licence plates. Their neighbours, mostly military, would have wondered if Len was hiding in Canada. They loved their son and were concerned about him. Colonel Walker told your grandfather, 'However you help my son, I'll be very thankful.' *That's* something to think about. He knew we were against war."

Len moved on to coastal towns in British Columbia, and Grandfather forwarded his mail to Vancouver, Victoria, Ucluelet and then Metchosin. Len returned to the United States several times, for a while avoiding the FBI, but eventually was caught and ended up in the "nut hospital," as he called it. Upon his release he lived with his parents. As I read letters that Len wrote to Grandfather, I can hear the agony and disillusionment in his voice.

> I don't know what will become of me—I haven't the faintest idea what is going to happen about this draft situation—and I don't really give a damn. If they want me—let them come and get me. (Just see if it does them any good!) My future is no further away than one hour. I am afraid to think any further ahead right now … I am a free man the FBI told me—all I have to do—is phone them every time I make a move—They call that freedom—to hell with them.[61]

Len decided to move to Canada to avoid a jail term. In another letter he wrote,

> Almost 2 years ago I met a Doukhobor and thought I knew him. But I had deceived myself. I did not know the Doukhobors from just meeting them and listening to their philosophy. It took time—much time to learn what a real Doukhobor is. I hope someday I might unsurface the "Doukhobor" that is within me. I know what it would take—I know how to do it—but Peter, I am NOT DOUKHOBOR ENOUGH TO MAKE myself search within for the ultimate truth. I am afraid to face myself—I am afraid to go to prison. I am not Doukhobor enough. I have convinced myself to stay here in Canada—and Fight this horrible war in the best way I know—by encouraging other young men like myself to leave America and come to Canada. God be with you.
>
> Love Len[62]

---

61.   Len Walker to Pete Maloff, undated correspondence, in the author's possession.
62.   Len Walker to Pete Maloff, undated correspondence, in the author's possession.

In March 1971, Len's wife, Arlene, sent my grandparents a letter. She introduced herself and told them about their new life. She had been born in New York twenty-five years ago. She wrote that after studying seven years to become a psychologist, she decided to give up her studies. She and Len met in Vancouver. From there they moved to the rural community of Metchosin on Vancouver Island, where they camped close to an old Indigenous burial ground. In the fall they found a cabin on a farm where they lived for a couple of years. There they grew a garden and gave birth to a daughter "by the warmth of a fire, without a doctor. It was the best night of my life!" Arlene wrote. Now they planned to live on a boat, but they needed to learn "about the capabilities of their boat and about navigation."[63]

Fearlessness and the willingness to try new adventures radiate from the pages of Arlene's letter. I tell Mother, "Their daughter would be forty-five now, Arlene seventy. It would be wonderful to meet them. Len was close—Grandfather was like a father to him."

Mother swallows. "He was, except for the drugs. Len tried to explain how smoking marijuana opened his mind ... to love ... to other ways of living. In this, Grandfather was disappointed in Len. He said, 'Sometimes people wake up, but they may wake up still groggy.'"

My uncle Walter stayed in contact with Len while they both lived in Vancouver. Eventually Walter moved to Hawaii, where he worked as a carpenter, and he asked Len to send his tools to him. A day after Walter received his tool box, a stranger knocked on Walter's door and asked for his packages. Under his carpentry tools, Walter found five large bundles of marijuana. Even years later, Uncle Walter said it gave him the shivers to think that he might have ended up in an American jail for this shipment of pot.

Grandfather's response was "Well, we have our *own* children and grandchildren to raise. Let them go their way."

---

63.   Arlene Walker to Pete Maloff, March 29, 1971, in the author's possession.

FINDING LEN WALKER

—⁓—

Fifty years after Len Walker became estranged from my grandfather, I found him again. During those intervening years I often asked people who had been involved in the American draft resistance movement if they knew Len Walker, the son of an American colonel who fled to Canada during the Vietnam War, but none recognized the name. For many years, my only clue about Len's fate was a letter, dated 1971, from his wife, Arlene, who said they were living in a boat on the coast. The prospects of locating Len changed with a chance meeting in 2018.

That summer, the fiftieth reunion of the Union of Young Doukhobors (UYD) attracted many of the five hundred or so young people who had participated in the Vancouver-based group since its origin in the ebullient sixties. The UYD had been formed by Jim Popoff and Gordon Bonderoff to provide an opportunity for Doukhobor youth living in the Lower Mainland to socialize together in support of their Doukhobor culture and beliefs, including non-violence and opposition to war. Those gathered were mostly of Doukhobor background, but non-Doukhobor friends and others of pacifist inclination were also welcomed. By 1970, Jim Popoff had met and befriended Ralph McGreal, an American who had come to Vancouver when he was only nineteen. Ralph was delighted to meet the Doukhobor youth who shared his feelings about war and participated with the UYD for a few years, even singing in the choir, despite speaking no Russian. At the reunion, when he gave a speech on how he had come to know the Popoff family and the Doukhobors, I thought of Len.

Later that evening I asked Ralph if he knew Len Walker. He said that he didn't recall ever having met him—but that he'd never had much to do with former Americans. As we continued to talk, after a pause, Ralph looked at me and said, "I get the feeling Len was of some importance to you. A friend of mine was involved in the Committee to Aid American War Objectors. I could ask him and get back to you."

A few weeks later he emailed me an article that a Len Walker had written a few years previously in a Vancouver Island newspaper. As I read the essay about his daughter's mediation work with First Nations, his words jumped out at me: "Back then I was known as the Colonel's son. Now, I am known as Tina's Dad."[64] Colonel as a father, Tina as a daughter, peace and reconciliation. This must be my man! However, when I emailed Len using the address at the end of the article, the email bounced back—address not found. It was with mixed emotions that I received this rejection. Thinking about Len had brought back memories of my teenage self and my family's role in helping draft resisters. I was disappointed, but I also felt a kind of relief—I would avoid dealing with the teenage infatuation I remembered and the uncomfortable emotions of an estrangement I did not understand.

Ralph was able to provide a post office mailing address and encouraged me to write again. "Over the past few years I contacted two people out of my distant past who were of considerable significance," he said. "I'd been quite uneasy about doing so, but overcame my fears and did it anyway, which turned out to be incalculably valuable and rewarding." A year later, I sent Len an artist card of the Kootenays and asked if he had known the Maloff family in the 1960s.

Shortly before Christmas, a letter arrived, and yes, it was from the Len Walker I had known. The response was heartfelt. "So very good to hear from you, Vera! ... I'm sitting here smiling at memories your letter has triggered, long buried in the mind's past."[65] As we continued to correspond, I learned some of what had transpired in Len's life in those fifty years.

First, he wrote about how he met the Maloff family. "A big bumble bee had hit my chest as I rode my motor cycle down the highway just where Peter was working in the garden." And life changed because of a bumblebee sting.

"I learned so many things living with the Doukhobor community. I became a vegetarian and raised my family that way too. ...

---

64.   Len Walker, "Island Tides Newspaper Inflames First Nations Gathering," *The Island Word*, June 12, 2015.

65.   Len Walker, letter to author, undated.

It was Peter who wrote a letter of introduction for me to take to Dr. Bernard Jensen at his Hidden Valley Health Ranch in California." Len travelled back to California, and on Grandfather's recommendation, Dr. Jensen gave him work at the ranch for room and board. He stayed for several months and learned about "being a knowledgeable vegetarian."

During the time of the Vietnam War, the FBI was hunting down draft resisters and the courts were sentencing young American men for lengthy periods of jail time for refusing to train for war. Of that time, Len does not speak. He says, "It is better not to bring those memories up. It was a difficult time." Eventually, Len made a tough decision. He broke ranks with his family and country and crossed the border into Canada.[66]

In Canada, I was to discover, Len became a man of many talents and careers—a child-care worker at an Indigenous residential school, an industrial first-aid attendant, a teacher, an assistant regional coordinator for a college, a gardener, a boat builder and an owner of a trucking business. Now that he is retired, he has bought a seven-acre farm, and he and his family are planning to grow a market garden. It was only later, when I read his book, that I was to learn of his role as a volunteer organizer in tsunami-ravaged Sri Lanka.

After a few emails, I felt I had to share the story I had written of Len's meeting with Grandfather Pete Maloff and their eventual alienation from each other. It was with trepidation that I sent him the chapter "Let Them Go Their Way," trusting that my version of the events would not end our correspondence and the friendship that I had come to value. Besides my teenage memories of a tall, handsome stranger living in a cabin behind our house and my mother's recollections, this story was of a young American man facing a momentous decision and an uncertain future. Perhaps as an author I had been unfair to him. Now Len would be in his seventies, I in my sixties. Could old events be accounted for?

I have to thank Len's wisdom in responding with humour. "Thank goodness I grew up," he wrote. "Nice story, about 90% true," and "Ha! What fun!"[67] which left 10 percent untrue. With a

66. Len Walker, email to author, January 1, 2020.
67. Len Walker, email to author, January 15, 2020.

huge sigh of relief that Len hadn't deleted my email and blocked further correspondence, I welcomed the chance to get our stories straight.

Where Grandfather had objected to his "numerous girlfriends," Len explained that the first woman who came with him to visit my grandparents was a platonic schoolmate. The second, Marti, was a girlfriend he met in Hawaii, and they lived together for a couple of years in Montreal. The third woman, Arlene, he married.

Mother tells me that Grandfather was scrupulous in his relationships with women. "If you follow my tracks, they are clean," he would say. It was one woman, Grandmother Lusha Hoodicoff, for him, and though life was turbulent because of Grandfather Pete's activism, they had a close, supportive relationship. But if he were alive, I might tease him, "Grandfather, times have changed—you were perhaps a bit old-fashioned."

As for the question of the marijuana, well, let's say that Walter's tool kit did contain "weed." It was sad, though perhaps inevitable, that this ended the relationship between Len and Pete Maloff that both had valued.

As I learned more about Len, I was astonished that, having been raised in a military family and with sisters married to men in influential careers in the US Armed Forces, he chose to protest against war.

Len explained, "I think it was the gift of growing up on military installations, first on the island of Guam and then later in Japan for four years. All that exposure to what Eisenhower called the Military Industrial Complex gave me a terrific insider view of the dishonesty and corruption and violence of governments. When speaking with Catholic priests about war and being told to *serve your country first*, then God ... All that stinking thinking I was very aware of at a very young age ... And then I met your granpa."[68]

Len sent me a book he wrote about his humanitarian work, *Tsunami Journey: Seventy Days in Sri Lanka.* The book begins with a quote by Albert Schweitzer: "You must give some time to your fellow men. Even if it's a little thing, do something for others—something for which you get no pay, but the privilege of doing it."

---

68. Len Walker, email to author, January 20, 2020.

Len assisted the people of Kulmanai, a coastal town of Sri Lanka where the 2004 Boxing Day Tsunami took more than five thousand lives and obliterated coastal villages. *Tsunami Journey* contains numerous letters in which medical staff at the hospital he worked out of and residents alike extended gratitude and appreciation for Len's service. The foreword by Dr. David and Mary Heaton explains Len's role there.

> Len is a man uniquely suited to assist the survivors. He was able to quickly establish a rapport with the government appointed leaders of the refugee camps, to assess the immediate needs, to request and purchase supplies, to warehouse, guard and to deliver them. ... We watched our dear friend Len develop a life-line connection with the community and the people.[69]

I chuckled to learn that, as he worked with the Canadian Disaster Alert Response Team and other disaster relief groups, Len prominently displayed the Canadian flag. Dr. Heaton said, "He was a great representative of the Canadian people."[70] Mr. K. Visara Devarakaj, on behalf of the people of Kulmanai, said, "May God bless your valuable service. I wish you and the people of Canada every success and good luck."[71]

The United States' loss was Canada's gain when Len Walker became a citizen of Canada.

Len dedicated the book to his wife, his daughters and the many people who assisted in the tsunami relief effort. And then I was astonished to read, "As well, I hold in fond memory my friend Peter Maloff Sr. of Thrums, BC, who encouraged me back in 1964 to visit Ceylon, his favorite place on earth."[72] When I asked him about this dedication, he wrote, "Peter made a great impression on me. He took me into his heart. He said to me once, 'you must go to Ceylon' ... and years later when I found myself in Sri Lanka one evening, I gasped as his words came into my head ... OMG!! I'm

---

69. Walker, *Tsunami Journey*, pp. 4–5.
70. Walker, *Tsunami Journey*, p. 4.
71. Walker, *Tsunami Journey*, p. 26.
72. Walker, *Tsunami Journey*, p. 9.

Len Walker kept the memory of Pete Maloff close to his heart for over fifty years.

here and it's just like he said it would be. I love the country and the people. In some small way everything that Peter taught me that he stood for ... that line of thinking I found to be with the Tamil people. I understood why he loved it so much there. He was a great man in my life, your grandpa."[73]

Reading these words brought my grandfather Pete Maloff back to life for me. I felt that Grandfather's struggle to change war into peace had made a difference in the life of one man and, through him, many others. It was as if Len was making up for the war his father, the colonel, had waged in the name of the United States of America. Instead, Len chose to take on a peacekeeping and service role in the name of Canada, dedicating this to the influence of a Doukhobor, Pete Maloff.

Echoes of my grandfather's life ring in my ears.

---

73.   Len Walker, email to author, January 29, 2020.

THE LAST CHAPTER

It is just before Christmas 2018. My mother lies partially paralyzed in the Kootenay Lake Hospital. She's had a stroke that has affected her right side. A fighter all her life, she struggles to regain movement, and even in the middle of the night, when she can't sleep, she does her exercises, lifting her arms and legs, moving her fingers as she is able. She thanks the nurses and aides for everything they do and beams when she sees us. "It's easy to give up," she says, "but you keep me going."

She has supported us, her family, all her life, and we are not ready to let her go. It would mean the end of her guidance, her stories and her life that has been harsh and, at the same time, rewarding. Her passing would be the end of an era. But when we visit, she does not reflect on the past. As she has done much of her life, she focuses on the day-to-day and says, "Tell me what's happening at home. How is everyone?"

I tell friends who phone asking about Mother that her mind is sharp. They respond, "Yes, we know that." They wish her well and say, "She is such a vibrant part of our community. We hope this is only a temporary setback. We know she will keep fighting."

I think about my mother's stories that have given me a connection to past generations. To her great-grandmother Malasha Androsova, who smuggled herself and her two young children on board a ship to Canada when her husband refused to give her permission to leave Russia. Great-Aunt Malasha Aseyeva, who was married at twelve, grew to love her husband and, even though she was pregnant, trekked through the Caucasus Mountains to visit him as he lay dying in an Azerbaijani *aul*. Grandparents Nikolai and Elizaveta Maloff, who married and lost a daughter in Russia; Nikolai was indentured to work in a Tatar village when he said "No!" to serving in the czar's army. Immigrating with the Doukhobors who came to Canada, they lived on farms in Saskatchewan, Oregon and California and then wandered between several idealistic communities in British Columbia, never finding a home to settle in. Perhaps they were searching for more, for traditions, beliefs and a culture that could not be easily recreated in this new land.

I ask Mother if she thinks the sacrifices her parents and grandparents made were worthwhile. "Well, life could have been easier!" she says. She thinks particularly about us, her children. If she could have had an education and a job that paid more money than selling her produce at local farmers' markets, our lives would have been better. But in the end, I see pride in how she speaks of the difficult years in her family—the straightening of her shoulders, the lift of her head. "You can't change the past," she tells me. She feels she has led an honourable life and is at peace.

We've had a heavy snowfall. Trees, their branches weighed down by wet snow, lay across the highway to Nelson where my cousin Sharon and I drove to visit her last night. She'd had an eventful day—therapy, a haircut, visitors—and though she doesn't look like she will pass on any time soon, she tells us, "I'm not afraid of dying. And who knows? I might live longer." She enjoys the moments, the taste of the cheese *nalyesnyeekee* I bring her, the warm hug of a male nurse who is able to lift her and set her down in a wheelchair, the visitors who bring flowers and make her smile.

On the way home, while we dodge branches and whole trees on the slushy highway, I think of the day decades ago, when she was in her fifties, I drove her down the Slocan Valley highway in the blue Mercedes her brother had given her. We were travelling to a schoolhouse in Vallican, where she was upgrading her math and English-language skills. The roads were icy, and as we rounded a sharp corner, a bear came tumbling down a steep bank and onto the narrow road. We were unable to stop, and the bear bounced off the right fender of the car and bounded into the forest. We drove on, hoping the bear was not badly injured.

That small schoolhouse class for Slocan Valley residents was Mother's opportunity to finally get an education, and she persisted, despite slippery roads and wildlife springing out of the forest. She said her teachers were interesting; she loved learning and was at the top of her class. Magazines and books, in both English and Russian, have always been her friends, and when I visit she comments on the viewpoints of the editors of *Iskra* and *Alive* magazines. I smile, give her a hug. Some losses are retrievable.

On a personal note, this journey I have taken to discover the history of my family has brought me to a deeper understanding of my roots. I have always been proud of my grandparents for speaking out against militarism, but it is in the details of their lives that I have learned of the cost of their outspokenness. That my grandfather Pete Maloff was prepared to serve time in prison when government dictates collided with his conscience, I find honourable and rare. And I have come to an acceptance of those who chose the easier route of accommodating to Canadian society's rules. Not all of us have the fortitude to face harsh penalties for acting on our beliefs.

Among my fellow Doukhobor friends whose families are of varied Doukhobor backgrounds, I notice the Sons of Freedom passion has kept their faith alive, while the Community and Independent roots have added reflection and pragmatism in their life choices. It took time, empathy and forgiveness on the part of many, but the fact that these factions have become reconciled is an achievement for which Grandfather Pete Maloff advocated.

Eighty years ago Pete Maloff was imprisoned and tortured for his refusal to support militarism. Today Canadian society allows more freedom of speech for those who speak in opposition to laws they feel they cannot support. And Canadians have begun to implement ways of mediating disputes other than raising arms against each other. My grandfather would have been happy to sit in the circles of restorative justice that are now being established to encourage compassion and forgiveness in our society.

The voices of the peacemakers have become respected. Pete Maloff, in the last years of his life, was called to share his vision with various groups including the Rotary Club in Trail, in peace rallies against chemical weapons being tested in Suffield, Alberta, and at the International Peace Garden between Manitoba and North Dakota.

I would like to believe that, in time, those speaking for peaceful resolution and justice will change how human beings and nations solve their conflicts. I have written this book to honour past generations of my family of Doukhobors; I end it with the dedication my grandfather Pete Maloff wrote at the beginning of his book, *Doukhobors, Their History, Life and Struggle.*

To all spiritual heroes, known and unknown, champions, heralders and martyrs, who perish on crosses, scaffolds, stakes, and in prisons, the participants of the past and present great historical procession—struggle against folly, hypocrisy, and universal evil—militarism. To all future pulsing hearts of world conscience, the vanguard and builders of universal brotherhood of all human beings in the world—I dedicate my work.

Pete N. Maloff 1948

My ancestors resisted becoming part of a military machine to solve disputes between people and nations. Though, in their time, challenging the Russian and Canadian authorities proved only to be a thorn in the side of a government bent on armed warfare, I believe that we, as human beings, must continue to raise our voices against hypocrisy and injustice in a non-violent manner. It is the way to create a just, peaceful community for our future.

Appendix

Letter from J. Macdonald, warden of the provincial jail in Nelson, BC:

The Government of The Province of British Columbia
Provincial Gaol
Nelson, BC

Thrums, BC
April 22, 1941
Mrs. Pete Maloff

Dear Madam;
I am in receipt of your letter of yesterday's date.

Your husband is in good health and although we do not allow prisoners convicted of certain offences the privilege of writing, I am in this instance allowing your husband to write you one letter and you will no doubt hear very shortly from him.

The laws of this country are very just and reasonable and if people complied with them they would have nothing to fear.

Yours obediently,
J. Macdonald
Warden

Letter from Lucy (Lusha) Maloff to Warden J. Macdonald:

Thrums, BC
April 25/41

J. Macdonald
Warden

Dear Sir:
Your kind letter I received. You cannot imagine how glad I was to receive both your and Pete's letter.

The stories about you were that you are a man with such an unkind heart, but with your kind deed you've not only made me ever so thankful to you, but I'm honestly telling you that you've changed my feelings towards you. Instead of thinking bad about you, I can only say that you are reasonable.

I do hope that you would understand us, Mr. Mcdonald, and would not consider us worse people than thieves and murderers, which do get the privileges of writing and receiving letters and even visits.

We are only trying to be just and honest and obey the laws of God as much as it is in our power, for this only reason we are being punished.

Once more I am thanking you ever so much.

I am yours very truly,
Mrs. Pete Maloff

Nelson B.C.
January 18, 1946
To: The Honourable St. Laurent.
Minister Of Justice
Ottawa, Ont.

Honourable Sir:

A humble appeal for the release of Doukhobors sentenced
for anti-war demonstration.

Humanity is sick of horror, of war, and the unspeakable
atrocities that certain men have visited upon the unarmed
and the innocent. Nor can the justice that is now being
meted out to them cleanse our thought of their crimes.
The world is still waiting for a wave of generosity or a
great wave of death; and we know that to the extent that
we find it in our hearts to forgive others, so may we be
forgiven, and receive the grace of God.

The last phase of the war ended on Jan. 1st. Therefore, could not some appropriate day be speedily found
on which to declare amnesty in favour of war resisters,
especially the Doukhobors of this province; the severity
of whose sentence seemed to us to partake of vengeance
rather than of justice.

I would ask you to regard the friends who have signed
below not numerically but as representatives of the many
men and women of good will who would go about their
daily chores so much the more happily could they believe that at least in Canada there is that generosity the
world stands in need of.

Your Obedient Servant
G.A. Butling and Friends

GLOSSARY

The following terms are transliterated from the original Russian spellings, as pronounced in customary usage by Doukhobors. The Doukhobors in Canada have generally spoken a unique and colourful dialect of Russian, which has been recognized by some scholars as a distinct Slavic language in its own right. The transliteration system utilized is essentially the one used by the Library of Congress, with a few exceptions. All consonants are pronounced as they would normally be in English, except where followed by an apostrophe or the letter *y*, in which case they should be pronounced in softened mode. The Russian *r* is rolled as in Scottish. The Russian language has ten vowels, and these are approximated by English equivalents, as follows: *a* and *ya*, as in *yawn*; *e* and *ye*, as in *yes*; *ee*, as in *feel*; *i*, as in *hill*; *o* and *yo*, as in *yore*; *u*, as in *tube*; and *yu*, as in *yule*. Russian also has a "semi-vowel," which is approximated by the sound of *y*, as in *you* or *boy*. To aid pronunciation, accent marks have been placed over vowels in this glossary to indicate stressed syllables.

— Jim Popoff

Many thanks to Jim Popoff for his invaluable assistance in compiling this glossary.

abchéennyeekee. Wild mushrooms.

akurátnaya. Proper; neat.

anhlyéekee. English speakers (also referred to anyone in Canada who wasn't a Doukhobor).

aúl. Tatar village.

ázbukee. Russian alphabet books.

bábushka/bábushkee. Grandmother/grandmothers.

bánya. Bathhouse; steam room.

béliy. White.

bésheniy. Wild.

Bístra ustaváy! Get up quickly!

bístraya. Quick.

Bokh pamahnyée nam. God help us.

borsh. Cabbage soup.

chórniy. Black.

daraháya. Dear.

dédushka. Grandfather.

Déla tahdá prapála. All would be lost.

delavóy muzhík. Usually implies a capable "go-getter" type of man.

Dóbriy dyen'. Good day.

Dóbriy véchir. Good night.

doch. Daughter.

dom nash blahadátniy. Our blessed home.

dyádya. Uncle; term of respect for an older man.

dyévachkee. Girls.

Eedyée! Come!

Eeshó umá nyee nabrálas'. Didn't have any brains yet.

Hde ti? Where are you?

hláwniy. Important man; the leader.

Hlyan', payékhalyee! There they go again!

Hóspadyee Bózhe. Dear God.

kalpák. Knitted toque.

kantóra. Office.

kásha. Porridge.

kastapráw. Doukhobor bone-setter.

kharashó. Good.

krasyéewa. Beautiful.

kusók. Piece.

lapshá. Homemade egg noodles used for special occasions such as weddings or funerals.

láptyee. Shoes made of rubber soles and crocheted hemp uppers.

lyeekárk/lyeekárka. Healer.

malényeeye. Prayer meeting.

metyólka. Broom.

na Kawkáze. In the Caucasus.

nalyésnyeekee. Cheese crepes.

naryázheniy. Well dressed.

nyee nash. Not one of us.

nyee pakaryáeetsa. Won't give in.

nyet. No.

Ótche. Lord's Prayer.

Oy, Hóspadyee! Oh, my God!

pakhót. Protest march; walk.

pasalómcheekee. Prayers.

pech. Masonry stove with a shelf on top to sleep on.

peerahée. Tart-like pastries with fruit and vegetable fillings, a Doukhobor staple.

píshkee. Buns; flatbread.

platók/platkée. Head scarf/scarves.

plow. Rice casserole made with raisins and melted butter.

prabábushka. Great-grandmother.

pradédushka. Great-grandfather.

prapavédawal. Preached; spreading the word.

prawadyéelka. Garden tool for making rows.

preeklyópka. Someone sticking to you, making a nuisance of themselves.

Preevét! Hello! Welcome!

preeyékhalyee. You've arrived.

prétkee. Ancestors.

raskóshniy. Luxurious; excessive; wasteful.

rassvét. Dawn; daybreak.

reebyónak. Baby.

sabáka. Dog; a derogatory term toward a person.

sadyées'. Sit down.

s dabróm. With peace in your heart; with goodness.

sennyéek. Hay barn.

shchável'. Sorrel.

Shto ti? What's with you?

Sláva Bóhu. Thank God.

smorchkée. Morel mushrooms.

stareechók. Father-in-law.

starúshka. Mother-in-law.

sud'bá. Fate.

sundúk. Chest made out of wood.

tyóta. Auntie, a respectful way to address an older woman.

Ukrepée menyá Hóspadyee. Strengthen me, Lord.

Usyó kharashó. Everything's okay.

vázhniy. Important; boss.

vényeek. Broom; when used in a *banya*, it is usually made of birch twigs.

Ya tut. I'm here.

zanavéska. Apron-like front overskirt used in traditional Doukhobor attire.

zapóy. Engagement party.

zhírnaya. Plump.

zhúzhaleetsa. Coal dump from steam engines.

BIBLIOGRAPHY

Frazier, Ian. *Travels in Siberia*. New York: Picador, 2011.

Jensen, Bernard. "In Memory of Pete Maloff." September 26, 1991. In the author's possession.

Jensen, Bernard. *World Keys to Health and Long Life*. Escondido, CA: Omni Publishers, 1975.

Lapshinoff, Steve. "Index of Sons of Freedom Children Placed with Independent and Community Doukhobor Families, 1933–1935." Compiled from BC Archives, GR 1725 [B-7622], Attorney General Correspondence, 1932, part 2. Retrieved from Doukhobor Genealogy Website, http://www.doukhobor.org/Piers-Children.pdf.

Lutz, Wayne. "The History of the Nelson Provincial Jail," Undated report including photographs. Touchstones Nelson Museum of Art and History, Nelson, BC.

Maloff, Peter N. *Doukhobors, Their History, Life and Struggle*. Unpaginated manuscript, translated by Peter N. Maloff from the original, *Dukhobortsi, ikh istoriya, zhizn' i bor'ba* (Thrums, BC: self-published, 1948). A major Russian-language work by a lifelong prominent Doukhobor activist, author and historian, the 607-page volume covers a survey of Doukhobor history and significant perspectives on the unfoldment of Doukhobor destiny in Canada, including analysis of the three major Doukhobor factions in Canada and prominent individuals in each. It includes dozens of vintage black and white photos, documents and correspondence, and a section devoted to an autobiographical perspective.

Maloff, Peter N. *In Quest of a Solution: Three Reports on Doukhobor Problem*. 2nd ed. Trail, BC: Hall Printing Ltd., 1957.

Maloff, Peter N. "P.N. Maloff's Address before the Rotary Club." Speech given at Crown Point Hotel, Trail, BC, October 29, 1968.

Rodgers, Kathleen. *Welcome to Resisterville: American Dissidents in British Columbia.*Vancouver: UBC Press, 2014.

Sulerzhitsky, Leopold Antonovitch. *To America with the Doukhobors.* Regina: Canadian Plains Research Center, 1982.

Tarasoff, Koozma J. *Plakun Trava: The Doukhobors.* Grand Forks, BC: Mir Publication Society, 1982.

Tarasoff, Koozma J. *Spirit Wrestlers Voices: Doukhobor Pioneers' Strategies for Living.* Ottawa: Legas Publishing, 2002.

Walker, Len. *Tsunami Journey: Seventy Days in Sri Lanka; A Story of Rebuilding.* Qualicum Beach, BC: Tsunami Haven Pre-Schools, 2005.

ACKNOWLEDGEMENTS

Our Backs Warmed by the Sun has been a work of love to honour my Doukhobor family, but it has been fostered and brought to life by a community of people. In the beginning my mother Elizabeth passed on the amazing stories about her Maloff-Hoodicoff family and Uncle Walter documented the family photos. Steve, my partner, encouraged me to write down Mother's stories and Grace Deveaux introduced me to a writing group started by Margaret Hornby, which supported my baby steps in writing. Among others, friends Nell Plotnikoff, Margrith Schraner, Natasha Knox, were cheerleaders when I shared my stories with them. Doukhobor historians, Jim Popoff, Koozma Tarasoff and Dr. Andrew Donskov unreservedly said, "It's about time Pete Maloff's story was told."

Winning first prize for "Porto Rico" in the non-fiction category of the Kootenay Literary competition gave me the credentials to apply for a grant with the Columbia Kootenay Cultural Alliance, allowing for an initial manuscript review with my kind and generous editor Anne DeGrace. Anne continued to skillfully mentor this book into its final publishing form. Uphill Writing group members, accomplished authors, Brian d'Eon, Ross Klatte, and Diana Cole, continued to guide my writing—gently critiquing, suggesting and encouraging—over the last five years.

All along my family supported the stories. My aunts Luba Rezansoff, Nadya Johnstone, and Annie Malahoff shared their experiences growing up in the family. Geraldine Soukerukoff gave me access to her research on the family tree. My four adult children, a major reason I wrote the book, were wholehearted supporters; Alena insisted I include a woman's perspective, Tamara photographed the author photo, Sasha had suggestions on the cover, and Robin asked questions I had to find answers for. My brother Ceral suggested historical information and sister Katya helped with the translation of Russian songs and the initial editing.

Iskra editors, Stephanie Swetlishoff and Barry Verigin, were enthusiastic about my first stories and the readers told me they wanted more. Susan VanRooy included a story on the Doukhobor experience in her West Kootenay Journal. Ernest Hekkanen, editor of *The New Orphic Review*, published "Let Them Go Their Way," a story about draft resister Len Walker who lived with our family in the 1960s. A fellow "peacenik" Ralph McGreal was able to locate Len Walker, as well as historical information on Pete Maloff's contacts in the 1920s in California. Thank you to Len for sharing his history and his love for my grandfather, Pete Maloff.

Photographs from the family albums were digitized by John Kalmakov and Peter Perepolkin.

Vici Johnstone of Caitlin Press selected my manuscript out of the myriad on her desk and provided the wonderful editorial and production team, Meg Yamamoto, Sarah Corsie, and Monica Miller who added their professional expertise.

Everyone graciously gave their time, knowledge and devotion to this book. A depth of gratitude and heartfelt thank you to all.

PHOTO TAMARA TERRY

VERA MALOFF was born into a Doukhobor family in the Kootenay valley of British Columbia. Her writing reflects the influence of her grandparents, who were active in the peace movement and befriended the American draft resisters, alternative healing practitioners, and social justice advocates who were regular visitors to their market garden farm. After retiring from a career in teaching, Vera began to record family stories passed down from generations. Her essays have been published in the Doukhobor magazine *Iskra*, in the *West Kootenay Journal* and in *The New Orphic Review*. Vera lives with her partner Steve in the community of Shoreacres on the Slocan River, where she continues the family traditions of gardening, singing in Doukhobor community choirs, and participating in peace gatherings and cooking groups.